Foundations of Representative Government in Maryland
1632–1715

T0381857

Publication of this book has been supported by a grant from the
Maryland State Archives
and the Hall of Records Commission,
Annapolis, Maryland.

Foundations of Representative Government in Maryland, 1632–1715

DAVID W. JORDAN

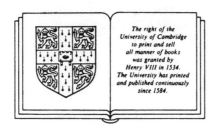

The right of the
University of Cambridge
to print and sell
all manner of books
was granted by
Henry VIII in 1534.
The University has printed
and published continuously
since 1584.

CAMBRIDGE UNIVERSITY PRESS

Cambridge

New York   New Rochelle   Sydney   Melbourne

PUBLISHED BY THE PRESS SYNDICATE OF THE UNIVERSITY OF CAMBRIDGE
The Pitt Building, Trumpington Street, Cambridge, United Kingdom

CAMBRIDGE UNIVERSITY PRESS
The Edinburgh Building, Cambridge CB2 2RU, UK
40 West 20th Street, New York NY 10011–4211, USA
477 Williamstown Road, Port Melbourne, VIC 3207, Australia
Ruiz de Alarcón 13, 28014 Madrid, Spain
Dock House, The Waterfront, Cape Town 8001, South Africa

http://www.cambridge.org

First published 1987
First paperback edition 2002

A catalogue record for this book is available from the British Library

Library of Congress Cataloguing in Publication data
Jordan, David William.
Foundations of representative government in Maryland,
1632–1715.
Bibliography: p.
1. Maryland – Politics and government – Colonial
period, ca. 1600–1775.   2. Representative government and
representation – Maryland – History.   I. Title.
F184.J67   1988
975.2′02   87-6630

ISBN 0 521 32941 8 hardback
ISBN 0 521 52122 X paperback

TO ANNA AND LEAH

Contents

Acknowledgments

The evolution of representative government in early America first captured my serious interest as a graduate student at Princeton University
and subsequently became a major concern of my doctoral dissertation,
prepared under the wise supervision of Wesley Frank Craven. That study
of the critical royal period of Maryland's colonial history soon led to a
more intensive focus on the earlier years of political development in that
colony, as well as to a closer examination of legislative institutions in
England and other colonies.

Much of the traditional literature on this subject seemed to focus narrowly on constitutional precedents gleaned from studies that paid too
little attention to social context. The few individuals who did appear in
these narratives or analyses were usually the most outstanding or notorious political figures. I became convinced of the value of broadening the
canvas to include the more typical participants in the development of
these institutions. My prosopographical analysis of the revolutionary
Convention of the Protestant Associators in 1689 and subsequent royal
assemblies persuaded me that much more should be attempted in collective biography. With support from the National Endowment for the
Humanities and the Maryland Hall of Records in Annapolis, I helped to
prepare a comprehensive biographical dictionary of every legislator in
Maryland from the founding of the assembly through 1789. The present
monograph integrates the gratifying results of that project with the rich
tapestry of recent social history. It is fitting that the conclusion of this
study follows closely upon the 350th anniversary of the first meeting of
the Assembly of Maryland.

In the course of years of pleasurable work on this subject, I have
incurred many debts. I thank the staffs of the numerous libraries and
archives both in this country and in England where I have conducted my
research, especially the highly efficient and cooperative personnel of the
Hall of Records and of Burling Library, Grinnell College. The Grinnell
College Grant Board helped to finance numerous research trips to Annapolis and London, and a fellowship from University House of the

University of Iowa freed me from normal responsibilities to devote an entire semester to preparing the original draft of this book.

It is impossible to recognize adequately the many individuals who provided inspiration, criticism, and other assistance. This book clearly draws heavily on the excellent work of many scholars, and the footnotes indicate that dependence. Many people made helpful comments on papers presented at various conferences or submitted to journals. I especially thank the editors of *William and Mary Quarterly, Maryland Historical Magazine,* and *The Historian,* as well as the editors of two collections of essays, *Law, Society, and Politics in Early Maryland* and *The Chesapeake in the Seventeenth Century,* for permission to adapt material that originally appeared in those publications.

A few individuals must be named separately. For two decades, Lois Carr has shared her unparalleled knowledge of the history and records of Maryland and frequently extended her hospitality during my research trips to Annapolis. This book, like almost all recent work on early Maryland history, owes much to her selfless dedication to other practitioners in the field. She provided particularly insightful commentary on drafts of this manuscript. Although she will undoubtedly disagree with some of its points, this book is immeasurably the better because of her advice. Don Smith and Randy Roth also constructively criticized numerous portions of this manuscript through various revisions.

I relied repeatedly on the staff of the Legislative History Project, especially Carol Tilles and Jane McWilliams. My former students Lisa Bowers, Steve Meyerhoff, and Janet Welsh made important contributions by refining and collating data and typing the manuscript. Emily Moore and Harry Bilger advised me on text processing. It has been a distinct pleasure and advantage to work with Frank Smith and his assistants at Cambridge University Press, and I appreciate the subvention provided by the Maryland Hall of Records.

Above all, I express my gratitude to Kay Jordan, who at successive stages in this project took notes, typed, and made trenchant criticisms of the entire manuscript. In innumerable other ways, she provided a congenial and supportive atmosphere for my work. Her encouragement and prodding were especially critical at several points.

My two daughters Anna and Leah have been affected by this project for all of their lives, often without really understanding what their father was doing on a particular summer trip or why he was crumpling another sheet of paper. They imbibed early, however, their parents' fascination with the political arena and the importance of individual involvement in the processes of government if they truly are to be representative. I dedicate this book to them with great love.

Introduction: "For the Good and Happy Government" of Maryland

On June 20, 1632, Cecilius Calvert, the twenty-seven-year-old second Lord Baltimore, received a proprietary charter for the vast domain in the New World that his father George Calvert had persistently sought for many years. King Charles granted to the Calverts and their heirs a princely territory of more than 10 million acres, to be called "Mariland" in honor of the queen, Henrietta Maria. Although the charter bestowed extensive prerogatives, Calvert's extraordinary dominion was not totally unchecked. Recognizing the growing expectations of the English to have an active voice in their own governance, the document also extended to the settlers of Maryland a critical responsibility "for the good and happy Government of the said Province." Lord Baltimore's power to "ordain, Make and Enact Laws, of what kind soever, according to their sound discretions, whether relating to the Public State of the said Province, or the private Utility of Individuals" required "the Advice, Assent, and Approbation of the Free-Men of the same Province, or the greater part of them, or of their Delegates or Deputies whom We will shall be called Together for the Framing of Laws."[1] Representative government in Maryland owes its origin and legitimacy to this clause of the Calverts' charter which made their province the first permanent English colony on the North American continent to provide from its founding for an assembly of resident freemen.

The Lords Baltimore welcomed the existence of an assembly in their colony. George Calvert had consciously introduced the provision for a legislature into his charter of 1623 for Avalon and carefully retained that commitment in his subsequent plans for Maryland.[2] Cecilius Calvert con-

1. Francis Newton Thorpe, ed., *Federal and State Constitutions, Colonial Charters and Other Organic Laws*, 7 vols. (Washington, D.C., 1909), 3:1669–77 (in Latin), 1677–89 (in English; quotations, 1679–80).
2. For the text of the Avalon charter, consult John Thomas Scharf, *History of Maryland from Earliest Times to the Present Day*, 3 vols. (Baltimore, 1879), 1:39–40.

curred in his father's intentions, as eventually did Charles Calvert, who succeeded to the proprietorship in 1675. However, these men never envisaged the assembly as a strong, countervailing force to their own proprietary rule. Eventual legislative power in the colonial government of Maryland was the result, not the intention, of the charter's provision for an assembly.

Neither George nor Cecilius Calvert left any extensive explanation of his political views. Their convictions on government are nonetheless clearly discernible. Both men subscribed to the cherished rights and privileges of what J. G. A. Pocock has conveniently summarized as "the ancient constitution," with the central place of Parliament in that arrangement of government. The first Lord Baltimore demonstrated repeatedly in his public career a commitment to the legislature as the fundamental agent of representative government in the English system. He personally served in three Parliaments before his public avowal of Catholicism in 1625 led to his withdrawal from elective politics. Cecilius Calvert's Catholicism also rendered him ineligible to serve in Parliament, but by all indications, he fully shared his father's convictions regarding the importance of that institution.[3]

The Lords Baltimore did not conceive of the projected colony of Maryland as a replica of Stuart England, however, nor any assembly there as a miniature Parliament. Their new settlement could provide neither the social structure nor other conditions necessary to sustain the current political system of England and the role that Parliament played in that polity. The formidable challenge of establishing an English society in the New World suggested to the Calverts more appropriate models in England of an earlier age or in contemporary Ireland.

George Calvert, with his own extensive experience in politics, desired the greatest possible sovereignty and flexibility in governing a colony. He early decided to become an independent proprietor rather than to proceed through the more restrictive organization of a joint stock company,

3. John D. Krugler is engaged in a modern study of both men. See particularly his articles "Sir George Calvert's Resignation as Secretary of State and the Founding of Maryland," *Maryland Historical Magazine*, 68 (1973), 239–54; " 'Our Trusty and Well Beloved Councillor': The Parliamentary Career of Sir George Calvert, 1609–24," ibid., 72 (1977), 470–91; " 'The Face of a Protestant and the Heart of a Papist': A Reexamination of Sir George Calvert's Conversion to Roman Catholicism," *Journal of Church and State*, 20 (1978), 507–31; and "The Calvert Family, Catholicism and Court Politics in Early Seventeenth Century England," *The Historian*, 43 (1981), 378–92. The best older biography is William Hand Browne, *George Calvert and Cecilius Calvert* (New York, 1890). See also J. G. A. Pocock, *The Ancient Constitution and the Feudal Law: A Study of English Historical Thought in the Seventeenth Century* (New York, 1967).

generally preferred by others for New World enterprises. Calvert pre-pared well for this new course, and his research located a promising precedent in pre-Tudor England, specifically in the palatinate of Durham during the 1300s. Calvert cleverly incorporated first into his charter for Avalon and more explicitly a decade later into the patent for Maryland the guarantee that the proprietor was to possess the equivalent powers that "any Bishop of Durham within the Bishopprick or County palatine of Durham in our Kingdome of England hath at anytime heretofore had" and that any interpretation of the charter's provisions should be "benefi-cial, profitable and favorable" to the proprietor. The founders of later colonies recognized the genius of Calvert's use of the bishop of Durham clause and frequently followed his example.[4]

This feudal model held many attractions. In addition to providing a "Royall Jurisdiction," the Durha.n precedent embodied a finely graded social order, upon which the Lords Baltimore also placed a high value. Such a system might encourage more men of wealth and status to invest in Maryland and facilitate a smoother transition to a prospering, stable province. The manor could become the basic social, political, and eco-nomic institution, with Maryland's lords providing leadership for this frontier community. Moreover, the Durham precedent ideally suited the purposes of the Calverts, who wanted to provide for the voice of the people in the political life of the colony but did not want proprietary authority much restricted by any expression of popular will. An assembly had gathered annually during the fourteenth century in Durham but sat without extensive legislative powers and possessed only limited control over taxation. Although barons and freemen had a voice in the govern-ment, the powerful bishop substantially circumscribed their role.

Acknowledging that the bishop of Durham clause conveyed powers obviously outmoded and intolerable in Stuart England, the Lords Balti-more claimed that these prerogatives were still timely and acceptable in a new colony across the ocean. Despite some strenuous objections to the terms of the charter, the king eventually concurred in its provisions. Two decades later, responding to renewed questions about this "Monarchical Government," Cecilius Calvert offered the clearest surviving expression of the family's philosophy. Although these powers "may not be conve-nient for any one man to have in England," he explained in 1652, "yet

4. See the respective charters and Gaillard Thomas Lapsley, *The County Palatine of Durham: A Study in Constitutional History* (Cambridge, Eng., 1924), especially 106–55; David B. Quinn, "Introduction: Prelude to Maryland," 11–25, in Quinn, ed., *Early Maryland in a Wider World* (Detroit, Mich., 1982); and Charles B. Andrews, *The Colonial Period of American History*, 4 vols. (New Haven, Conn., 1934–38), 1:308–12; 2:276–85.

they are necessary for any (whether one man or a Company) that undertakes a Plantation, in so remote and wild a place as Mariland, to have them there." The laws of the colony, he carefully continued, still had to have the consent of an assembly, "be consonant to reason, and be not repugnant or contrary, but, as neare as conveniently may bee, agreeable to the Laws of England." In Calvert's opinion, this provided the necessary check on what were otherwise essential deviations from contemporary English practices.[5]

The English experience in Ireland also influenced the founders of Maryland. George Calvert became a peer of Ireland in 1625 and owned a baronial estate there. In 1614, he had served on a special royal commission to examine the grievances of the Irish Parliament, which King James had summoned in 1613. The knowledge Calvert gained on this royal assignment undoubtedly returned to mind in the planning for his colonies. England's approach to the control of Ireland depended heavily on its colonization by numerous Englishmen of wealth and prominence and on the creation of new feudal estates for these immigrants. The first Lord Baltimore had even considered settling permanently in Ireland himself before he turned his attention more fully to America.[6]

This model remained before the Calverts through their continuing involvement in Ireland and through the activities of their good friend and adviser Thomas Wentworth, earl of Strafford, who served as lord deputy of Ireland from 1632 to 1640. Wentworth's views of the Irish Parliament, which sat again in 1634 with both Catholic and Protestant members, illuminate the attitudes of the Calverts as well. As Wentworth explained to the Irish Council, although the king called a Parliament in deference to the ancient ways, "he had absolute right and power to collect all the revenue he required without the consent of anybody and that their business as councillors was to trust their sovereign without asking questions."[7] The

---

5. Clayton Colman Hall, ed., *Narratives of Early Maryland, 1633–1684* (New York, 1910), 173–74; William Hand Brown et al., eds., *Archives of Maryland*, 72 vols. to date (Baltimore, 1883-), 1:264 (cited hereafter as *Archives*). On the Calverts' intentions, in addition to the works cited in note 4, see particularly Russell R. Menard, "Economy and Society in Early Colonial Maryland" (Ph.D. diss., University of Iowa, 1975), especially 1–56, and John D. Krugler, "Lord Baltimore, Roman Catholics and Toleration: Religious Policy in Maryland During the Early Catholic Years, 1634–1649," *Catholic Historical Review*, 65 (1979), 49–75.

6. David Beers Quinn has influentially noted the importance of Ireland; others ably extend his work in K. R. Andrews, N. P. Cranny, and P. E. H. Hair, eds., *The Westward Enterprise. English Activities in Ireland, the Atlantic, and America 1480–1650* (Liverpool, 1978). Richard Bagwell, *Ireland Under the Stuarts and During the Interregnum*, 3 vols. (London, 1963), 1:108–17, discusses the Parliament of 1613–15 and Calvert's role.

7. Bagwell, *Ireland Under the Stuarts*, 1:211–314 (quotation, 212). Krugler, "The Calvert

Calverts were to voice similar sentiments about their government in Maryland. Like Wentworth, they saw no inconsistency in concurrently championing the rights of the English Parliament while also laboring to keep another legislature in a more subordinate role.[8]

Other models from the New World undoubtedly affected the Calverts' early thinking about the role of freemen. Rudimentary assemblies had evolved in Virginia, Bermuda, and Massachusetts from the structures of the joint stock companies that had founded the respective colonies. These institutions remained frail and their futures uncertain in 1632. Even so, if the Calverts were to compete successfully for immigrants, they had to offer no less an opportunity for the participation of freemen, especially since the awesome powers of a Catholic proprietor might initially discourage some prospective colonists.[9]

The Calverts, in implementing their philosophy on popular participation, resembled earlier English monarchs who had summoned the first Parliaments. Those rulers had set out not to establish a counterforce to their own power, but rather to acquire assistance and an endorsement of actions. However, just as discussion in Parliament led eventually to opposition and a limit on authority, so it would be with Maryland's assembly.[10] Gradually, the freemen and their representatives came to expect an influence far surpassing that which the Calverts ever intended. The only model most of these Englishmen knew was their perception, however precise or accurate, of the Parliament of their own day. In fact, many early Marylanders displayed an astonishing knowledge of current parliamentary procedures and powers and the latest political developments in the mother country. Popular awareness of such issues was mounting throughout the English-speaking world. Following the Parliament of 1628, with its famous Petition of Right, debate over the proper place of that institution remained at the center of political discussion for the next

Family," 380–84, 388–90; and J. P. Cooper, ed., *Wentworth Papers, 1597–1628* (London, 1973), especially 291.

8. Wentworth's actions have puzzled historians who wish to categorize him neatly as a royalist or parliamentarian. Conrad Russell disputes the arguments of a court-country dichotomy among members of Parliament in this era and considers Wentworth in a more sophisticated fashion. I believe the same explanations apply to the Calverts. See Russell's "Parliamentary History in Perspective, 1604–1629," *History*, 61 (1976), 1–27, and *Parliament and English Politics, 1621–1629* (Oxford, 1979).

9. Andrews, *Colonial Period*, Vol. 1, extensively discusses the joint stock companies' roles in the governance of these colonies. Michael Kammen, *Deputyes & Libertyes. The Origins of Representative Government in Colonial America* (New York, 1969), 12–26, is also pertinent.

10. G. R. Elton, "The Body of the Whole Realm," in *Parliament and Representation in Medieval and Tudor England* (Charlottesville, Va., 1969), 16–17.

two decades, the very critical years of Maryland's founding and the start of its own representative assembly.[11]

Immigrants to the Calverts' Chesapeake colony naturally wanted to replicate desirable aspects of the world they had left behind.[12] They especially brought the convictions of contemporary Englishmen engaged in a critical political debate. Liberties under assault in England, as King Charles tried to rule without a Parliament in the 1630s, assumed a special currency for colonists subject to a Catholic proprietor claiming monarchical powers himself. It is no wonder that the settlers of Maryland over the next century were to appeal to the precedent of Parliament and attempt in their assembly to emulate the House of Commons to a degree probably unmatched elsewhere in the New World.[13]

These political concerns surfaced almost immediately in the young colony. Settlers quickly asked "what Laws the Province should be governed by." By common understanding, the charter and instructions to the governor, as well as English common and statute law, were to provide the basic foundation for government, but some colonists wanted this understanding explicitly stipulated in legislation passed by their own assembly. Perhaps, others pondered, some provisions of English law were more appropriate and desirable than others, and local circumstances might require some unique statutes. Whatever their respective opinions on such questions, most freemen readily concurred that they should play a central role through the assembly in resolving these differences and in determining what the colony's laws were to be. Most freemen did not accept the proprietor's proposition that his bills would always necessarily make "wholesome laws and ordinances," nor were they anxious to acknowledge further or to enhance his powers. Rather, they desired a firm recognition of the role of the local assembly in keeping with their understanding of the position of Parliament with respect to the king.[14]

These sharply opposing perspectives on the Maryland assembly came

11.   D. M. Hirst, *The Representative of the People? Voters and Voting in England Under the Early Stuarts* (Cambridge, Eng., 1975) and Russell, *Parliament and English Politics*, argue persuasively for the existence of an involved and enlightened citizenry in early seventeenth century England.

12.   These themes of persistence and replication of English practices and beliefs have been explored by David Grayson Allen, *In English Ways: The Movement of Societies and the Transfer of English Local Law and Custom to Massachusetts Bay in the Seventeenth Century* (Chapel Hill, N.C., 1981), and by T. H. Breen in numerous essays, many recently collected in *Puritans and Adventurers* (New York, 1981).

13.   Mary Patterson Clarke, *Parliamentary Privilege in the American Colonies* (New Haven, Conn., 1943), 21 (particularly n. 15).

14.   *Archives*, 1:9, 10; 2:23; 3:50–51, 53. The application of English laws long remained a subject of debate. See George Leakin Sioussat, *The English Statutes in Maryland*, The Johns Hopkins University Studies in Historical and Political Science, Nos. 11 and 12 (Baltimore, 1903).

into open conflict in the 1630s and persisted for decades thereafter. The dimensions of the debate and the specific issues in dispute were transformed over the years, as Charles Calvert succeeded his father as third Lord Baltimore, as conditions altered both in the colony and in the mother country, and as the profile of the colony's population and particularly the membership of the assembly likewise changed. Through the 1680s, proponents of a more active and representative assembly battled vigorously with two proprietors and their deputies over general procedures and prerogatives as well as particular legislative issues, and elected delegates futilely fought for a predominant role in the proceedings of the assembly. Gains were slow in coming, for the Calverts successfully withstood most pressures for many decades. Not until the overthrow of proprietary authority in the revolution of 1689 and the imposition of royal government in Maryland for a generation thereafter did the assembly realize the earlier claims of its supporters. Governors appointed by the Crown regarded the introduction of English parliamentary practices as both normal and desirable, and ironically these royal placemen aided the advancement of representative government.

No direct line of development, no steady "winning of the initiative" characterizes the history of the legislature in Maryland. Rather, it followed an irregular pace of development.[15] The eventual shape of the assembly in its institutional forms and practices owes much to the model of Parliament, but the evolution of representative government in the colony also derives significantly from developments far removed from the political debates of the mother country. Demographic, economic, and social influences with a timing of their own profoundly influenced the course of Maryland's political history, as did the particular and often peculiar personalities of individual colonists. Collectively, these forces of both the Old World and the New, the impersonal and the decidedly human factors interacted to shape the assembly from its first meeting in February of 1634/35 until 1715, by which time that legislative body had assumed most of those fundamental features and powers it was to possess through the years of the American Revolution.[16]

15. The phrase comes from Wallace Notestein's celebrated essay, *The Winning of the Initiative by the House of Commons* (London, 1925). Recently, historians have postulated that the ascendancy of Parliament occurred later, less steadily, and without so conscious a dichotomy between the legislature and the Crown as usually argued. See particularly G. R. Elton, *Studies in Tudor and Stuart Politics and Government*, 2 vols. (Cambridge, Eng., 1974), and works cited in note 8. J. H. Hexter surveys this revisionist literature in "The Early Stuarts and Parliament: Old Hat and the Nouvelle Vague," *Parliamentary History*, 1 (1982), 181–215.

16. All dates falling between January 1 and March 25, the start of a new calendar year in Old Style dating, will be rendered with a slash mark, as here in "February of 1634/35."

PART I

"In the Infancy of This Plantation": 1632–1660

1

"A Country. . .Newly Planted"

The government established is a monarchicall forme and (under his Majestie) successive in my Lord and his issue, assisted by a councell of select men chosen from among the Master Adventorors and a parl[i]am[en]t to be called when occasion shall require all the freeholders.

> "A Short Treatise sett downe in a letter written by R. W. to his worthy friend, C. J. R.," 1635

Bee it Enacted by the Lord Prop^r wth the advise & consent of the Counsell & Burgesses of this province now assembled That this p^{r}nt assembly during the continuance thereof bee held by way of Upper & Lower howse to sitt in two distinct roomes a part, for the more convenient dispatch of the busines therein to bee consulted of . . . .And all Bills that shall bee passed by the s^d Two howses of the maior part of both of them, & Enacted or Ordered by the Gou^r shall bee Lawes of the province after publicon thereof, under the hand of the Gou^r & the Great Seale of the s^d Province as fully to all effects in Law as if they were advised & assented unto by all the ffreemen of the province personally.

> An Act for the Settling of this present Assembly, 1650

The *Ark* and the *Dove* departed from England on November 22, 1633, with the first settlers destined for Maryland. It was late winter before the weary passengers, between 150 and 200 in number, sailed into Chesapeake Bay. After stopping briefly in Virginia, the colonizing party proceeded up the Potomac, described by one of the men as "the sweetest and greatest river I have seene, so that the Thames is but a little finger to it." The vessels landed at St. Clement's Island on March 25, where the immigrants immediately erected a large cross, planted the English standard, and held a worship service. Governor Leonard Calvert, his deputies, and the local Indians soon agreed upon a more suitable site down river for establishing the English settlement. Reboarding the vessels, the colonists sailed for several more miles to "a very commodious situation for a Towne." There, "upon the 27. day of March Anno Domini 1634, the Gouvernour tooke possession of the place, and named the Towne Saint Maries." The actual settlement of Maryland was underway.[1]

1. Hall, ed., *Narratives*, 39–41, 72–74. One colonist later claimed "neere 200 people" embarked on the ships (ibid., 70). Some 128 swore allegiance at departure, but the ships took on an unknown number of Catholics farther down the channel. Some passengers died en route. See Andrews, *Colonial Period*, 2:286–88.

The Calverts nurtured ambitious dreams for this new colony. They hoped to enhance the fortunes of their family and of other colonists while providing an attractive haven for English Catholics, advancing missionary work among the heathen Indians, and augmenting the glory and power of England and the king in America. Building carefully upon his previous colonial experiences in Avalon and Virginia, George Calvert had retained the fundamental features of the Avalon charter but had altered the form of landholding from tenure in capite to that of free and common socage, which afforded him greater rights and fewer obligations. New provisions enabled him to erect churches and chapels and to exempt Maryland completely from the English laws of mortmain; the Catholic church and its adherents were not to suffer the restrictions currently imposed in England and in Virginia, where Lord Baltimore's religious beliefs had presented such an obstacle to his settlement in 1629.[2]

Cecilius Calvert had fashioned more specific plans for implementing the family vision. The second Lord Baltimore's Conditions of Plantation promised all initial investors the rights to 2,000 acres of land for every five men between the ages of sixteen and fifty brought into Maryland. Landed estates of this size would become manors with their resident lords able to hold courts leet and courts baron. Individuals paying their own way and transporting fewer than five persons would receive less munificent plantations without feudal privileges. The proprietor further advertised liberal trading privileges and other incentives to attract investors.[3] His promotional literature portrayed a New World paradise where adventuresome colonists would enjoy "a quiett life sweetened with ease and plenty." In this new Promised Land, virtually everyone would "live like princes."[4]

Calvert's grandiose blueprint suffered a crippling blow before the *Ark* and the *Dove* ever left Gravesend. The venture failed to attract the anticipated volume of investors; indeed, the proprietor "found very few who were inclyned to goe and seat themselves in those parts." The response of the Catholics was quite disappointing. Although the Jesuit order transported thirty settlers, the Catholic laity proved surprisingly uninterested in leaving England, despite the many restrictions on them there. Nor were

2. Hall, ed., *Narratives*, 20. On the Calverts' earlier colonial ventures, see Thomas J. Hughes, *History of the Society of Jesus in North America, Colonial and Federal*, 4 vols. (London, 1907–17), Text, 1:176–202; and Thomas D. Coakley, "George Calvert and Newfoundland: The Sad Face of Winter," *Maryland Historical Magazine*, 71 (1976), 1–19.

3. Hall, ed., *Narratives*, 6, 91–92, 95–96; *Archives*, 3:47–48.

4. John D. Krugler, ed., *To Live Like Princes* (Baltimore, 1976), particularly 30–31 (quotations); Hall, ed., *Narratives*, 5–10; *A Declaration of the Lord Baltimore's Plantation in Maryland*, Maryland Hall of Records, 350th Anniversary Document Series (Annapolis, Md., 1983).

many disposed to underwrite the migration of other individuals who were willing to go. Even fewer Protestants enlisted, either as investors or as free colonists. The acknowledged risks of any colonial venture, and in this instance the additional uncertainty of association with a Catholic proprietor, discouraged much voluntary participation from Protestants.[5]

The original colonizing party included only seventeen Gentlemen Adventurers, probably all Catholics. A smaller number of passengers were free immigrants of moderate means, and most notable in this limited category were three Jesuits heading their order's mission to Maryland. Colonists paying their own passage, much less those migrating with families or transporting a retinue of servants, journeyed in greater numbers during the 1630s to New England than they did to the Chesapeake.[6]

The overwhelming majority of passengers on the first two ships and on most vessels thereafter were indentured servants. Indeed, an estimated 70 to 85 percent of all immigrants to Maryland during the seventeenth century arrived in servitude. Predominantly young, unskilled males, they were to provide essential labor in Maryland, but their numbers initially offered little consolation to the proprietor for the absence of more affluent settlers.[7]

The earliest immigrants, whether new lords of manors, independent freemen, or servants, confronted a common task upon reaching Maryland. They shared the challenge of clearing and planting the land and of erecting shelters, first caves or crude temporary structures and then gradually more permanent dwellings. Adaptation to a new environment and the cultivation of adequate food supplies, much less a commercial crop for export, became an almost all-consuming experience. Despite the publication in England of glowing reports of Maryland's progress, the actual experiences of the first colonists bore no resemblance to the promised "quiett life sweetened with ease and plenty."[8]

5. *Archives*, 5:267; John Bossy, "Reluctant Colonists: The English Catholics Confront the Atlantic," 149–164, in Quinn, ed., *Early Maryland*; Hughes, *History of the Society of Jesus*, Text, 264–69.
6. Menard, "Economy and Society," 24–47.
7. Lois Green Carr and Russell R. Menard, "Immigration and Opportunity: The Freedman in Early Colonial Maryland," 206–42, and James Horn, "Servant Emigration to the Chesapeake in the Seventeenth Century," 51–95, in Thad W. Tate and David L. Ammerman, eds., *The Chesapeake in the Seventeenth Century* (Chapel Hill, N.C., 1979).
8. For contemporary reports, see *The Calvert Papers, Number One*, Maryland Historical Society, Fund Publication No. 28 (Baltimore, 1889), and Hall, ed., *Narratives*, especially 25–119. Standard secondary surveys include Aubrey C. Land, *Colonial Maryland* (Millwood, N.Y., 1981); Andrews, *Colonial Period*, 2:274–379; Wesley Frank Craven, *The Southern Colonies in the Seventeenth Century, 1607–1689* (Baton Rouge, La., 1949), Vol. 1 of Wendell Holmes Stephenson and E. Merton Coulter, eds., *A History of the South*; Newton D. Mereness, *Maryland as a Proprietary Province* (New York, 1901); and Russell R. Menard and Lois Green Carr, "The Lords Baltimore and the Colonization of Maryland," 167–215, in Quinn, ed., *Early Maryland*.

The primary obstacle to survival and success was never the indigenous population. Colonists promptly established peaceful relations with the Piscataways and other natives in the immediate area. On numerous occasions aid from the Indians proved critical in sustaining the weak settlement. Serious conflicts eventually arose, especially with the Susquehannahs, but there was no insurmountable problem in the initial years of the settlement.[9]

Debilitating illnesses posed a far greater challenge "in the infancy of this plantation." A frightful death rate ravaged successive shiploads of immigrants who quickly succumbed to what the English labeled the "seasoning," a strange malady that afflicted new arrivals. Survivors still faced an often unhealthy future. Perhaps 40 percent of the servants through the middle decades of the century never completed their term of indenture. Lord Baltimore's colonists rapidly perceived the fragility of life in the seventeenth century Chesapeake world.[10] Death proved no respecter of persons, either. The proprietor's brother George Calvert and at least five other prominent settlers died in the first few years. The unhealthy climate and discouraging conditions persuaded an additional seven of the original seventeen Gentlemen Adventurers to abandon Maryland in the first decade. Servants and poorer freemen rarely enjoyed that option.

Despite a continuing influx of new settlers, the province's total population probably never exceeded 500 persons before 1649, and at one point in the mid-1640s it almost certainly plummeted below 100. Maryland's slow growth also derived from the nature of the early population. Throughout the 1630s and beyond, men outnumbered women 6 to 1 among immigrants sailing from London to the Chesapeake. This shortage of women seriously discouraged any prospects of marriage. Those few men fortunate ever to marry usually did so at an older age than was customary among English people. The scarcity of family units and the slowness of traditional households to appear in the province compounded the proprietor's prob-

9. J. Frederick Fausz, "Present at the 'Creation': The Chesapeake World That Greeted the Maryland Colonists," *Maryland Historical Magazine*, 79 (1984), 7–20; James H. Merrill, "Cultural Continuity Among the Piscataway Indians of Colonial Maryland," *William and Mary Quarterly*, 3rd ser., 36 (1979), 548–70; and Hall, ed., *Narratives*, 42–45, 73–75.

10. Carville V. Earle, "Environment, Disease, and Mortality in Early Virginia," 96–125, in Tate and Ammerman, eds., *Chesapeake in the Seventeenth Century*; Darrett B. Rutman and Anita H. Rutman, "Of Agues and Fevers: Malaria in the Early Chesapeake," *William and Mary Quarterly*, 3rd ser., 33 (1976), 31–60; Lorena S. Walsh and Russell R. Menard, "Death in the Chesapeake: Two Life Tables for Men in Early Colonial Maryland," *Maryland Historical Magazine*, 49 (1974), 211–27; Carr and Menard, "Immigration and Opportunity," 208–9. Thomas Copley used the phrase "infancy of this plantation" (*Calvert Papers, Number One*, 159), as did the assembly in 1663 (*Archives*, 1:487–88).

lems in establishing both a well-ordered society and a growing population. Not until 1649 did any appreciable number of settlers arrive with families, and these were usually people relocating from Virginia.[11]

Circumstances of a political nature also threatened the colony's progress. Residents of a trading outpost on Kent Island, settled by William Claiborne from Virginia, refused to recognize the Calverts' authority. Marylanders employed armed force to subjugate the island's settlement of ardent Protestants in 1637/38, and during the subsequent two decades proprietary officials had to deploy already overextended resources to maintain a precarious authority there.[12]

Meanwhile, not everyone in the small settlement around St. Mary's willingly obeyed the proprietor's deputies. Inevitable disagreements aligned many settlers against the absent Lord Baltimore, and several of the leading investors quarreled repeatedly with some of the proprietor's most important policies. By 1652, no surviving original immigrant of wealth remained in the province. Similarly brief and divisive residences characterized the experiences of an additional thirteen colonists of comparable status who arrived before 1648 and to whom Baltimore looked anxiously for assistance. Only one of these individuals, Thomas Gerard, persisted in Maryland as long as ten years, and recurring opposition to Lord Baltimore eventually resulted in Gerard's own exile to Virginia. The proprietor searched in vain during these critical early years for a stable, dependable leadership to support Leonard Calvert and subsequent governors. Acrimony among his most prominent colonists set no positive example for the majority of Marylanders, and the failure of the settlement to unite placed the entire enterprise in peril. The colony came to the brink of collapse during the "time of troubles" in the 1640s when Claiborne's supporters and internal dissidents joined in their opposition. Lord Baltimore's deputies always ruled in uneasy fear of such combined assaults, one of which finally succeeded in deposing proprietary government for four years in the following decade.[13]

11. See Menard, "Economy and Society," 153–224, 396–422; also his "Population, Economy, and Society in Seventeenth Century Maryland," *Maryland Historical Magazine*, 79 (1984), 71–92, and "Immigrants and Their Increase: The Process of Population Growth in Early Colonial Maryland," 88–110, in Aubrey C. Land, Lois Green Carr, and Edward C. Papenfuse, eds., *Law, Society, and Politics in Early Maryland* (Baltimore, 1977).

12. Hall, ed., *Narratives*, 53–61, 150–56; *Archives*, 3:16–23, 24–44, 65–67, 68–70; Nathaniel C. Hale, *Virginia Venturer: A Historical Biography of William Claiborne, 1660–1677* (Richmond, Va., 1951).

13. Russell R. Menard, "Maryland's 'Time of Troubles': Sources of Political Disorder in Early St. Mary's," *Maryland Historical Magazine*, 76 (1981), 124–40, and David W. Jordan, "Maryland's Privy Council, 1637–1715," 65–73, in Land et al., eds., *Law, Society, and Politics*, provide helpful introductions to these difficult years.

Struggling against both nature and human enemies, the small band of early colonists labored for their livelihood. They directed their energies extensively toward the cultivation of oronoco tobacco. The Chesapeake tobacco industry was experiencing a second boom period in the mid-1630s. Although prices for the exported leaf had fallen to between five and six pence per pound from the price of two to three shillings commanded in the early 1620s, the growth and export of tobacco still returned an attractive profit for planters. With the settlement of Maryland, the quantity of tobacco shipped from the Chesapeake increased dramatically.

Initially, colonists cultivated this valuable product primarily to the enrichment of a few men, for landownership remained highly concentrated over the first decade. In 1642, for example, sixteen manors comprised 83 percent of all patented land, and the small coterie of manor lords basically controlled as well the available capital in the colony and held the indentures of most servants. About three-quarters of the free Europeans, 136 of 172 men, owned no land and possessed little if any personalty. The few landowners beyond the lords of the manors had generally acquired singly or in partnership small plantations rarely exceeding fifty acres, little as yet cleared or planted.

Gradually, a larger proportion of the free population established plantations and households of their own. Under the terms of successive Conditions of Plantation, a freedman upon satisfaction of his indenture became entitled to the rights to fifty acres of land. With the scarcity of labor, a prudent, industrious individual, once free, could save in a reasonable period sufficient income to pay the fees for surveying and patenting his fifty acres and for acquiring seeds and implements. The price of tobacco remained sufficiently high through the 1660s for such a man even to acquire his own indentured servants to assist in clearing land and producing more tobacco. Many eventual property holders in seventeenth century Maryland followed this route to become substantial freeholders. By midcentury, some contemporaries were describing Maryland as a favorable place for a poor man to advance economically, and so it was if the poor man were fortunate to live sufficiently long to make the transition from servant to freeholder.[14]

14. Menard, "Economy and Society," 63–101; his essays, "From Servant to Freeholder: Status Mobility and Property Accumulation in Seventeenth Century Maryland," *William and Mary Quarterly*, 3rd ser., 30 (1973), 37–64, and "The Chesapeake Tobacco Industry, 1617–1730: An Interpretation," in Paul Uselding, ed., *Research in Economic History: A Research Annual*, 5 (1980), 109–77; and his collaborations with Lois Carr, "The Lords Baltimore and the Colony of Maryland" and "Immigration and Opportunity," and with John J. McCusker, *The Economy of British America, 1607–1789* (Chapel Hill, N.C., 1985), 117–43. An instructive contemporary account, John Hammond's "Leah and Rachel," appears in Hall, ed., *Narratives*, 281–308.

Early Marylanders, though concentrating primarily on physical survival and economic advancement, also established those rudimentary political institutions necessary to serve their immediate concerns. Since most lived in an area close to the center of the settlement, the emerging government was simple and small-scaled; little distinction existed between levels of jurisdiction. The county of St. Mary's, first explicitly mentioned in 1637, functioned as both the local and the provincial government. The governor, or lieutenant general as his commission formally titled him, exercised the final administrative and judicial authority in the colony and headed the militia, but Lord Baltimore had also appointed Thomas Cornwaleys and Jerome Hawley to assist as commissioners. In 1637, the proprietor made more explicit the responsibilities of these men and John Lewger, who became the three original members of his lordship's Privy Council in Maryland. Following the precedent of such a body in the old bishopric of Durham, the council advised the governor, officiated in his absence or illness, and among other duties served as the earliest justices of the St. Mary's court. After the governor, the councillors held the greatest immediate power over the settlers in Maryland.[15]

A more extensive structure of government evolved as the population dispersed and the needs of the province increased. The individual hundred, a common subdivision transferred from England, became Maryland's counterpart to the parish in Anglican Virginia and Barbados and the township in Puritan New England and quickly surpassed in importance the manor, which had been more prominent in the proprietor's original schemes. Although a few manors established their own courts and other agencies, these institutions had largely disappeared by 1660, supplanted by other bodies that corresponded more closely to those of contemporary rather than medieval England.[16]

Slowly, the county became the critical level of authority. The problem of governing the subdued Kent Island particularly spurred this transition. Leonard Calvert first experimented with making the island a hundred of the distant St. Mary's County, but sometime between 1640 and 1642 he designated the area as a distinct second county with two hundreds of its own and a separate court. For another decade, the St. Mary's County administration with five hundreds and the provincial structures of government stayed closely intertwined. With further migration northward, however, the hundred of Providence eventually became the county of Anne Arundel by act of assembly in 1650, and four years later the legislature also created the county of Patuxent, soon to be called Calvert. As a

15. Hall, ed., *Narratives*, 16; *Archives*, 3:49–55.
16. Donnell M. Owings, "Private Manors: An Edited List," *Maryland Historical Magazine*, 33 (1938), 307–34; *Archives*, 53:lxi-lxv, 627–37.

consequence, a fuller complement of courts and administrative agencies evolved on both the county and provincial levels. For example, St. Mary's acquired its own separate and subordinate court, and the governor and members of the council became the justices of a superior Provincial Court.[17]

In staffing these structures, Lord Baltimore and Governor Calvert preferred to rely on the Gentlemen Adventurers and like individuals who followed in later ships. Such men possessed the education, status, and experience likely to satisfy the proprietor's expectations and to command the deference of other colonists. Early officeholders Cornwaleys, Hawley, Robert Wintour, George and Robert Evelyn, and Giles and Fulke Brent, all well-educated descendants of families that had provided members of Parliament or justices in their respective shires throughout England, contrasted sharply with the vast majority of settlers, who neither came from a tradition of such public service nor had acquired much education.[18]

The number of positions, however, quickly exceeded the available supply of gentlemen. Soon, modest freemen and even former servants were occupying the local offices and eventually even the highest provincial posts. For example, Robert Philpott, William Coxe, and Thomas Allen, who became commissioners of Kent in 1637 with powers equal to those of a justice of the peace in England, would never have anticipated filling such an office in the mother country. Thomas and James Baldridge, possibly former servants, served successively as sheriff and coroner of St. Mary's in the late 1630s, and Nicholas Gwither, definitely a freedman, followed them in those two positions within a decade. During the 1650s, an illiterate former servant, Daniel Clocker, officiated as a justice of the peace of St. Mary's County, one of at least sixteen bondsmen who had immigrated to Maryland by 1643 and eventually served as justices in the colony's courts. Such men became the backbone of local government, and during these early years, Lord Baltimore even extended commissions for

17. David W. Jordan, "Elections and Voting in Early Colonial Maryland," *Maryland Historical Magazine*, 77 (1982), 242–43; Lewis W. Wilhelm, *Local Institutions of Maryland*, Johns Hopkins University Studies in Historical and Political Science, Nos. 5–8 (Baltimore, 1885); Edward B. Matthews, *The Counties of Maryland: Their Origins, Boundaries and Election Districts*, Maryland Geological Survey, Special Publications, Vol. 6, Part 5 (Baltimore, 1907); *Archives*, 53:xi–lx. For comparable developments in another colony, see Warren M. Billings, "The Growth of Political Institutions in Virginia, 1634 to 1676," *William and Mary Quarterly*, 3rd ser., 31 (1974), 225–42, and "The Transfer of English Law to Virginia, 1606–1650," 215–44, in Andrews et al., eds., *The Westward Enterprise*.

18. See entries for these individuals in Edward C. Papenfuse, Alan F. Day, David W. Jordan, and Gregory A. Stiverson, eds., *A Biographical Dictionary of the Maryland Legislature, 1635–1789*, 2 vols. (Baltimore, 1979–85).

the council to former servants Robert Vaughan and Robert Clarke and to John Price, an illiterate freeman of modest origins.[19]

Much responsibility in these early years devolved upon Leonard Calvert himself. Government remained largely personal during his thirteen-year administration; he interacted directly with most colonists, adjudicating their disputes, patenting their land, and addressing problems that were typical of a young settlement. He could easily summon the freemen together for any necessary business affecting the entire colony. Accordingly, Cecilius Calvert had instructed his brother to gather all immigrants upon arrival in Maryland for a reading of the patent and other important documents and for a communal subscribing of an oath of allegiance to King Charles, as the official commencement of government in Maryland.[20]

Governor Calvert presumably followed a similar procedure on subsequent occasions when he had important information to disseminate. The first assembly, convened in February of 1634/35, probably met in this fashion. At least three of the initial seven assemblies were such general meetings with all freemen called to attend. Each of these open gatherings followed the arrival in Maryland of new Conditions of Plantation or a new commission reconstituting the government. Whenever such basic changes occurred, authorities apparently reconvened the whole body politic. This was government in its simplest, most direct form for matters affecting everyone, and this procedure adhered closely to the important precedent of the bishop of Durham and his regular meetings with barons and freemen in a nonelected, unicameral assembly.[21]

The problem of including in such meetings the residents of Kent Island prompted the first departure from this pattern. The second assembly was in temporary recess when Leonard Calvert captured Kent in 1637/38; it was obviously impractical for most of the islanders to journey across the bay and attend in person when the assembly reconvened. A few accepted the governor's invitation to come to St. Mary's, but the majority of freemen instead elected delegates to represent them at what was otherwise a general meeting.[22]

Freemen on the Western Shore, despite close proximity to the capital, also early declined to attend personally or to remain for the duration of an assembly. Illness kept some individuals away, and the primitive conditions under which the meetings were held discouraged others. The

19. *Archives*, 3:61–63; Menard, "From Servant to Freeholder," 43–47; Papenfuse et al., eds., *Biographical Dictionary*.
20. Hall, ed., *Narratives*, 20; *Calvert Papers, Number One*, 131–40.
21. For these new Conditions of Plantation and new commissions, see John Kilty, *The Land-holder's Assistant and Land-Office Guide* (Baltimore, 1808), 29–59, and *Archives*, 3:47–55, 99–101, 108–16.
22. Hall, ed., *Narratives*, 153; *Archives*, 1:3, 6, 15, 19, 22.

weather could be quite unpleasant during the winter months, which authorities generally favored for convening these assemblies. On an individual basis, then, some freemen in St. Mary's appointed proxies for all or
parts of assemblies open to every freeman.[23]

Participants quickly observed that such inclusive gatherings could be
unwieldy for conducting important business and concluded that a smaller
body might work more effectively; not everyone was equally well suited
to the tasks of preparing bills, debating, and conducting other business.
Freemen at the second assembly in 1637/38 eventually selected a committee of five men to consider the proprietor's proposed legislation, and the
full assembly adjourned until the committee was ready to report sometime later.[24]

The virtues of smaller meetings became apparent as the colonists experimented further with a limited elected membership, but the alternatives
also frequently confused the public. The proprietor always wanted certain men to be present, so the governor extended a special writ of summons to the current councillors and lords of manors; they attended each
legislature through a peculiar right to be present, like the barons of
Durham and certain members of the early Parliaments. Voters did not
always understand these writs and occasionally elected men already summoned. Other misunderstandings also arose. For an elected body scheduled to meet in 1638/39, Leonard Calvert instructed the freemen of the
various hundreds to "chuse from amongst themselves two or more dis-
creet honest men to be their deputies or Burgesses." When the legislature
convened, two other men asked to attend because they did not assent to
the election as held; the assembly obligingly allowed them to take seats as
voting members. "An Act what persons shall be called to every General
Assembly," approved later in this session, provided for subsequent
elected bodies but made no provision for anyone to attend who might
disagree with a particular election.[25]

Elected assemblies with smaller memberships became increasingly the
practice during the 1640s, while attendance at the occasional open meeting declined noticeably. At one such gathering in 1642, 19 men cast
proxies for at least 138 eligible freemen who chose not to be present.

23. *Archives*, 1:2–24. Seven of the first ten meetings convened in the winter. See also Lois
     Green Carr, " 'The Metropolis of Maryland': A Comment on Town Development
     Along the Tobacco Coast," *Maryland Historical Magazine*, 69 (1974), 124–27, and
     Susan Rosenfield Falb, "Proxy Voting in Early Maryland Assemblies," ibid., 73
     (1978), 217–25.
24. *Archives*, 1:10, 12.
25. Ibid., 27–32, 74–75; Jordan, "Elections and Voting," 239–40. In 1641, a freeman
     dissenting to an election was denied a voice in his own person (*Archives*, 1:105).

Earlier open assemblies had attracted 56 freemen in 1637/38, not counting those attending on special writs, and 53 individuals in 1641/42.[26]

With plantations spreading over a wider geographical area, it became
increasingly difficult to attract all eligible freemen to the capital, but no
standard procedure existed for a permanent alternative. William Stone,
one of Leonard Calvert's successors as governor, attempted some clarifi-
cation in January 1649/50. For the next assembly, freemen should agree
either to send proxies, with no man holding more than two, or to elect
burgesses; some minor stipulations were made on the number of possible
representatives. Stone desired a greater certainty of attendance and a
system acceptable to the majority of the freemen. The latter throughout
the colony preferred the elective system, with all but three hundreds
choosing two burgesses each. Thereafter, Lord Baltimore settled on the
elective form of organization, although he controlled the conduct of elections in a manner not always pleasing to the populace.[27]

Throughout these formative years, freemanship alone determined the
eligibility for participation in the political process. Any distinction of
owning land, heading a household, possessing a minimum degree of
wealth, or adhering to a particular set of religious beliefs proved less
important in early Maryland than simply being free as opposed to owing
time under an indenture. Gentlemen and recent freedmen, the well educated and the illiterate voted side by side and sat together in the assembly.
For example, an election in St. Clement's Hundred in 1640 involved
seven voters, four of whom were illiterate. Only two of the men present
would have qualified for the suffrage in contemporary England, and none
would have been a plausible candidate for election. The voting proceeded
informally; as the returned writ noted, "We thereby being but a small
Company in number make election of Lieutenant Robert Vaughan." The
new delegate was a former servant who had but recently been appointed
the local deputy of Thomas Gerard, the major landowner in the hundred
and already summoned to attend the upcoming assembly on a special
writ. Perhaps most striking about this and other elections was the mutual
participation of Catholics and Protestants.[28]

Indeed, restrictions on political participation in these early years were
notably rare, and the few that existed were consistent with English precedents. For example, the Assembly of 1637/38 excused three Jesuit priests
from attendance; by canon and civil law, they could not try cases of blood,

26. Papenfuse et al., eds., *Biographical Dictionary*, 1:15–19.
27. *Archives*, 1:259, 260–61.
28. Ibid., 89.

and this assembly was also serving as a court. A decade later, Cuthbert Fenwick successfully challenged the presence of Nicholas Gwither, who was not yet a freeman. Newcomer Thomas Weston learned in 1642 how liberally the colony interpreted the term "freeman." Despite his confession that he was "no freeman because he had no land nor certain dwelling here &ca," the assembly voted that he was qualified to sit. Such liberality did not extend, however, to a freewoman, even if she were a substantial property holder, as the formidable Margaret Brent discovered when Governor Thomas Greene rebuffed her effort to attend in 1647/48.[29]

The smallness of the colony, the informality of its procedures, and the liberal criteria for voting and officeholding ensured a more fluid political arena than prevailed elsewhere in the English-speaking world. Possession of a forty-shilling freehold had been required for the right to vote in county elections in England since 1429. In the early seventeenth century, this stipulation effectively disfranchised the majority of adult males. Despite growing demands for a broader suffrage, no significant increase in the size of the electorate occurred until the latter half of the seventeenth century. Substantially greater wealth was always expected of anyone standing for election, and oath requirements further restricted the eligibility of Catholics to serve in Parliament.[30]

All English colonies in the New World initially developed more generous provisions for the suffrage than existed in the mother country, and whatever restrictions did slowly materialize in America still qualified a larger percentage of the free adult male population to vote and hold office. Only in Maryland, however, could Catholics fully participate. Elsewhere, as in England, oath requirements effectively excluded non-Protestants, especially from sitting in assemblies.[31]

Despite the broader participation of freemen and the greater percentage of adult males who qualified to serve as representatives, colonists throughout the New World tended whenever possible to elect men clearly perceived as their superiors in economic status, education, and experience. In Massachusetts, a distinct political elite quickly emerged from among the more affluent settlers, and by the early 1640s, a remarkable

29. Ibid., 1:2, 5, 16–17, 170, 215, 218; Hughes, *History of the Society of Jesus*, Text, 1:382–83.
30. Richard L. Bushman, "English Franchise Reform in the Seventeenth Century," *Journal of British Studies*, 3 (1963), 36–56; Hirst, *The Representative of the People?*, 29–105.
31. Edmund S. Morgan, *American Slavery, American Freedom: The Ordeal of Colonial Virginia*, (New York, 1975), 145; B. Katharine Brown, "The Controversy Over the Franchise in Puritan Massachusetts, 1954 to 1974," *William and Mary Quarterly*, 3rd ser., 33 (1976), 212–41; Richard S. Dunn, *Sugar and Slaves: The Rise of the Planter Class in the English West Indies 1624–1713* (Chapel Hill, N.C., 1972), 92–93; Andrews, *Colonial Period*, 2:313–14.

continuity of leadership prevailed that was to persist through two subsequent generations. To a slightly lesser extent, a similar pattern soon characterized the political life of Barbados. Well before 1660, a few family names dominated the major offices, both appointive and elected, in that colony.[32]

Such continuity among a few men and their families did not appear until much later in the Chesapeake settlements, nor did successful candidates there initially stand so visibly above the general electorate in wealth or ability. The composition of the populations of both Maryland and Virginia and the extraordinarily high death rates in these colonies frustrated for some time the development of a well-knit political community or the persistence in office of any appreciable number of individuals. The rapid turnover of settlers also meant that despite the small number involved, freemen might be choosing from among relative strangers with little knowledge of one another's backgrounds, character, or ability. The proprietor in Maryland encountered extreme difficulty as did the Crown in Virginia, even in filling the small provincial council with men deemed suitable by most current criteria for such authority. Since these councillors received special writs to attend the assembly, voters had to look elsewhere in selecting their representatives, and obvious choices frequently did not exist.[33]

Consequently, for some time in Maryland and Virginia the freemen usually cast their votes for men who resembled themselves, individuals of brief residence in the colony, landless or just acquiring a small plantation, poorly educated and of modest social origins. As late as midcentury in Lord Baltimore's colony, most settlers remained newcomers who had arrived less than five years earlier. With so little to distinguish voters from

32. Timothy H. Breen and Stephen Foster, "The Puritans' Greatest Achievement: A Study of Social Cohesion in Seventeenth Century Massachusetts," *Journal of American History*, 60 (1973), 5–22; Robert Emmet Wall, Jr., "The Membership of the Massachusetts General Court, 1634–1686," (Ph.D. diss., Yale University, 1965); Dunn, *Sugar and Slaves*, especially 97–100; and "Some Records of the House of Assembly of Barbados," *Journal of the Barbados Museum and Historical Society*, 10 (1943), 173–87.

33. The late emergence of a stable elite in Virginia is an important theme of Morgan, *American Slavery, American Freedom*; Sigmund Diamond, "From Organization to Society: Virginia in the Seventeenth Century," *American Journal of Sociology*, 63 (1957–58), 457–75; and Bernard Bailyn, "Politics and Social Structure in Virginia," 90–115, in James Morton Smith, ed., *Seventeenth Century America: Essays in Colonial History* (Chapel Hill, N.C., 1959). However, Jon Kukla argues for the appearance of a reasonably stable leadership by the late 1650s in "Order and Chaos in Early America: Political and Social Stability in Pre-Restoration Virginia," *American Historical Review*, 90 (1985), 275–98. Lois Carr also believes chaos has been overemphasized, particularly with respect to local government; see "Sources of Political Stability and Upheaval in Seventeenth-Century Maryland," *Maryland Historical Magazine*, 79 (1984), 44–70.

one another and so few colonists who might plausibly expect deference from the electorate, freemen widely shared the responsibilities of service in the assembly. There seemed little reason to return the same individuals to subsequent assemblies and perhaps even a disinterest in doing so; assembly service, if not shared, might become onerous. Those in attendance suffered personal inconvenience, and delegates usually received minimal reimbursement for expenses. Even had some freemen wished to serve in numerous assemblies or had the voters desired to reelect these men, few colonists enjoyed sufficient health and longevity to become veteran legislators.[34]

Richard Lusthead and David Wickliff typify most burgesses of these early years in Maryland. Transported to the colony as a servant in 1634, Lusthead completed his term of indenture by 1637/38 and won election in 1640 to represent Mattapanient Hundred. Illiterate and Roman Catholic, he appears to have owned no land at the time of his selection. He died within two years of sitting in that assembly. Wickliff, in contrast, immigrated to Maryland as a free adult in 1636. A Protestant, he owned fifty acres when his neighbors in St. George's Hundred sent him to the assembly in 1638/39. They returned him as a burgess again in 1642, but Wickliff died less than a year later.

Lusthead and Wickliff were among ninety-seven men elected to the legislature through 1660. Lusthead, in serving only one term, resembled fifty-eight other delegates, comprising 61 percent of the total elected membership. Wickliff, as a veteran of two assemblies, was one of twenty-one men, or 22 percent, elected no more than twice. Only four individuals first elected during these years attended more than four assemblies as a delegate, and only an additional thirteen men sat as representatives in three or four legislatures (see Appendix A).[35]

A low incidence of recurring service was a pervasive characteristic of membership in the Maryland assembly in these years. Although legislatures generally met for only one session and full elections occurred on the average every two and a half years, few assemblies experienced much carryover in personnel. Recurring service does not generally appear until

34. Menard, "Economy and Society," 145–46, 216, on the rapid turnover of population. In July 1642, delegates from St. Mary's received a daily allowance of 40 pounds of tobacco, with delegates from Kent Island receiving additional tobacco for the hiring of a boat (*Archives*, 1:142–43). The stipend varied from one assembly to another. In 1649, delegates received 10 pounds of tobacco per day "for losse of their time" plus 16 pounds per diem "for their diet," whereas in 1650, there was a standardized per diem allowance of 50 pounds of tobacco (ibid., 237, 284). The intention was only to cover minimal expenses. Virginia provided a basic 150 pounds of tobacco per day for each burgess, and Massachusetts allowed two to three shillings, or the equivalent of 20 to 30 pounds of tobacco. See Morgan, *American Slavery, American Freedom*, 208.

35. Papenfuse et al., eds., *Biographical Dictionary*, 1:15–23.

the five elected assemblies of the 1650s. Fourteen of the seventeen delegates elected more than twice sat in 1654 or later, with most of their
legislative service actually coming after 1660. These men tended, significantly, to be more affluent than the usual burgesses of this period and
represented the vanguard of an important group of successful freemen
settling in Maryland.

Longevity of service in the assembly was somewhat more common
throughout the first two and a half decades among those men specially
summoned by the governor to attend the assemblies. Thirty individuals
received these special writs through 1660, and nine men, or 30 percent,
accumulated experience in five or more assemblies. Again, however,
many of these nine gentlemen, including Philip Calvert, who eventually
served in an unusual stretch of ten legislatures, first sat in the later years
of this period. Despite slightly greater carryover among these nonelected
legislators, seventeen men, or 57 percent, still attended no more than two
assemblies, death and departure from the colony most often abbreviating
their service (Appendix B).

With turnover so pervasive then among both elected and nonelected
delegates and with recurring participation limited even with inclusion of
the membership of the open assemblies, few Marylanders accumulated
much experience that they could apply to future service. The governor,
especially through the years of Leonard Calvert's tenure, and occasionally a councillor or two provided the primary continuity from one assembly to another. Frequently, they alone knew firsthand what a preceding
legislature had or had not accomplished or attempted. The continuing
inexperience of most delegates inclined them to defer generally to these
appointed officials for direction or left the elected delegates at a disadvantage when they did disagree.

Other factors divided members of these early assemblies into two
rather clearly defined groups. A few individuals of considerable wealth,
status, and education formed one mode; these men were overwhelmingly
Catholic in religious persuasion and almost invariably attended the assembly on a special writ. The more numerous portion of any legislature
consisted of men of modest means and origins, frequently former servants, less well educated, and predominantly Protestant; elected members
exclusively comprised this group for most of the assemblies in question.
Titles conveniently identify this division; very few of the larger group of
legislators merited a "Mr." before their names upon arrival in Maryland
or for many years thereafter, but the members of the smaller category
usually carried the designation "Gent." or even "Esq." from their first
appearance in the colony.

A more detailed examination of the sixteen men, excluding Governor

Leonard Calvert, who comprised the first elected assembly in 1638/39 illustrates well these membership patterns. Five colonists attended on a special writ, nine persons served as elected delegates, and two additional men, as earlier noted, claimed a separate voice in this assembly.[36] Reflecting the profile of the population at large, all members of this legislature fell within a rather limited age range, with only one man known to be older than forty and the average in the midthirties. There the similarities ended. All those on special writ were identified as gentlemen and each was a Catholic. Two had attended university in England and the others were also impressively educated. Three definitely possessed more than 1,000 acres in the colony, as did probably a fourth, and the recently arrived secretary of the province, John Lewger, already owned 200 acres and a number of profitable patronage positions. Each of his four colleagues held at least one other public office.

Only one elected member, Thomas Gerard, in any way resembled these men. A wealthy Catholic with a Protestant wife and children, Gerard had arrived in Maryland the year before, bringing five servants with his family. Lord of a new manor of more than 1,000 acres, Gerard would attend subsequent assemblies on a special writ himself. Otherwise, the elected delegates in 1638/39 presented a decidedly different profile. None currently held another position of importance, and six of them never would. At least two and probably four owned no land, and two others possessed 100 acres or less. One delegate had 200 acres, and the landed estate of only one representative besides Gerard approached 500 acres. Five elected members could not sign their names; literacy was probable but unproved for two others. Again, Gerard alone had any appreciable education. Five delegates were Protestant; religious affiliation cannot be determined for three men, but Gerard, again the exception, was the only known Catholic elected to this assembly. Robert Clarke and Cuthbert Fenwick, who claimed the additional seats, were Catholics and enjoyed the support of powerful figures in Maryland, but otherwise as recent freedmen they currently could claim neither wealth nor distinguished origins themselves.

Table 1 illustrates the persisting chasm in these early legislatures between those summoned by special writ and those chosen by the electorate. A serious split became discernible as early as 1642. That July, representative Robert Vaughan "in the name of the rest desired that the house might be Seperated & the Burgesses to be by themselves and to have a

---

36. John Boteler of Kent also received a writ but did not serve. His summons was a futile gesture by Leonard Calvert to woo a prominent Protestant supporter of William Claiborne.

Table 1. *Profile of elected assemblies, 1638/39–1659/60*

Assembly	Total members	Religion			Landownership (acres)					Education			
		Catholic	Protestant	Unknown	None	1–100	101–500	501+	Unknown	Well educated	Literate	Illiterate	Unknown
1638/39													
Special writs	6	5	1	0	0	0	2	3	1	5	0	0	1
Elected	9 (2)[a]	1 (2)[a]	5	3	2 (1)[a]	2	2	1	2 (1)[a]	1	1 (2)[a]	5	2
1640–41													
Special writs	6	6	0	0	0	0	1	3	2	4	2	0	0
Elected	13[b]	4	4	5	2	4	2	3	2	2	7	1	3
1642													
Special writs	9	6	0	3	0	0	2	3	4	6	3	0	0
Elected	10	1	6	3	0	5	3	2	0	0	3	3	4
1649													
Special writs	5	2	3	0	0	0	2	3	0	1	3	1	0
Elected	9	3	2	4	0	3	2	3	1	0	7	2	0
1650–51													
Upper house	9	3	6	0	0	0	2	7	0	3	5	1	0
Lower house	14 (1)[c]	3 (1)[c]	9	2	0	0	8	5 (1)[c]	1	0	7 (1)[c]	7	0
1654													
Elected	16 (2)[c]	0	16 (2)[c]	0	0	1	5	8 (2)[c]	2	0 (1)	16 (1)[c]	0	0
1657													
Elected	10	0	10	0	0	0	3	7	0	0	9	1	0
1658													
Upper house	8	3	5	0	0	0	1	7	0	4	3	1	0
Lower house	16	3	10	3	0	0	5	10	1	1	14	1	0
1659/60													
Upper house	8	3	4	1	0	0	1	7	0	4	3	1	0
Lower house	27 (1)[c]	2 (1)[c]	18	7	0	0	12	14	1 (1)[c]	0	24 (1)[c]	2	1

[a] Numbers in parentheses represent two additional freemen, Robert Clarke and Cuthbert Fenwick, who were not elected but claimed and received seats.

[b] Three men—Catholics John Lewger, Giles Brent, and Cuthbert Fenwick—sat in this assembly, both as elected members and by virtue of special writs, and are counted in both categories.

[c] Numbers in parentheses represent a delegate elected to fill a vacancy.

negative," but the governor refused.[37] Differences over the colony's defense policy apparently sparked this incendiary request. At the previous assembly a majority had voted that a proposed march against some Indians not be left to the discretion of the governor and council, and in the assembly before that a majority had also declined to provide the financial support sought by Leonard Calvert for such an expedition.[38] Opposition to higher taxes influenced the burgesses, but by 1641 religious tensions rendered some Protestants uneasy over the prospect of critical decisions regarding the use of the militia resting with the exclusively Catholic leadership.[39] In 1642, Vaughan and others also resented special writs going to nine men, who with the governor exactly matched the number of elected delegates. Previously, the burgesses had always comprised a substantial majority.

This assembly in 1642, though not implementing Vaughan's request, did move toward bicameralism in agreeing that a quorum should consist of ten members, of whom the governor and at least six elected delegates had to be present. Prior rules on a quorum had not differentiated between elected and nonelected members.[40] Later in this session, a delegate objected that a critical bill had not been approved "by the major part of Burgesses as it ought to be," but a careful review clarified that the rule had stipulated that a majority of the burgesses was necessary only for a legal house, not for passage of an act. The challenge itself reflected the sharpening awareness by some members that the legislature, although unicameral, nonetheless consisted of two bodies with quite separate allegiances.[41]

For many Marylanders, the model of Parliament with its House of Commons distinct from the House of Lords had greater relevance than the Durham assembly for a legislature in which several members present by virtue of their titles as lords of manors and privy councillors seemed a group apart from those individuals present by virtue of the votes of freemen. Division on bills by no means always fell along these lines, but the pattern generally held, and some vocal burgesses, in concluding that every bill should command a majority of the votes of the elected members before becoming law, were edging ever closer to the procedures of Parliament.

Explicit analogies to Parliament had been invoked as early as 1635 and, surprisingly, in the first instance in a pamphlet employed by the proprietor for promotional purposes.[42] However, the word "Parliament"

37. *Archives*, 1:130–31.
38. Ibid., 107, 118.
39. Ibid., 119; 4:35–38; Hughes, *History of the Society of Jesus*, Text, 1:539–47.
40. *Archives*, 1:131–32. On earlier practice, ibid., 91.
41. Ibid., 141.
42. Krugler, ed., *To Live Like Princes*, 37–38.

never appears in the charter itself, and Lord Baltimore and his immediate subordinates usually employed less suggestive language, such as "the general assembly." Nonetheless, many resident Marylanders quickly adopted the terminology of English politics that encouraged associations with the various rights, powers, and privileges of Parliament.[43]

The journal of the Assembly of 1637/38, the first gathering for which a full record survives, shows an unmistakably conscious effort to emulate Parliament. A majority of those present immediately claimed, like the members of Parliament, immunity from arrest during the period of the assembly's sitting, for both themselves and those for whom they held proxies. When the legislature adjourned for a few days, the freemen ruled "the priviledge of parlam'" temporarily void. Members adopted other customs of the House of Commons, among them the procedure of reading a bill three times on separate days before a final vote. Meeting times were similar, and members further determined that any one speaking should first uncover his head, as was done in Parliament. This assembly also established a bar, in keeping with the English practice, and assumed judicial functions, like Parliament, in trying a case of alleged piracy.[44]

Subsequent assemblies built upon this pattern. In 1638/39, a bill asserted possession of the same rights and privileges "as the house of Commons within the Realm of England at any time heretofore assembled in that Kingdom," and members launched their lengthy struggle to acquire control over the frequency and duration of meetings. Elections and representation should also occur, the assembly proposed that same year, "in the same manner and to all the same intents and purposes as the Burgesses of any burrough in England in the Parliament." However, neither these two bills nor thirty-one others ever received final approval, probably because Leonard Calvert opposed so strong an assertion of legislative initiative by members of the assembly. Meanwhile, the tendency to associate the local assembly with Parliament reached beyond the members to the general public itself. In 1641, for example, the freemen of Mattapanient Hundred asked a fellow colonist "to answer for us at the Parliament."[45]

Sensitively attuned to the latest developments in the struggles between the king and Parliament in England, freeman argued unsuccessfully in

43. Neither Cecilius nor Leonard Calvert is known to have used explicit parliamentary references. Proprietary deputy John Lewger, usually careful to refer only to "the General Assembly," did once speak of "such Parliament, or Assembly." See Hughes, *History of the Society of Jesus*, Documents, 1:161.
44. *Archives*, 1:1–24, especially 4–5, 8, 10 (quotation), 12, 13, 14, 16. On Parliament's practices and procedures, see J. E. Neale, *The Elizabethan House of Commons* (New Haven, Conn., 1950).
45. *Archives*, 1:32–33, 75, 81–82, 106 (quotation).

1641/42 that their own assembly could not be adjourned or prorogued without the "Consent of the house." Months earlier, Parliament had obtained the king's approval for legislation prohibiting the adjournment, prorogation, or dissolution of the current Parliament without its consent. Also conscious of the recently passed Triennial Act in England, the Assembly of 1642 actually succeeded, against the governor's wishes, to have laws in the colony remain in effect for only three years from the time of passage. Throughout the 1640s, the assertions of parliamentary parallels further escalated.[46]

Knowledge of these critical precedents arose from several sources. At least three and probably four influential members of these early assemblies were the sons of members of Parliament and no doubt had learned much about the legislature of England through discussions in their homes.[47] Several other men possessed sufficient education or experience to have an appreciable knowledge of parliamentary lore, now readily available within literate circles on both sides of the Atlantic. Some Marylanders undoubtedly had access to books, such as William Lambarde's *Notes on the Procedures and Privileges of the House of Commons* (1584), Sir Thomas Smith's *The Commonwealth of England: And the Manner and Government Thereof* (1640), and John Selden's *The Privileges of the Baronage of England* (1642).[48] The inventory for Thomas Adams, who sat in the Assembly of 1640–41 and was censured in October of 1640 "for some indecent speeches touching the Lord Proprietor," mentions a "small book of presidents [precedents]." Leonard Calvert's library contained at least thirteen volumes that presumably assisted in the proper conduct of duties. Inventories later in the century identify important volumes on government, and by 1681 assembly members definitely had sufficient resources for a "Serious Examination of the

46. Ibid., 117 (quotation), 177–80, 182–98 (body of laws); Samuel Rawson Gardiner, ed., *The Constitutional Documents of the Puritan Revolution, 1625–1660* (Oxford, 1951), 144–55, 158–59.
47. The ancestral members of Parliament included George Calvert, the father of Leonard; Sir William Cornwaleys (MP for Oxford, Suffolk, in 1614), the father of Thomas; James Hawley (MP for Andover in 1586), the father of Jerome; and Sir Edward Wintour (MP for Newport, Cornwall, in 1586 and Gloucester in 1589 and 1601), almost certainly the father of Robert. Thomas Cornwaleys's grandfather (MP for Norfolk in 1604) also served with George Calvert on the royal commission to Ireland in 1614.
48. Pocock, *The Ancient Constitution*; Hirst, *The Representative of the People?*; and Warren M. Billings, "English Legal Literature as a Source of Law and Legal Practice for Seventeenth Century Virginia," *Virginia Magazine of History and Biography*, 87 (1979), 403–16, discuss this literature.

best records and Authorities of the Customs and usages of the Commons house of England (the only Rule to walk by.")[49]

Marylanders learned within a matter of months of critical political developments in England. Information spread orally from ship captains and the continuing stream of new immigrants, as well as by imported "news. books" and "monthly Mercurys." Incidental comments in surviving records as well as explicit references in the assembly journals attest to an avid interest in the English political scene and similarly intensive debates in Maryland on many of the same subjects.[50]

The growing assertiveness of the elected members of Parliament in the 1640s in turn influenced the assembly in Maryland. Its delegates temporarily achieved one objective in 1646, when the provincial legislature sat in two separate houses, the lower chamber, composed only of elected representatives, regarding itself as a "whole house of Commons." Unfortunately, a partial journal does not indicate how and why this important change occurred. The next assembly, convened in 1647/48, returned to the one-house organization.[51]

The sense of a separate identity among the burgesses and of particular powers residing in the elected membership persisted in these years of political uncertainty. In the unicameral legislature of 1649, the first committee appears with its members drawn exclusively from the elected delegates.[52] The ultimate split occurred the following year, when the Assembly of 1650 officially organized as two houses, "to sit in two distinct roomes a part." The upper chamber consisted solely of members of the current council on special writs. The lower house contained only the elected representatives. Any legislation had to pass both houses before going to the governor for final approval. The proprietor actually found much to commend this division within the assembly, for in many ways the new arrangement appeased vocal representatives while still effectively protecting his interests; in a single-house legislature, Calvert potentially commanded only a minority of the votes and might be readily defeated,

---

49. Susan Rosenfield Falb, "Advice and Assent: The Development of the Maryland Assembly, 1635–1689" (Ph.D. diss., Georgetown University, 1976), 9–22, investigates the transatlantic exchange of ideas. She found 84 assemblymen serving before 1689 who owned books other than the Bible. On Adams, see *Archives*, 1:92, and the comment from the Assembly of 1681 (ibid., 7:123). By 1704, more sophisticated delegates were regularly consulting English laws and wanted copies of new acts of Parliament as soon as possible (ibid., 26:122, 152).

50. *Archives*, 5:278, 303–4, 319, 509–12: 10:38; 15:245–46; 17:31, 55, 56; 23:500.

51. Ibid., 1:208–10, 211–33, 239 (quotation). The separation in 1646 may have been influenced by its convenor Edward Hill, who had recently served as speaker in the bicameral legislature of Virginia.

52. Ibid., 237.

but through a separate upper house he was assured of another possible veto in addition to the governor's and his own separate negatives. In acquiescing, Lord Baltimore exemplified the strategy inherent in his father's maxim: "The Conquering Way sometimes is yielding."[53]

This institutionalizing of bicameralism roughly paralleled contemporary developments in the legislatures of three other English colonies. The assemblies of Barbados, Virginia, and Massachusetts also comprised two rather distinct groups sitting by virtue of a separate authority, although the social and religious differences were not as great as in Maryland. Bicameralism appeared in 1639 and 1643 in Barbados and Virginia, respectively, with a less precise division into two totally separate chambers than was to characterize the process in Massachusetts in 1644 and in Maryland.[54]

In important sessions of the 1650s, the Assembly of Maryland assumed that fundamental bicameral structure it would retain, with only a few exceptions, through the remainder of the colonial period.[55] Ironically, by this time the membership of the two houses actually differed socially and economically to a lesser extent than in earlier assemblies. More diversity now prevailed within each house in wealth, religious affiliation, educational attainment, and degree of previous political experience (see Table 1). Cecilius Calvert had been unable to maintain a truly distinctive council. Moreover, political circumstances at home and abroad had dictated the inclusion of more Protestants among the ranking officers of the colony. Consequently, in the upper houses of 1650–51, 1658, and 1659/60 non-Catholics comprised at least one-half of the members. The individuals invited by special writ to sit in these legislatures included several men of moderate wealth and low social origins. The rapid promotion of new immigrants with any appreciable affluence also meant the presence within this currently less exclusive political circle of several men with literally no previous experience in Maryland's governance. The predominance of such

53. Ibid., 272–73. George Calvert's remark is quoted in Krugler, "The Calvert Family," 382.
54. Kammen, *Deputyes & Libertyes*, 12, 22–23 (quotation), 27; Robert Emmet Wall, Jr., *Massachusetts Bay: The Crucial Decade, 1640–1650* (New Haven, Conn., 1972), 41–92. Considerable debate exists as to whether the lower house in Virginia actually sat regularly as a separate body before the 1680s. For the most recent opinion – that it was separate – see Jon Kukla, "Robert Beverley Assailed: Appellate Jurisdiction and the Problem of Bicameralism in Seventeenth Century Virginia," *Virginia Magazine of History and Biography*, 88 (1980), 415–29.
55. For organizational changes in Maryland, especially the evolution of the speaker's office, see *Archives*, 1:261, 273–74, 276, 277, and Donnell MacClure Owings, *His Lordship's Patronage. Offices of Profit in Colonial Maryland* (Baltimore, 1953), 137. Chapters 2 and 4 below discuss the unicameral legislatures that briefly met between 1654 and 1658 under the commonwealth government, the rebellious Assembly of 1659/60, and the Convention of the Protestant Associators from 1689 to 1692.

novices contrasted sharply with the profiles of contemporary councils and upper houses in Massachusetts, Barbados, and Virginia.[56]

Meanwhile, a larger pool of available talent had emerged in the colony for service in the lower house. For example, at least twelve of the sixteen elected members of the Assembly of 1658 currently possessed more than 400 acres, while none owned less than 200. Only one burgess was even of questionable literacy. At least six delegates had held some previous office of importance, such as justice of the peace. The subsequent Assembly of 1659/60 contained an even more experienced membership. Among the twenty-eight delegates, at least sixteen had previously served as a justice, four had officiated as sheriff, and eight had held a militia office. Fourteen men owned more than 500 acres and no one possessed less than 150 acres. Just two representatives were illiterate, and most members demonstrated a greater degree of education than simply the ability to sign their names.

Such characteristics among the membership, with a few individuals in particular beginning to contribute some modest degree of continuity and experience to the assembly, were starting to affect noticeably the conduct of business within the lower house. Meanwhile, the legislature had survived two tumultuous decades and in the process had evolved many of the distinctive organizational features it was to carry through the next century. Elected delegates, although meeting now in a separate chamber, had not yet achieved a truly independent voice or effective representative government. Many battles lay ahead, with victory in many respects still half a century away. Nonetheless, the early settlers of Maryland had laid a substantial foundation in the face of considerable obstacles.

56. Jordan, "Maryland's Privy Council," 68–71. Most councillors in Virginia had resided ten to twenty-five years before appointment and virtually all had held prior offices. See Billings, "Growth of Political Institutions," 239–40; see also the works cited in note 32.

2

"Divers Occurences & Difficulties"

Wee being bound therunto by the Lawes both of God and man Doe recognize and acknowledge your Lordship's just title and right unto this province by the grant and donation of the late King Charles of England . . . and doe allsoe recognize and acknowledge your Lordshipp to bee true and absolute Lord and Proprietary of this province. And doe humbly submitt unto all power jurisdiction and Authority given granted and confirmed unto your Lordship and your heires in and by the said Grant and donation, and doe hereby submitt and obleige us our heires and posterityes for ever until the last dropp of our blood bee spent, to mayntaine uphold and defend your Lordship and your heires Lords and proprietarys of this Province in all the Royall Rights Jurisdictions Authorities and preheminences given granted and confirmed unto your lordship by the said grant and donation . . . .

An Act of Recognition of the Lawfull and undoubted right and title
of the Right Honble Cecilius Lord Baron of Baltimore, 1650

Forasmuch as the strength of the Lord Proprietary of this Province doth consist in the love and affection of his people on which hee doth resolve to relye upon all occasions for his supplyes both by sea and Land not doubting of their duty and Assistance upon all Just and Hono^ble occasions, Bee it therfore enacted by the Lord Proprietary with the Advice and Assent of the upper and lower house of this present Assembly that noe Subsidies ayde Customes taxes or impositions shall hereafter bee layd assessed, leavyed or imposed upon the freemen of this Province or on theire Merchandize Goods or Chattles without the Consent and Approbation of the freemen of this Province their Deputyes or the Major parte of them, first had and declared in a Generall Assembly of this Province.

An Act Against raysing of Money Within the said Province Without
Consent of the Assembly, 1650

Cecilius Calvert presided over the new province of Maryland as "absolute Lord and Proprietary" for four decades. This continuity of leadership, extraordinary for any seventeenth century colony, enabled him to accumulate the experience, connections, and stature in imperial affairs that served well the family's venture in the New World. Lord Baltimore's longevity as proprietor is somewhat misleading, however, with respect to the internal development of Maryland, since he always remained in England and across the Atlantic no individual of comparable ability spans the early decades with such permanence and effectiveness. Although Calvert's extended tenure proved critical for protecting the colony in its external relations, the turnover of administrative deputies less astute than the absentee proprietor more profoundly influenced the evolution of government and politics within Maryland.

There, Leonard Calvert and his successors as governor directly confronted the rising demands of the colonists and their frequent disagreements. Occasionally concurring with local wishes and other times forced by circumstances to acquiesce or take sides on divisive issues, these officials presided over a population that placed increasing emphasis on the general assembly's role in governance and insistence on the people's possession of all the traditional liberties and privileges of Englishmen. During those years when the colony was without an effective proprietary deputy, the freemen particularly sought a stronger voice in decision making.

Lord Baltimore was fortunate in having his brother Leonard serve as governor for most of the initial thirteen years of settlement.[1] Only twenty-seven at the time of appointment, he demonstrated a remarkable poise and ability for one in so unenviable a position. He had to respond forcefully to a variety of unexpected situations, yet Lord Baltimore delegated few discretionary powers. Moreover, the proprietor's precise directives were not always feasible to implement. Leonard Calvert had to obey instructions conceived in remote England or to improvise alternatives that might offend his superior. The governor and his successors had to learn by experience how flexible they could be in deviating from proprietary orders. Such challenges had emerged as early as the transatlantic voyage, when Calvert, whether under duress or by personal conviction, violated his brother's explicit instructions by changing the ship's course of travel, by permitting Catholics to worship openly, and by subordinating proprietary concerns to the economic interests of some colonists.[2]

Divergence from orders occurred frequently thereafter, but Calvert also learned that such actions could greatly anger the proprietor. The governor's instructions made no provision for calling an assembly, although the charter clearly acknowledged a role for such a body in the colony. Responding most likely to pressures from the freemen, Calvert convened a legislature in 1634/35, which passed the first laws for Maryland. Lord Balti-

1. No good biography of Leonard Calvert exists, but see Papenfuse et al., eds., *Biographical Dictionary*; Clayton Colman Hall, *The Lords Baltimore and Their Maryland Palatinate* (Baltimore, 1904); and John Bailey Calvert Nicklin, "The Calvert Family," *Maryland Historical Magazine*, 16 (1921) 50–59, 189–204.
2. *Calvert Papers, Number One*, 131–40, and Hall, ed., *Narratives*, 16–23, 29–45.

more, upon receiving word of this body, promptly disallowed all its statutes and plainly reiterated the limited role any future assembly should play
in Maryland. To make certain Leonard Calvert grasped the seriousness of
his breach of trust, the proprietor also dispatched John Lewger to Maryland as his personal agent and the colony's secretary.[3]

Lewger brought from Cecilius Calvert a draft set of laws. If the colony
wanted legislation, the proprietor would provide it from England. He
desired the assembly, among other business, to enact restraints on the
activities of the Jesuits in Maryland, to sanction less generous provisions
for subsequent immigrants, to revise trading privileges in ways that
would benefit the proprietor, to impose quit rents due annually on all
land patented in the colony, to assure the Calverts of undisputed control
over all land transactions in the province, and to pass local laws addressing major criminal offenses. Lord Baltimore, not wishing English legislation automatically to apply in Maryland, especially penal laws that
would affect Catholics, preferred a selective local enactment of statutes,
particularly those concerning criminal behavior.

When Leonard Calvert dutifully summoned a second assembly in late
January of 1637/38 to approve the proposed code of laws, he set in
motion an angry struggle within the colony. Factions rapidly coalesced
around the powerful personalities of Lewger and Thomas Cornwaleys.
These two men staked out firm positions on either side of the governor,
who tried to moderate their extremes. Especially in dispute were the
questions of whether the freemen or the Calverts were to draw up the
laws of Maryland and whether English laws, civil and criminal, should
transfer to the colony.[4]

Lewger, who had recently resigned from an Anglican curacy and con-
verted to Catholicism, depended totally for his livelihood upon Lord
Baltimore, a former classmate at Oxford. Calvert found Lewger's views
and impressive talents particularly helpful in promoting proprietary interests and especially in addressing delicate church-state problems in Maryland. The two friends belonged to that wing of the Catholic church that
sought a compromise with Protestants and supported limits on the claims
to temporal authority of the more militant papists.[5] By the late 1630s, the

3. The first assembly met on February 26, 1634/35. No journal survives, but a later
    reference to this assembly mentions "wholesome lawes and ordinances then made"
    (*Archives*, 1:23). For Lord Baltimore's response, ibid., 3:50–51.
4. Ibid., 3:51; 1:1–24. Lois Green Carr, "Extension of Empire: English Law in Early
    Colonial Maryland," paper presented at Conference on Maryland, A Product of Two
    Worlds, St. Mary's City, Maryland, May 17–20, 1984, provocatively discusses some of
    these differences.
5. Papenfuse et al., eds., *Biographical Dictionary*; Hughes, *History of the Society of Jesus*,
    Text, 1:350–62.

evolving role of the Jesuits was disturbing the proprietor. His father, by exempting the province from English laws that restricted the rights of religious bodies and other corporations to hold property, had provided special opportunities for the Catholic church in Maryland. Cecilius Calvert probably always favored a tighter rein on Catholic priests; certainly, by 1637 he was resolved to control the zealotry of the Jesuits and to limit their economic and political role in the colony. Through investments and rights assigned by other settlers, the priests already held claims to at least 28,500 acres, and they had expected this land to be exempted from any financial, military, or other obligations. Moreover, emboldened by their greater freedom abroad, the Jesuits were aggressively proselytizing among both the Protestants and the Indians and were accepting gifts of land directly from the natives. These activities showed a flagrant disregard for proprietary instructions to keep the practice of religion a private matter, and the mission's independent relations with neighboring tribes threatened to undercut the governor's authority. Lord Baltimore, like most prominent English Catholics of his day, was accustomed to a more cautious, subordinate priesthood. Worried about the suspicious attitudes harbored by uncompromising Protestants in the mother country and nearby Virginia, the proprietor resented deeply any threat the Jesuits might pose for the survival of Maryland and for the Calverts' undisputed control within the province.[6]

Baltimore was currently lobbying to protect his charter from attacks by its numerous Protestant opponents. An oath of allegiance to the king, stipulated in instructions to the first settlers, had been one tactic to defuse such opposition, and Calvert further concluded that a demonstration of effective control over the Jesuits was also clearly advisable. Lewger almost certainly drafted the proposed laws for Lord Baltimore and definitely worked industriously for their enactment in Maryland. His presence particularly alarmed many Catholics, for Lewger was developing a following among numerous Protestants whose antipathy to the Jesuits he cleverly encouraged.[7]

Cornwaleys, Lewger's strongest opponent, was in contrast beholden to

6. Ibid., 236–343, and Documents, Vol. 1, *passim.*, provide the most complete discussion of the Calverts' religious ideas and the early activities of the Jesuits in Maryland. See also John D. Krugler's three essays, "The Calvert Family, Catholicism and Court Politics," "Lord Baltimore, Roman Catholics and Toleration," and " 'With Promise of Liberty in Religion': The Catholic Lords Baltimore and Toleration in Seventeenth-Century Maryland," *Maryland Historical Magazine*, 79 (1984), 21–43.
7. Hall, ed., *Narratives*, 20 (oath). Cornwaleys expressed concern after the assembly lest Lewger "proves not tooe Stiff A maintayner of his own opinions" and added that the secretary was "Somewhat tooe forward in Suggesting new businesses for his owne imployment" (*Calvert Papers, Number One*, 179).

no one, including the proprietor. Descended from a family whose status paralleled that of the Calverts, Cornwaleys had invested heavily in Maryland. His wealth and abilities made him indisputably after Leonard Calvert the most powerful man in the colony. Both as an ambitious entrepreneur whose trading interests were endangered by the proposed legislation and as an ardent defender of the Jesuits, Cornwaleys found ample cause to oppose many of the bills placed before the second assembly. Most likely, he had been a driving force in the prior legislative gathering.[8]

When the freemen actually met to act on Lord Baltimore's laws, Cornwaleys quickly marshaled support and defeated the proposed code by a vote of 37 to 14 when it was considered as a whole. His tactic forced the governor to allow the assembly to take up the bills individually and eventually both to amend and to initiate legislation. In subsequent voting on numerous procedural and substantive issues, the membership sharply divided into the camps led by Lewger and Cornwaleys; both they and the governor engaged in adroit manuevering over the next two months. Forty bills finally received substantial support. The text of only one statute survives, the Act for Attainder of William Claiborne, so it is impossible to determine the exact nature of this voluminous legislation or the degree to which it finally diverged from the proprietor's drafts. The substance of at least some of his proposals was salvaged, as several later accounts clearly argued. Leonard Calvert reported that despite earnest efforts to have the code passed as instructed, "he could not effect it, there were so many things unsuitable to the peoples good and no ways conducing to your profitt." Some of the laws managed to get by, and others newly drafted, the governor explained, were just as good.[9]

The legislation addressed concerns that were characteristic of a young colony. Acts involved land issues more than any other subject, but statutes also treated questions of defense, the economy, criminal codes, allegiance to the Crown, support of the proprietor, and the liberties of the people. There is no indication of any time limitation imposed on these laws. Clearly, several statutes implemented some of the important changes that

---

8. Papenfuse et al., eds., *Biographical Dictionary*; Sebastian F. Streeter, *Papers Relating to the Early History of Maryland*, Maryland Historical Society, Fund Publication No. 9, (Baltimore, 1876), 124–217; and Harry Wright Newman, *The Flowering of the Maryland Palatinate* (Washington, D.C., 1961), 188–89.
9. For contemporary accounts of this session, see letters from Leonard Calvert, Thomas Copley, and Thomas Cornwaleys to Cecilius Calvert, all written in April 1638, in *Calvert Papers, Number One*, 157–69, 169–81, and 182–86. This assembly has interested many historians, particularly Streeter, *Papers*, 15–92; Bradley T. Johnson, *The Foundation of Maryland and the Origins of the Act Concerning Religion of April 21, 1649*, Maryland Historical Society, Fund Publication No. 18 (Baltimore, 1883), 36–55; Hughes, *History of the Society of Jesus*, Text, 1:380–427, and Elihu S. Riley, *A History of the General Assembly of Maryland, 1635–1904* (Baltimore, 1905).

Cecilius Calvert had announced in his new Conditions of Plantation in 1636.[10] The original settlers, like all subsequent immigrants, now owed rent on their land and had other extensive obligations either newly imposed or previously misunderstood. These new provisions meant, for example, that some individuals might have to relinquish acreage already in their possession, and everyone had to accept certain restrictions on any future sale or disposal of land. The law for support of the proprietor also reversed an earlier guarantee to the initial investors of free trade with the Indians, thus denying several colonists an enterprise that many considered essential to their well-being, especially since barter in certain commodities was the only means of local exchange. Much of this legislation obviously restricted the Jesuits' activities and influence in the province.

Cornwaleys immediately conveyed his disgruntlement to the proprietor. The trading restrictions hurt both his pride and his purse; he boasted that "few in the Colony will deny but that the Generallety was les in debt, necessary Goods more Plentifull and better Cheape" under his predominant control of the trade with the Indians and his furnishing of essential supplies to other colonists. Cornwaleys had never been much interested in agriculture; "Yr Lop: knowes I came not hither for toe plant Tobacco," he reminded Calvert in 1638, and vowed that if he had no other way to support himself but by "Planting this Stincking Weede of America, I must desert the Place." Cornwaleys noted that the new laws explicitly contradicted the original conditions under which he had immigrated. The angry councillor reserved his strongest words, however, for the proprietor's and the assembly's incursions on the rights and liberties of the Catholic church, as Cornwaleys perceived them. "Security of contiens was the first Condition that I expected from this Government," he asserted; "I will rather sacrifice myself and all I have in defense of God's honor and his Churches right than willingly Consent toe anything that may not stand with the Good Contiens of a Real Catholick."[11]

In battling for the rights of the Jesuits, other settlers, and himself, Cornwaleys became the primary challenger of Lord Baltimore's stipulations about the functioning of the assembly and the legislation it might pass. Opposition from so formidable a figure created a climate in which less powerful men might also venture to resist the Calverts, and Cornwaleys actively sought their support. He turned especially to the "Real Catholicks" who might similarly defend the rights of the Catholic church

10.   For these Conditions of Plantation, see *Archives*, 3:47–48.
11.   *Calvert Papers, Number One*, 169–81. Leonard Calvert, aware of Cornwaleys's feelings and his important economic contributions, urged Lord Baltimore to accommodate the councillor with at least some portion of the Indian trade (ibid., 190, 197, 209; *Archives*, 3:57).

against encroachment by the secular government. He received valuable support from Cuthbert Fenwick, his former servant who later became a trustee for the Jesuits, and from Robert Clarke, another former servant, whose proxies for the three Jesuit priests were denied by the Assembly of 1637/38, thereby establishing the principle of full exclusion of clergy from seats in the colonial assembly. The presence of both Fenwick and Clarke at the Assembly of 1638/39, as freemen not assenting to the election of Thomas Gerard and Francis Gray from St. Mary's Hundred, constituted a continuing effort to dilute probable votes against the interests of the Jesuits in that important third assembly.[12]

Some Catholics hesitated to oppose the Calverts too strenuously. Thomas Greene, for example, typified several coreligionists who voted against many of the proprietary bills but nonetheless resigned themselves to accepting most enacted measures. Over the next decade Greene proved to be the bellweather of moderate Catholic sentiment. As Protestant challenges mounted in England and America, he would finally become more assertive in his Catholic views and eventually oppose the proprietor. In 1638, however, he was not so outspoken.[13]

Other colonists proved more susceptible to the Jesuits' arguments that good Catholics could not lend their votes to legislation that attacked or restricted the church without in the process incurring serious penalties, perhaps even excommunication. The papal bull *In Coenae Domini*, issued annually on Holy Thursday, forbade the citing of ecclesiastical persons before a lay tribunal, prohibited the imposition of taxes on ecclesiastical property without permission of the Pope, and proscribed all judges who took part in any capital or criminal causes against ecclesiastics. Father Thomas Copley outlined the implications of *Bulla Coena* in a letter to Lord Baltimore of April 3, 1638, and it was much discussed among Marylanders.[14]

Lewger, finding such arguments gaining support among Catholic freemen, prepared a series of cases addressing the responsibilities of local magistrates and assemblymen in the "divers occurences & difficulties which we meete with here." He particularly discussed the proper role of a good Catholic "in a country (as this is) newly planted, and depending wholly upon England for its subsistence, where there is not (nor cannot be until England be reunited to the Church), any ecclesiastical discipline established, . . . nor Spiritual Courts erected, nor the Canon Laws ac-

12. *Archives*, 1:1–84, especially 5, 29, 32.
13. *Calvert Papers, Number One*, 159; also, *Archives*, 1:5, 8, 19, 22, 32; Newman, *Flowering of the Maryland Palatinate*, 213–18.
14. Hughes, *History of the Society of Jesus*, Text, 1:436–37; *Calvert Papers, Number One*, 166.

cepted, nor ordinary or other Ecclesiastical persons admitted (as such), nor Catholick religion publickly allowed; and whereas three partes of the people in foure (at least) are hereticks." Lewger's cases circulated among church officials as the controversy grew in Maryland.[15]

As Lewger astutely noted, scarcely a fourth of the colony's population was Catholic, and despite the Jesuits' boasts of success in converting Protestants, the proportion of non-Catholics was steadily increasing. Not even a united Catholic minority could proceed as it might wish with respect to Protestants, given the current climate of official and private opinion on both sides of the Atlantic. As it was, that Catholic minority was divided in sentiment, and whenever religious problems arose in Maryland, proprietary authorities always sided with the Protestant position.[16]

The submission of Kent Island in 1637/38 added to the population more non-Catholics with no cause to embrace Lord Baltimore or his policies, but neither were these Protestants disposed to favor the Jesuits. Consequently, both factions of the Catholic minority were bidding for the support and votes of Protestants, a political reality that further encouraged a more active debate within the assembly and a more assertive role for the legislature. Protestants did not consistently adopt a common position, but usually aligned with Cornwaleys's faction on procedural questions, especially in favoring legislative initiative in the assembly, and with the proprietary group on many specific bills. For example, most Protestants welcomed restrictions on Jesuits and wanted the mission to accept the same obligations placed on other landholders. Protestants, wishing a broader transfer of English laws, responded most anxiously to the bills affecting perceived liberties or extending powers that were too broad and discretionary to the colony's almost exclusively Catholic officeholders.[17]

Protestants lacked a natural leader in these early assemblies. In that vacuum, some individuals assumed a greater prominence than they might ordinarily have commanded. Francis Gray, a carpenter and one of the few Protestants of moderate wealth, served in three assemblies, but thereafter the discontented representative moved to Virginia. Robert Vaughan, a former servant of Leonard Calvert, had a more lasting impact. He eventually served in at least eight legislatures, a remarkable accomplish-

---

15. Hughes, *History of the Society of Jesus*, Documents, 1:158–61. See also Johnson, *Foundation of Maryland*, 69–80; *Calvert Papers, Number One*, 164–65.
16. On Jesuit proselytizing, see Hall, ed., *Narratives*, 119–20, 130. Krugler, "Lord Baltimore, Roman Catholics and Toleration," 59–64, and *Archives*, 4:35–39 and 1:119, explore relations between Catholics and Protestants.
17. Andrews, *Colonial Period*, 2:302–7 and Craven, *Southern Colonies*, 196–98, 202–3, discuss Kent and the situation there. On voting patterns, see *Archives*, 1:9, 11, 22, 92, 93, 94, 95, 137, 139, and Falb, "Proxy Voting in Early Maryland Assemblies," 217–25.

ment for the period, and held numerous positions of responsibility, culminating in appointment to the council in 1648. Although an ardent defender of Lord Baltimore, Vaughan still did not hesitate to oppose the governor or Lewger on particular issues, as he did in vigorously defending the rights of the freemen, especially to initiate legislation, and in early efforts to create a two-house legislature.[18]

Amid this growing divisiveness, Leonard Calvert worried lest the various factions be forced into adopting a treasonous position. He worked assiduously to effect compromises and to contain discontents within manageable boundaries. For example, Calvert implemented his brother's policy against the influential Jesuits less rigidly than Lord Baltimore desired. Regarding as unwise some of the proposed legislation periodically forwarded to America, the governor occasionally encouraged attempts to defeat the bills. He allowed some initiative within the assembly and held firmly only to what he considered critical issues or procedures. Calvert patiently defended his actions in correspondence with the proprietor and sympathetically represented the actions of most dissident colonists. The governor perceived the serious threat to local peace posed by Lord Baltimore's program, a theme that he, the Jesuits, and Cornwaleys all stressed quite effectively in their letters to England. Leonard Calvert failed, however, to appreciate the mounting external threats to the colony; not until he returned to England for consultation with Lord Baltimore in 1643 did the governor fully comprehend the pressures behind the proprietor's attempts to curb the Jesuits and the Catholic church in Maryland.[19]

In these struggles, Cecilius Calvert continued to disapprove any acts passed by the assembly. The legislation of 1637/38 probably died because of his opposition to the amending of bills and the initiating of new laws by the assembly and his concurrent negotiations with the Catholic church. Poor phrasing of the laws may also have influenced the proprietor's position. Cornwaleys had advised Lord Baltimore to be "more wary in Confirmeing then wee have beene wise in Proposeing," and Father Copley had reported that some colonists doubted the validity of the laws because the procedures followed in passing them seemed questionable.[20]

Lord Baltimore sternly instructed the next assembly to ensure passage of the original portfolio of bills, unamended. However, a new commission to Leonard Calvert did permit the governor to approve laws not

18. Papenfuse et al., eds., *Biographical Dictionary*; see also *Archives*, 3:59–60, 76, 95, 127, 198.
19. *Calvert Papers, Number One*, 157–211 (especially 158) and *Archives*, Vols. 1 and 3, *passim.*, provide the basic information for the years of Leonard Calvert's leadership. Later, he did pursue a more vigorous policy against the Jesuits. See Hughes, *History of the Society of Jesus*, Text, 1:546–47.
20. *Archives*, 3:50–51; *Calvert Papers, Number One*, 161, 171 (quotation).

originating with the proprietor, so long as these acts were not contrary to the laws of England. Calvert was not to employ this power casually. Accordingly, the legislation considered by the third proprietary assembly appears to have been Lord Baltimore's code minus its provisions on manors and landholdings.[21]

This first elected legislature convened on February 25, 1638/39, at St. John's, the home of Secretary Lewger.[22] After organizing, the members approved "An Act for Establishing the house of Assembly and the Laws to be made therein." It called for an electoral model of government, with the burgesses "to supply the places of all the freemen consenting or subscribing to such their election in the same manner and to all the same intents and purposes as the Burgesses of any borough in England and the Parlyament." Any acts passed and approved by the lieutenant general would have the same force as if Lord Baltimore and all the freemen had been present and voting for the legislation. The assembly then considered thirty-six bills that because of persisting differences never passed the required third reading. To salvage something from the meeting, the delegates on the last day approved "An Act ordering certain Laws for the Government of this Province." This ordinance incorporated the substance of eleven of the earlier bills plus two or three points not readily identifiable in the previously considered legislation. The act was to endure until the end of the next assembly or for only three years if no assembly were called sooner. These actions constituted still another rebuff to the proprietary code, and the new limitation reflected a clever parliamentary maneuver to expand the power of the assembly by ensuring another meeting soon.[23]

The third and fourth paragraphs of the makeshift statute, loosely borrowing language from Magna Carta, promised to the "Holy Church" within the province, to the "Lord Proprietor," and to the inhabitants of Maryland all of their respective "rights and liberties." The phrasing concerning the church and English rights was sufficiently enigmatic to satisfy all parties. Colonists were to take an oath of allegiance to the king. There were loose provisions for judicial business and the maintenance of law and order, and Lewger acquired oversight of testamentary matters. Other portions briefly addressed questions of defense, a fee schedule for services, settlement of just debts, the planting of tobacco and corn, and a

21. *Archives*, 1:27, 31; 3:51 (commission); *Calvert Papers, Number One*, 187.

22. Garry Wheeler Stone, "St. John's: Archeological Questions and Answers," *Maryland Historical Magazine*, 69 (1974), 146–68, discusses this site of several early assemblies.

23. *Archives*, 1:25–84 (journal of this assembly), especially 82 (quotation); Thomas Bacon, ed., *The Laws of Maryland, at Large with Proper Indexes . . .* (Annapolis, Md., 1765), Acts 1638, Chaps. 1–2.

customs duty on exported tobacco. Finally, any subsequent assembly was to consist of "the Lieuten' General & Secretary (or his Deputie) and Gentlemen Summoned by Speciall writt & one or two Burgesses out of every hundred (at the choice of the freemen)."[24]

It is unclear what transpired further at this assembly, beyond the obvious refusal of the membership to enact the proprietor's laws as drafted, and at least four burgesses even opposed the general ordinance. Among the bills introduced had been several defining crimes and punishments, and others highly objectionable to the Jesuits – bills affecting marriages, oaths to the proprietor, land claims of the Catholic church, and the rights of priests to "travel freely among the Indians doing missionary work." The influence of Catholics in defeating these measures seems unmistakable. Father Copley later sent his Jesuit superiors an account of the assembly; Provincial General Edward Knott responded in delight on "that state of tranquillity which has ensued on the rejection of the laws by the delegates, as well the uprightness of that magistrate, who desiring to be reckoned a Catholic will, I trust, determine on no measure against ecclesiastics without referring to the Chief Pastor."[25]

The next assembly convened in October of 1640. An elected body in accordance with the ordinance of 1638/39, it too gathered at St. John's. The orders of procedure adopted by this meeting demonstrate a growing sophistication and increasing adherence to parliamentary practices. For example, in case of a tie vote, the members now determined that the measure under consideration would not pass. In the previous assembly, under similar circumstances, the side on which the governor voted had prevailed. The assembly clearly was attempting to restrict the power of the chief executive within the legislature.[26]

This session was also contentiously divided, most bills failing to gain majority support or suffering Leonard Calvert's ultimate objection. The governor's vote within the assembly had been rendered no more powerful than the voice of another member, but he retained the right of veto as Lord Baltimore's principal deputy. The members and governor eventually agreed on ten acts. Most noteworthy was the statute that again enigmatically guaranteed the church "all her Rights liberties and Franchises wholy and without Blemish." Other laws pertained to less controversial issues

24. *Archives*, 1:83–84. The phrase in Magna Carta says "that the English Church shall be free, and shall have her rights entire, and her liberties inviolate." The Maryland statute read, "Holy Churches within this Province shall have all her rights and liberties."
25. Quoted in Hughes, *History of the Society of Jesus*, Text, 1:458. See also Hughes's discussion of this assembly (ibid., 449–58).
26. *Archives*, 1:85–99, covers this session. On previous procedure in the case of ties, ibid., 33.

such as fencing, corn crops, and clothes due to servants at the conclusion of their indentured terms. No legislation addressed courts or criminal jurisdiction.[27]

Again, Lewger had most consistently advocated the proprietary position, for even Leonard Calvert had failed to support a proposed Act on Greater Crymes. In the temporary absence of Cornwaleys, then in England, Giles Brent had assumed the mantle of leader of the opposition. Brent had arrived in Maryland in 1638 with his brother and two sisters, all devout Catholics from a prominent English family who became substantial landowners in the colony. Brent had quickly won preferment to the posts of treasurer and commander of Kent Island, but the proprietor learned from this assembly that he could not totally depend upon this influential colonist's support either.[28]

A second session, with fewer delegates attending in an effort to reduce costs, met the following August. The governor again encountered poor luck in gaining approval of key bills. One for confirmation of his lordship's patent was denied by all but Calvert and Lewger, who secured only one additional vote for a bill that would have authorized a military expedition against some Indians. Three acts did pass, one regarding runaway servants, one establishing a standard of measures, and finally an act on causes testamentary, introduced by Brent and opposed by Lewger. These statutes, like most of those passed in 1640, were to be in effect for two years only.[29]

Four successive legislative gatherings had declined to approve the major bills proposed by Lord Baltimore. A majority of freemen had withstood pressures to endorse the princely powers claimed by the proprietor or to enact without amendment his proposed laws. A majority of colonists would neither pass local statutes concerning major crimes nor any legislation that would restrict the rights and privileges of the Catholic church otherwise protected by the charter. A frustrated Lord Baltimore now resorted to more arbitrary means of accomplishing his objectives. For example, he initiated measures to have secular clergy replace the recalcitrant Jesuits in Maryland and instructed his brother to grant them no more land patents.[30]

27. Ibid., 96 (quotation) and 96–99, for text of the other acts.
28. Papenfuse et al., eds., *Biographical Dictionary*, and files on the Brents, Legislative History Project, Hall of Records.
29. *Archives*, 1:101–10; Bernard C. Steiner, *Maryland During the English Civil Wars*, Part 1, Johns Hopkins University Studies, No. 24 (Baltimore, 1906), 18.
30. Hughes, *History of the Society of Jesus*, Text, 1:477–501, on the proprietor's relations with the Jesuits and his new actions. The governor, on orders, had already seized the Jesuits' mission at Mattapany, a gift from the Patuxent Indians; it later became the residence of the third Lord Baltimore.

New Conditions of Plantation followed in November of 1641. The first four paragraphs once more reduced the size of land grants and doubled the annual rents due to the proprietor. New sections applied the law of mortmain to Maryland and called for colonists to take a special oath of allegiance. If implemented, these provisions would immediately deprive the Jesuit mission of all land previously acquired from the Indians or from other colonists, would threaten other property claimed by the priests through their own headrights, and would frustrate any attempts to disobey the proprietor or threaten his authority.[31]

Lord Baltimore presented these measures to Catholic officials in England, while Lewger and Leonard Calvert disclosed them privately to the Jesuits and other individuals in Maryland. The proprietor and his deputies were worried about possible threats of excommunication under the terms of the *Bulla Coena*; proprietary actions had already seriously alienated members of the Calvert family in England. Negotiations quickly floundered, and during this impasse, only the first four paragraphs of the revised Conditions of Plantation were made public in the colony.[32]

An exasperated Lord Baltimore now refused permission for any Jesuit replacements or new personnel to travel to Maryland until church officials endorsed his latest policies. In a letter to Leonard Calvert the proprietor poured out his increasing animus against the Catholic clergy, complaining that the Jesuits were amassing a "greate deale of Land" from the Indians and railing against their other activities. Baltimore's writing had then been interrupted by the arrival of news of still further Jesuit successes in immigrating to Maryland without his permission and of the governor's approval in 1641 of the Jesuits' placing some land in trust with a layman. Resuming the letter two days later, the proprietor wrote in even less temperate tones, referring sarcastically to the clergy and expressing a wish for the "expulsion of such an enemy."[33]

Shortly after receiving this angry letter, Leonard Calvert journeyed to England to confer personally with his brother on the religious issue and the dangerous splits it was promoting in Maryland. In three assemblies over the past seven months, Protestants had displayed heightened impatience with the dominance of Catholics and the absence of tangible support for the religious endeavors of non-Catholics. It was in these meetings that Robert Vaughan and other Protestants had displayed such a keen awareness of contemporary parliamentary developments, pressed for

31. Ibid., Documents, 1:162–68.
32. *Archives*, 3:99–101 (for version released in the colony); Hughes, *History of the Society of Jesus*, Text, 1:501–21.
33. Hughes, *History of the Society of Jesus*, Text, 1:527–50; *Calvert Papers, Number One*, 211–20.

separate houses and for control over the frequency of meetings and their adjournment, and formed the first committees of grievances.[34]

The continuing debate through these assemblies – indeed, the primary impetus for so many legislatures in so short a period – was a proposed expedition against the Susquehannah Indians, which Governor Calvert greatly desired but the majority of members opposed. Anxious to avoid a more burdensome levy, they explicitly did not want any expedition left solely to the discretion of the governor and the council. Calvert asserted that the decision whether to march against the Indians was his, not the assembly's, but he tacitly acknowledged a need for the legislature to approve the funding. Finally, freemen at the general meeting in September of 1642 proved more amenable and despite the opposition of Cornwaleys passed two acts, one providing for the desired expedition and a second providing for defense in case of an invasion. When Calvert issued a proclamation four months later for the actual expedition, he sought to gain further support by appointing Cornwaleys to head the expedition and by promising that the proprietor would cover all costs except for the soldiers' pay.[35]

Calvert regretted having to leave the colony in the spring of 1643 with "divers jealousies and feares abroad." He had vetoed much of the legislation passed at these three meetings, and his primary subordinates – Lewger, Cornwaleys, and Giles Brent – were unwilling to work cooperatively in the governor's absence. Lewger, the most loyal councillor, was too widely disliked to be an effective acting governor. Cornwaleys refused to take an oath as councillor under a necessary new commission. Although Brent had recently been suspended from his offices and charged by Lewger with disloyalty, Calvert saw no alternative to naming Brent, albeit reluctantly, as deputy chief executive in the governor's absence. The prospects were not encouraging.[36]

Brent officiated through the autumn of 1644. During his tumultuous tenure, disputes over English politics further polarized the population. Some colonists, Brent among them, staunchly upheld the cause of King

34. *Archives*, 1:111–98, cover the sessions of March 21–23, 1641/42, July 18 to August 2, 1642, and September 5–13, 1642. Maryland still had only Catholic places of worship at this time, although Protestants had limited use of one of those chapels. Hughes, *History of the Society of Jesus*, Text, 1:539–41.
35. *Archives*, 1:118, 130–31, 139, 171, 174, 179, 180, 182, 196–98 (acts); 3:128 (proclamation). Cornwaleys complained about the exemption of Leonard Calvert and his servants from the levy and was also angry over the Calverts' treatment of the Jesuits and himself regarding some transfer of property and protested bills of exchange. In 1644, Cornwaleys finally carried his grievances to court (Hughes, *History of the Society of Jesus*, Text, 1:544–45).
36. Calvert had left Maryland by April 15, 1643 (*Archives*, 3:124–25, 128, 130–31; 1:179; 4:125–64.

Charles; others, including Cornwaleys and Catholic councillor James Neale, supported the parliamentary party and, like Lord Baltimore, now accepted the need for some moderation on the part of Catholics in Maryland. Brent precipitated a crisis in January of 1643/44 with the attempted arrest of Richard Ingle, a Protestant mariner who had allegedly committed high treason in speaking against the king, but Neale and Cornwaleys assisted Ingle in escaping. When Brent angrily suspended Neale from the council, virtually expelled Cornwaleys from the province, and a few months later discharged Lewger from his positions, the structure of government in Maryland almost completely crumbled.[37]

Leonard Calvert returned the following fall and futilely attempted to reestablish order. He dismissed Brent and convened an assembly in February of 1644/45. Only a single act, a statute of one year's duration for defense of the province, survives. Within days of the assembly's close, with the full outbreak of what has subsequently become known as Ingle's Rebellion, the colony definitely required defense. This "plundering time" or "time of troubles," as it was variously called by contemporaries, left Maryland without an effective government for more than two years and almost wiped out the colony.[38]

Ingle, who was in Maryland only during the initial weeks of the rebellion that bears his name, primarily provided a rallying point for other Protestants, especially on Kent Island, who had long-standing grievances of their own against Lord Baltimore's government. Rebels seized the estates of some Catholics, and, ironically, Cornwaleys particularly suffered at the hands of the locals and of Ingle, who by 1645 had absconded with £200 worth of goods entrusted him by his earlier rescuer. Leonard Calvert and many other Marylanders, both Catholics and Protestants, were forced to seek refuge in Virginia. They launched a successful expedition from that neighboring colony a year later to recapture the Western Shore, but Kent Island remained for some time under the control of the rebels, who aligned with William Claiborne, still seeking personal revenge against the Calverts.[39]

37. Ibid., 3:127–28, 131–32, 160, 166–67; 4:231, 232–34, 237–39, 241, 245–52, 258. No assembly is known to have met during Brent's tenure (*Archives*, 3:135, 139).

38. For contemporary descriptions, see ibid., 1:238; 4:365, 421; on the Assembly of 1644/45, ibid., 1:205; and on Brent's dismissal, ibid., 4:301. Historical accounts include Edward Ingle, *Captain Richard Ingle, The Maryland "Pirate and Rebel," 1642–1653*, Maryland Historical Society, Fund Publication No. 19 (Baltimore, 1884), and Menard, "Maryland's Time of Troubles," 124–40.

39. *Archives*, 3:166–67, 169–71, 195. One report asserts that Calvert was taken prisoner and expelled from Maryland. "A Description of the Province of New Albion," in Peter Force, ed., *Tracts and Other Papers Relating Principally to the Origin, Settlement, and Progress of the Colonies in North America* (Washington, D.C., 1838), 2:6.

It is impossible to reconstruct fully the political developments of these years. At some point in the early spring of 1646, Captain Edward Hill of Virginia traveled to Maryland, apparently under instructions from the Virginia assembly. He was persuaded, allegedly by a rump membership of the council, to officiate as deputy governor in Calvert's absence. Some colonists questioned the legality of the appointment, but the Protestant Hill still assumed control and issued writs for the election of a new assembly. The rebel party enthusiastically welcomed his actions and apparently dominated that legislature when it convened. Calvert, after reestablishing his own authority in December of 1646, met the same assembly in what was probably its second session. A later legislature, seeking to undo the work of the Assembly of 1646, asserted that "the whole House of Commons (two or three only excepted) consisted of that Rebelled Party and his [Leonard Calvert's] Professed Enemies." Lord Baltimore subsequently disallowed the legislation passed under Hill as "very prejudicial to our Rights and Royal Jurisdictions" but allowed to stand the few acts legislated in the session presided over by his brother.[40]

Leonard Calvert lived less than six months after this assembly disbanded. With the governor's death, Lord Baltimore lost his most effective deputy in the colony. Leonard Calvert had been the only Catholic, indeed probably the only person of any religious persuasion in Maryland, capable of exercising any semblance of accepted authority. Calvert had often been ineffective himself, but it is hard to conceive of anyone in the colony who might have performed better. On his deathbed, the governor appointed his old friend Thomas Greene as his political successor.[41]

The original company of adventurers and Catholic gentlemen, with the exception of Greene, had now effectively disappeared and an era in the colony's history was over. Cornwaleys had returned to England, as had Lewger, and the council had so dwindled in number that it had virtually ceased to exist during the chaos of the previous three years. Greene had few resources with which to rebuild a Catholic leadership, but he was also personally disinclined to look favorably on Protestants as likely candidates for major positions of responsibility. Accordingly, Greene reappointed Giles Brent as councillor, and along with the erratic Thomas Gerard these men constituted the provincial government for the next two years. Each man was controversial and easily aroused opposition; collec-

40. *Archives*, 4:321–22; 3:188, 219–21 (second quotation); 1:220, 221, 239 (first quotation), 266. One of the approved acts stipulated that the governor and chief judge were to administer all justice, criminal and civil, "according to the Lawes of the Province," and otherwise according to the "sound discretion" of the officials with no explicit obligation to enforce English law.
41. Ibid., 3:187–98. Calvert died on June 11, 1647.

tively, they provided a weak, untrustworthy group upon whom the proprietor had to rely and to whom the diminished band of colonists were supposed to look for enlightened leadership in these troubled times.[42]

The declining effectiveness of Catholic leadership received further confirmation when Greene convened an open assembly on January 7, 1647/48. Attendance was low, since most surviving freemen relied on proxies. Protestants outnumbered Catholics, and Greene could depend on the consistent support of only four members. Brent, who arrived late in the session, actively opposed the proprietary legislation and personally championed the grievances of the colony. Among the complaints were discontent over high charges for support of soldiers and military expeditions and a strong reaction against taxation for those earlier defense expenditures that Leonard Calvert had reputedly planned to underwrite from his own and the proprietor's estates, an action Lord Baltimore had never sanctioned. Greene opposed the grievances, but the majority of freemen easily defeated the bill for support of the government. Cecilius Calvert subsequently denounced the grievances as seditious and unjust, disallowed several acts passed by this body, and dismissed Brent from the council.[43]

Greene soon aggravated already tenuous situations. He discharged Robert Vaughan as commander of Kent and thereby removed the one Protestant loyal to the proprietor and still capable of commanding the allegiance of the colonists on the island. More serious was Greene's unbounded determination to defend the cause of King Charles. The governor's defiant opposition to the parliamentary party contradicted Lord Baltimore's current policy of careful accommodation.[44]

Lord Baltimore had long been committed to a greater liberality in religious matters than prevailed in England or elsewhere in the colonies. His charter, his instructions to his officers, his antipathy toward the militancy of the Jesuits all attested to his philosophy of moderation and toleration, as well as to a strategy of calculated pragmatism in these

42. Ibid., 4:313–488. Calvert named Margaret Brent to oversee his personal affairs, an appointment the assembly later defended even while denying her request for a voice in the assembly (ibid., 215, 238–39). On Gerard, see Papenfuse et al., eds., *Biographical Dictionary*, and Edwin W. Beitzell, "Thomas Gerard and His Sons-in-Law," *Maryland Historical Magazine*, 46 (1951), 189–206.
43. *Archives*, 1:213–33, 267–70; 3:211–13.
44. Vaughan had accused "the Greene Gouvenor" of partiality in the administration of justice. Greene reinstated Vaughan shortly thereafter. See ibid., 3:197–98; 4:439 (quotation), 440, 441, 449–50, 459; see also Bernard C. Steiner, *Maryland During the English Civil Wars*, Parts 1 and 2, Johns Hopkins University Studies, No. 25 (Baltimore, 1907), his *Maryland Under the Commonwealth: A Chronicle of the Years 1649–1659*, ibid.; No. 29 (Baltimore, 1911), and Johnson, *Foundation of Maryland*, 102–16.

uncharted waters. Now, while making adroit concessions to the influential Puritan merchant community in London, he also moved vigorously
both to provide sufficient protection to his fellow Catholics and to alleviate the fears of uneasy Protestants.

For some time Calvert had actively recruited Protestants to settle in the
colony. In 1648 and 1649, in response to renewed overtures, several
hundred Protestant dissenters journeyed northward from Virginia to relocate in Maryland.[45] Simultaneously, Lord Baltimore placed the leadership
of his colony firmly in the hands of Protestants. William Stone, a prominent Virginian with influential connections in the powerful London merchant community, became governor. In the summer of 1648, the proprietor dispatched Thomas Hatton from England as the new secretary of the
colony and elevated to the council Vaughan and John Price, local non-
Catholics. Protestants now occupied the principal offices of the provincial government, although the council continued for a brief while to
include two Catholics, Greene and John Pile, in subordinate roles.[46]

Accelerating already extensive efforts to attract more wealthy Protestants to Maryland, Lord Baltimore issued immediate commissions for the
council to such men when he heard of their intentions to migrate or
hoped thereby to influence them to settle in his colony. The next five
appointments to the council went to Robert Brooke, William Eltonhead,
William Mitchell, Edward Gibbons of New England, and Job Chandler
of Virginia. Eltonhead and Chandler, like Stone, had especially important
ties in England, and Gibbons, who apparently never accepted Calvert's
offer, was much respected in Massachusetts.[47]

Once on the scene, Stone implemented additional measures to quell
opposition. A series of appointments at the governor's discretion, but no
doubt ordered by Calvert, placed each county under the primary authority of Protestants as commanders and also as justices. The ranking officials of the Provincial Court now had to swear they would not trouble or
molest, directly or indirectly, any professing Christian or disturb the free
exercise of religion of any Catholic loyal to the proprietor. While satisfy-

45. *Archives*, 3:207; Hall, ed., *Narratives*, 235–36, 245–55; Krugler, "Lord Baltimore,
Roman Catholics and Toleration."
46. *Archives*, 3:198, 201–18; 4:376–78; Harry Wright Newman, *The Stones of Poynton
Manor* (privately printed, 1937). Robert P. Brenner, "Commercial Change and Political Conflict: The Merchant Community in Civil War London" (Ph.D. diss., Princeton
University, 1970), is most helpful on the London merchants, one of whom was
Thomas Stone, uncle of the new governor.
47. *Archives*, 3:237–41, 242, 250–52, 261–64, 271–72, 275–76. Chandler's brother
Richard was a frequent witness before English authorities on colonial issues. On all
these men, see Papenfuse et al., eds., *Biographical Dictionary*, and files of the Legislative History Project.

ing critics, the proprietor was also anxious not to leave Catholics without protection. He sought a true toleration of all Christians in the colony.[48]

What Calvert did not desire was any continuation of the aggressive and divisive activities of the Jesuits. A final effort to reach an accommodation with the Catholic hierarchy in England proved futile. Consequently, new Conditions of Plantation issued in the summer of 1648 officially included those provisions Calvert had not fully implemented after 1641 and in effect escheated much of the property of the Jesuits; Lord Baltimore attempted in other ways to counter the trusteeships he knew they had devised to protect some of their land.[49]

The Jesuit mission was in no condition to battle the proprietor as it had done before. Its leading lay Catholic supporters had died, left Maryland, or been discredited. The operation of five missionaries that had thrived before Ingle's Rebellion had in effect disbanded, and church authorities in Europe hesitated to reinvest. Father Thomas Copley returned to Maryland at the end of the decade but met frustration in his efforts to collect rents and to acquire title to 20,000 acres he claimed were still due to the Jesuits. When Copley died in 1652, the Jesuits at last tacitly surrendered. As the vicar-general remarked, "Let him [Calvert] give us soules; the rest he may take to himself." Even so, through secret trusts the Jesuits kept at least indirect control of some land.[50]

Lord Baltimore still desired legislative endorsement of proprietary policies and statutory acknowledgment of the wide-ranging powers he claimed under the charter. He wanted nothing less than to achieve the permanent legal code earlier assemblies had repeatedly denied him, particularly, he thought, through the intrigues of "those of the Hill there," as he sarcastically referred to the Jesuits. Calvert dispatched sixteen bills that he requested the assembly to enact as permanent laws, "without any alteration, addition or dimunition." It required two assemblies before Lord Baltimore obtained his desired statutes and completed his strategy for buttressing the charter, enhancing his authority, and protecting the colony.[51]

Governor Stone convened the first of these two assemblies on April 2, 1649. Six of the nine burgesses in this relatively inexperienced assembly had not previously served in any office, and four men had been in Maryland three years or less. The membership reflected the colony's depleted population and precarious existence. Among the elected members, only Catholics Cuthbert Fenwick and Robert Clarke had previously served as

---

48. *Archives*, 3:214, 216–17, 256, 257, 259–60.
49. Ibid., 196–97, 221–28, 230.
50. Hughes, *History of the Society of Jesus*, Text, 2:17–45 (quotation, 44–45), Documents, 1:217; *Archives*, 3:258, 259.
51. *Calvert Papers, Number One*, 216 (first quotation); *Archives*, 3:220–21.

elected delegates or even played any appreciable role in earlier open meetings, although Catholics Greene and Pile and Protestant Robert Vaughan, among five men attending on special writs, did provide some additional experience. The gathering included five known Catholics, five known Protestants, and four men whose religious affiliation is uncertain.

The experienced "old guard" assumed the major role in deliberations. Fenwick, Clarke, and Greene possessed the knowledge reflected in the subsequent maneuvering, and as Catholics historically close to the Jesuits, they remained the most concerned about the implications of many of the bills. Lord Baltimore later decried those individuals, unnamed, who had misled the major part of the legislature into opposing much of the proposed code on the grounds of the proprietor's disregard for their liberties, when in fact, Calvert asserted, these men had opposed him for other secret reasons. He disparaged the "Deceiptful Suggestions of Subtile Matchiavilans pretending Religion, and an extraordinary care of the Peoples liberty . . . to alienate their affections from the present Government."

Objections had surfaced to those bills recognizing the charter, requiring an oath of fidelity to Lord Baltimore, and affecting land acquired from the Indians, all issues directly involving the Catholic church and the Jesuit mission. Citing the need for a short meeting, since planting time was at hand, and lamenting so many laws "so long and tedious containing withal so many Branches and Clauses," members of the assembly proposed for the moment to select from the proprietor's bills only those "most necessary and best Suitable to our present Condition." The delegates disregarded the other bills as "not Convenient or as we Conceive it just to Pass." The assembly eventually enacted twelve laws, seven of which came completely or in large measure from the proprietor's package. Heading the statutes was the celebrated Act of Religion, the most famous bill to pass the Maryland assembly in the colonial period. It legislated the guarantees that Lord Baltimore had explicitly extended through oaths of officers and promises in the past year and that he had implicitly upheld since the founding of the colony. Other acts addressed relations with the Indians, awarded an export duty to the proprietor, established some punishments for crimes, and regulated several aspects of the economic life of the colony.[52]

The next April, a new assembly organized itself into two separate houses. Besides being bicameral, this legislature significantly differed from its predecessor in containing a decided majority of Protestants. The fourteen delegates included only three known Catholics and possibly a

52. *Archives*, 1:235–55, contains all that survives of the records of this assembly, the journal of the last day, the laws enacted, and a letter from the assembly to Lord Baltimore explaining the session's actions. For the proprietor's response, ibid., 265.

fourth, and just two Catholics sat in the upper chamber. Their status became questionable when Stone tendered, for the first time, an oath to be sworn by all assemblymen that required full secrecy regarding the body's deliberations. The Catholics balked and eventually only two, one in each house, participated actively in this session.

Once seated, the delegates heard a reading of the proprietor's response to the legislature's actions of the previous year. Lord Baltimore dissected the arguments raised against him and his proposed laws. The major portion of the letter carefully rehearsed his powers and prerogatives, reminding the members of the assembly of their proper place in obedience to him. "Wee Knowe full well," Calvert had written,

> our Right to that Province doth not stand in neede of any Confirma-
> tion thereof by Act of Assembly there, for our Charter above men-
> tioned, and our deare purchase of our Right to that Province, by the
> expense of great sumes of money with much sollicitude and travaile,
> (whereby that Collony was first begun and preserved) entitles us
> sufficiently thereunto, But wee have Great Reason to wonder that
> any well affected person there, not seduced by Eviell Councell should
> be backward in concurring to a publick Act of Recognition of our
> Rights there.

He reiterated his indisputable right to assemble the freemen in whatever manner he desired without any regard for what the assembly itself might wish or might attempt to legislate. Calvert had concluded with his presumption that "the Assembly there will make noe further Scruple of Consenting to all the said Lawes as wee sent them."

Whether as a result of this chastening or because some of the most adamant resisters were now missing from this legislature, the Assembly of 1650 obliged the proprietor by enacting the remaining proposed statutes. New laws recognized Lord Baltimore's charter and authority, instituted an oath of allegiance from all settlers, and established an act of oblivion regarding the recent rebellion. Two especially important statutes, however, acknowledged that no money could be raised in Maryland without the assembly's consent and that no colonist had an obligation to assist or to aid in any war unless the assembly had given its prior endorsement. Other legislation, not part of the proprietary package, addressed a variety of civil and criminal matters, provided for money to be raised for government expenses and relief for the poor, established a table of fees, treated economic questions requiring attention in a colony finally beginning to grow, and included at least two private bills, the first to be approved by the assembly. None of this legislation carried a time limitation.[53]

53. Ibid., 1:257–308 (quotation, 265).

Within five months, Calvert approved eighteen of the laws passed by the two assemblies, sixteen of the statutes being his proposed bills or slightly modified legislation. A few years later, he endorsed another ten acts. Maryland now had a substantial body of permanent statutes, and the proprietor had finally obtained his desired legislation – legislation that had been in dispute since 1637. In turn, the assembly had also firmly secured acknowledgment of its sole authority to tax and to compel military service, and the proprietor had accepted organization of the legislature into two separate houses.[54]

The same assembly met again the following year in a second session, but thereafter not until 1658 was another proprietary legislature to convene in the colony.[55] Lord Baltimore's success in England in maintaining satisfactory relations with the parliamentary government and in protecting his charter proved insufficient when the primary threats came not from militant Catholics unhappy in a colony too Protestant, but from militant Protestants who could no longer abide any role for Catholics in Maryland and who coveted for themselves this colony of a Catholic proprietor. In September of 1651, Richard Bennett, William Claiborne, and two other individuals obtained power from Parliament as agents to reduce the colony of Virginia, which had remained faithful to the deposed king. Lord Baltimore managed to keep any specific mention of Maryland out of their commission, but ambiguous wording, perhaps cleverly inserted by his enemies, authorized the agents "to reduce all the plantations within the Bay of Chesapeake." Employing this phrase, Bennett and Claiborne, after subduing Virginia by the late winter of 1651/52, proceeded to Maryland, where on March 27 they removed the incumbent officers and appointed a new council, retaining only Protestants Robert Brooke and Job Chandler from the proprietor's most recent commission.

Contending forces maneuvered for power over the next few years. Stone, swearing that he was loyal to the Commonwealth, which recognized Cecilius Calvert's charter, reached some temporary accommodation in 1652 with his adversaries, who then reinstated the governor and other Protestants; as a concession, Stone ceased for the time being to issue any writs in the name of Lord Baltimore. The proprietor, less pleased with this arrangement, lobbied vigorously in England for a restoration of his full authority. Favorable responses to his appeals and the ascendancy of Oliver Cromwell as lord protector encouraged Baltimore to have his deputies become more assertive. Accordingly, Stone ended any association with the parliamentary commissioners on March 2, 1653/54, while

54. CO5/729, Public Record Office, London, is a list of the laws of Maryland with the proprietor's approval or veto. See also *Archives*, 1:317–18, 322–28.
55. Only the legislation survives from this assembly (*Archives*, 1:309–23).

being careful to profess his continuing obedience to the Commonwealth. Many influential Protestants, especially within the nonconformist community, joined with Bennett and Claiborne to overthrow the proprietary government that summer and establish a commonwealth in Maryland. The initial ten commissioners came predominantly from among former Virginia residents, including William Fuller appointed as the de facto chief executive. By the end of March 1655, the new officials had effectively crushed all remaining opposition in Maryland.[56]

Two unicameral assemblies, in keeping with the current parliamentary model, convened under this government, the first in October of 1654 and the second in September of 1657. Membership of both legislatures was totally Protestant, with even participation as voters expressly denied to Catholics and any others who had "born arms against the Parliament."[57] Disregarding their relative inexperience as lawmakers, these men energetically refashioned the political life of Maryland. The Assembly of 1654 assumed the right to issue writs for elections, formerly a proprietary prerogative, and passed a statute that subsequent legislatures were to be called a minimum of "once in every three years," achieving a victory denied the elected membership throughout the 1640s. The busy assembly enacted forty-five statutes in 1654, and its successor in 1657 passed another eleven laws. These assemblies recognized the lord protector of England as the supreme authority in Maryland, revised desired legislation, explicitly repealed ten acts – including the Act Concerning Religion and statutes affecting Claiborne – and passed some new laws, particularly to address drunkenness, swearing, profanation of the Sabbath, and adultery. Pursuing further the model of the contemporary Parliament, the Assembly of 1654 drew verbatim from that body's Instrument of Government, dated December 16, 1653, for a new act depriving Catholics of their freedom of religion.[58]

These commonwealth assemblies had little lasting impact, however. By November of 1657, Lord Baltimore had marshaled sufficient support within the English government to have the colony restored to his control. Governor-designate Josias Fendall carried the authorizing papers as quickly as possible to Maryland, where the surrender of the parliamentary commissioners was completed on March 24, 1657/58. Writs were

56. Steiner, *Maryland Under the Commonwealth*, 53–105, and *Archives*, 3:264–316 and 10:159–412, cover this confusing period. Hall, ed., *Narratives*, 161–308, reproduces important pamphlets printed by contending factions.

57. *Archives*, 1:339–56 and 357–65, for what remains of the records of these two assemblies, and 3:313, on requirements for voting or service.

58. See Gardiner, ed., *Constitutional Documents of the Puritan Revolution*, 405–16, especially Chaps. 25 and 37.

issued immediately for the election of a new proprietary assembly to gather at St. Leonard's in Calvert County on April 27, 1658.[59]

This assembly contrasted considerably with its immediate predecessors. First, it restored bicameralism and the use of special writs. Second, devoted proprietary adherents sat in the same house with recent proprietary enemies, just as Catholics and Protestants were serving together again in the assembly. The members quickly endorsed the change in government but also approved articles stating that no participant on the losing side of the recent struggles was to suffer any political penalty. Officers of the previous regime were to receive all fees still justly due to them, and most legislation from 1654 and 1657 not directly affecting the lord proprietor remained in effect. An article signed in England but missing, probably by accident, from the assembly's version had specifically reendorsed the Act Concerning Religion of 1649. The assembly gratefully accepted these terms of surrender as conducive to the "peace of the Province." In the next week or so, the two houses also approved ten statutes, most of them temporary laws, to reinstate legislation earlier repealed by the commonwealth assemblies, but this session reenacted as well the recent government's law on drunkenness and several other acts. The proprietor declared the permanent legislation of the Assemblies of 1649 and 1650 automatically in effect once again.[60]

The "peace of the Province" was not so pervasive as the assembly implied, however, nor could the proprietor easily erase hard feelings even with the very generous terms of the surrender agreement. New commissions for justices and other officers of the various counties excluded by and large the leaders of the commonwealth government and aroused further animosities. Among the population at large, passions still ran high against the proprietary government and especially against any renewed role of Catholics. At the first opportunity, these disgruntled Marylanders tried to reassert their commonwealth form of government. In the words of one unfriendly observer, "A company of weak-witted men which thought to have traced the steps of Oliver [Cromwell]" attempted a "pigmie rebellion."[61]

The first step toward that rebellion came with the election of another assembly in the winter of 1659/60. Freemen of the Upper Western Shore almost exclusively returned former leaders of the discredited commonwealth government. These men carefully plotted with sympathetic allies

59. *Archives,* 3:323–40; 41:61; Steiner, *Maryland Under the Commonwealth,* 112–16.
60. *Archives,* 1:367–77, for the legislation of this session. See also ibid., 3:342, 343–44.
61. For commissions, see ibid., 348–52, and records of the respective county courts, on deposit in Hall of Records. The quotation comes from George Alsop, "A Character of the Province of Maryland, 1666," in Hall, ed., *Narratives,* 381.

from other counties to seize control of the government. They successfully asserted leadership in the lower house, and after securing the support of a majority of the representatives announced that the elected membership considered itself "to be a lawfull Assembly without dependence on any Power in the Province." Conferences with members of the upper house ensued. A subsequent vote revealed that Governor Fendall and at least two other councillors, Thomas Gerard and Nathaniel Utie, were sympathetic to the delegates' claim, if not actual conspirators in introducing it. In opposition, Philip Calvert, Baker Brooke, and John Price professed their loyalty to Lord Baltimore and their conviction the "Burgesses are not the supreme power." Fendall, while reserving the right of a governor to a "casting voice" for the proprietor or his deputy in the assembly and explaining that no governor could on his own confirm laws, observed that the charter had intended for freemen through themselves or their deputies to pass the laws.

The representatives invited the governor and council to take seats as part of a single chamber. The speaker would then surrender his place to the governor, although the power of adjourning and dissolving would remain with the elected members. Fendall agreed to sit with them under these terms, with himself as representative of the proprietor having a double vote. Philip Calvert and Baker Brooke refused to cooperate.[62]

Only a decade earlier, elected members had finally obtained a bicameral legislature to assure the freemen of a countervailing voice against the powerful wishes of the dominant proprietary party and its agents present on special writs. Now, with a growing Protestant and antiproprietary sentiment in the colony and the elected lower house potentially in the ascendancy, the very existence of a separate upper house, under Baltimore's control, offset the wishes of the majority of the electorate. Some colonists were now determined to abolish that house with its powerful, nonelected membership.

The rebels remained in authority less than a year. Reassembling as a one-house legislature, the participating members of the Assembly of 1659/60 repealed all former acts, passed a statute providing against disturbances in the government, and approved other laws necessary to govern. A council composed of Gerard, Utie, Robert Slye, and John Hatch assisted Fendall, with William Fuller also a powerful accomplice. This group soon foolishly alienated many settlers not firmly bound to either

62. *Archives*, 1:381–91 (journal of assembly); 3:404; 41:427; Bacon, *Laws of Maryland*, Assembly of 1659, notes. A few days later, the legislature in Virginia issued a similar pronouncement, but there as in Maryland this governing experiment lasted only a year. See Jon Kukla, "Political Institutions in Virginia, 1619–1660" (Ph.D. diss., University of Toronto, 1980), 205–13.

side and enabled Philip Calvert, leading the remnants of the proprietary party, to regain effective control of the provincial government by November of 1660.[63]

The lord proprietor was not disposed to be so generous as he had been three years earlier. He barred most of the guilty members of the assembly for seven years from holding office or from having a vote in elections, except for William Burgess, who had played a helpful role in ending the rebellion. Fendall, Gerard, and Hatch suffered permanent ineligibility to vote or sit in the assembly. Fuller fled the province to prevent arrest and eventually settled in South Carolina, where he subsequently sat on that colony's council. Other individuals who had sided with the rebels lost temporarily or permanently their appointive offices.[64]

The restoration of Charles II in England and Cecilius Calvert in Maryland ended in both places the overt rule of the militant Protestants, although these individuals were to continue to exercise in the colony a far greater influence and role in government than their counterparts could effect in England. Mother country and colony now entered upon an era of executive dominance with a temporarily weakened role for the respective legislatures. The assembly in Maryland, like the Parliament, had made significant strides during the previous decades in asserting its privileges and in gaining critical acknowledgment of some fundamental powers, particularly the right to approve any taxes and to initiate as well as to amend bills. The Maryland legislature had increasingly identified with Parliament, especially with the House of Commons. The stage was now set for more explicit parallels to be drawn. Meanwhile, residents of both the mother country and the colony were looking forward to a period of welcomed respite after years of turmoil and uncertain political authority.

63. *Archives*, 3:387–98; Alsop, "Character of the Province of Maryland," 381.
64. *Archives*, 3:399–401, 404–10; 41:427–29, 447–50, 492.

PART II

"Lord Baltimore's Politick Maximes": 1660–1689

3

"For the Most Part Good Ordinary Householders"

Once every year within this Province is an Assembly called, and out of every respective County (by the consent of the people) there is chosen a number of men, and to them is deliver'd up the Grievances of the Country; and they maturely debate the matters, and according to their Consciences make Laws for the general good of the people; and where any former law that was made, seems and is prejudicial to the good or quietness of the Land, it is repeal'd. These men that determine on these matters for the Republique, are called Burgesses, and they commonly sit in Junto about six weeks, being for the most part good ordinary Householders of the several Counties, which do more by a plain and honest Conscience, than by artificial Syllogisms drest up in gilded orations.

George Alsop, "A Character of the Province of Maryland," 1666

Now when any thing in the Popish chamber is hatched that must have a Country cloack, warrants issue forth to every County to choose 4. men ... These are called Deligates, but the Country calls them Delicats, for thy gladly com to sutch Christenings at St. Marys, where there is good cheere made, and the poore Country payes every time, one two or more hundred thousand pounds of tobacco for it. For there is many Items: and item for chancellors fees; item for secretary fees etc: and the more Assemblies the oftener it goes about, all dae thy nothing els, but argument fees uppon fees, and continue temperary lawes as thy call them ... this thy call Acts of Assembly, but the Country calls them, dissemblings, and abreptive procured acts.

"Complaint from Heaven with a Huy and crye," 1676

The struggling survivors of Lord Baltimore's young colony still clustered primarily along the Lower Western Shore of the Chesapeake Bay at midcentury, but Maryland was entering a period of substantial growth. The harsh years of the initial settlement slowly gave way after 1660 to an era of consolidation and expansion and the maturing of emerging institutions.

New patterns of migration from continental Europe, Ireland, and Africa accompanied resettlement from other colonies and from England as Maryland became more heterogeneous in its composition. These new colonists, who contributed to a 6000 percent increase in population over the next three decades, continued the vital stream of immigrants, which ultimately totaled some 34,000 people by 1681. Even so, the presence then of only 19,000 to 20,000 colonists dramatically illustrates the persistent precariousness of life in this Chesapeake province.

White indentured servants, as before, comprised the bulk of the new arrivals. The proportion of servants among the immigrants probably declined slightly between 1660 and 1689 but still far surpassed that of free settlers. Although servants provided the major source of labor, during these decades the province also imported its first appreciable number of blacks to augment the work force. By 1681, between 1,000 and 1,600 Afro-Americans, coming primarily from the Caribbean Islands, had been transported into Maryland; as with white colonists, young, single men far outnumbered women, children, or older males in the black immigrant population.

For a brief time, families became somewhat more common among the free, white newcomers. Beginning with the Virginians relocating in Maryland at midcentury, wives and children more frequently accompanied the free male settlers; an estimated one-third of the immigrants between 1658 and 1667 arrived with other family members, but this pattern largely disappeared soon thereafter. Nonetheless, these few families helped to redress the imbalanced sex ratio and to expand the number of traditional households. Earlier immigrants were now also enjoying greater success in establishing households, starting families, and increasing the ties of kin relationships in the colony. Although deaths still exceeded births, some native-born Marylanders were finally suggesting the permanence of this colonial venture and lending a significant creole influence to the society.

Somewhat more settlers also arrived during these years with capital sufficient to purchase land, acquire labor, and develop productive plantations more quickly than had been the common experience previously. Again, the figures remained small in comparison with the much larger influx of servants and poor freemen, and like family groups these more affluent immigrants did not arrive in consistent numbers over the entire period, but they too joined with more successful Marylanders from earlier years of settlement to fill a void in the economic and social structure of the province. A small contingent of younger sons of English gentry and merchants also settled in Maryland with resources that usually overshadowed the wealth of most established settlers.[1]

This growth of population with its accompanying demand for land pushed settlement beyond the limited boundaries that had previously marked the colony's presence. Settlers initially migrated northward along

1. The best sources for the changes in population are the many studies by Russell Menard, especially "Economy and Society," 153–205, 213–24, 335–95, and Arthur E. Karinen, "Maryland's Population: 1631–1730," *Maryland Historical Magazine*, 54 (1959), 365–407.

the Patuxent and Severn rivers, into the new counties of Anne Arundel, Calvert, and Charles. In the early 1660s, the movement of population shifted across the Chesapeake Bay, with the consequent extension of Kent County to areas on the Eastern Shore and the establishment of a new Talbot County. The preference of colonists not "to build nere each other," as the proprietor explained in 1678, "but soe as to have their houses nere the Watters for conveniencye of trade," dictated a more scattered population as settlers scouted out unpatented land along rivers, creeks, and inlets. This search soon carried them southward on the Lower Eastern Shore, with the settlement of what became Dorchester and Somerset counties by 1671, and farther north to the head of the Chesapeake Bay, with the creation of Baltimore and Cecil counties by 1674.[2]

The overwhelming majority of colonists remained economically preoccupied with growing oronoco tobacco. George Alsop observed in 1666 that "Tobacco is the only solid Staple Commodity of this Province." In the middle decades of the century, tobacco production expanded at a remarkable rate as planters increased the amount of land under cultivation and more impressively doubled the quantity of tobacco one person could grow in a year, from about 700 pounds in the 1630s to more than 1,500 pounds by the 1660s. At the end of that decade, Maryland and Virginia were exporting annually 15 million pounds of tobacco.

Earlier booms in the tobacco industry had created a golden age of high prices and rich profits, but any expectations of sustaining these levels substantially faded during the second half of the century. By the 1670s, planters were receiving only about a penny per pound for their tobacco, but greater productivity and reduced costs still enabled the market to grow and planters to enjoy profitable returns. Demand in the mother country reached its saturation point in the 1680s, especially as export duties raised the cost for consumers and restricted the popular market. Wartime conditions in the Atlantic soon increased transportation costs and further discouraged growth in markets outside England. Consequently, what had been cyclical problems in the mid-1660s and mid-1670s became in the following decade pronounced long-term difficulties with the onset of a thirty-year period of stagnation.

These conditions affected most directly the prospects for upward mobility of freedmen and immigrants of modest means. By the 1670s, their

2. *Archives,* 5:226 (quotation). On new areas of settlement, see Lorena S. Walsh, "Charles County, Maryland, 1658–1705: A Study of Chesapeake Social and Political Structures" (Ph.D. diss., Michigan State University, 1977); Paul G. E. Clemens, *The Atlantic Economy and Colonial Maryland's Eastern Shore: From Tobacco to Grain* (Ithaca, N.Y., 1980); and Carville V. Earle, *The Evolution of a Tidewater Settlement System: All Hallow's Parish, Maryland, 1650–1783,* University of Chicago, Department of Geography, Research Paper No. 170 (Chicago, 1975).

economic situation had suffered serious deterioration, and many men henceforth encountered staggering obstacles in establishing themselves as householders and landowners. Those who succeeded required many more years to accomplish this goal than had their predecessors. Less fortunate colonists either remained laborers and tenant farmers or sought a better life in another colony, usually Pennsylvania or the Carolinas.[3]

Just after midcentury, however, before the economy experienced its worst dislocations, a society of striking opportunity and equality briefly prevailed in Maryland. Prospects then were still quite encouraging for any freedman or poor immigrant; high wages for labor enabled an enterprising individual to save enough money in a reasonable period to pay the fees for obtaining a patent, at least to the headright claim of rights to fifty acres, and in time usually for much more land. The proportion of tenant farmers declined temporarily in the province, and small planters clearly predominated among the free population. The majority of landowners possessed between 100 and 500 acres, only a small proportion of the planters owning either much larger or smaller plantations. Ownership of labor was similarly widespread, few settlers possessing many servants or slaves. Inventories of the estates of deceased Marylanders clearly indicate that the distribution of wealth during these years was more equitable than at any other time in the century. After the 1660s, a slowly widening gap began to appear, and by the close of the century, clusters of wealthier and poorer colonists had become more noticeable.

Even with this surprisingly equal distribution of land and property, few Marylanders enjoyed many of the normal accoutrements of wealth possessed by even the average seventeenth century Englishman. Inventories rarely included items that provided comfort, color, or diversion from the hard, drab life of most settlers. Homes provided protection against the worst elements of the environment, but did little beyond that. Furnishings were simple and sparse, clothing plain and practical. Personal property was minimal, and privacy almost an unknown concept. Only a very few colonists transcended this prevailing life style.[4]

3. Alsop, "Character of the Province of Maryland," 363; Menard, "Economy and Society," 278–335, 490–92, and also "The Chesapeake Tobacco Industry, 1617–1730: An Interpretation," especially 142–55; Carr and Menard, "Immigration and Opportunity"; Lorena S. Walsh, "Servitude and Opportunity in Charles County, Maryland, 1658–1705," 111–33, in Land et al., eds., *Law, Society, and Politics*; and Russell R. Menard, Lois Green Carr, and Lorena S. Walsh, "A Small Planter's Profits: The Cole Estate and the Growth of the Early Chesapeake Economy," *William and Mary Quarterly*, 40 (1983), 171–96.
4. Gloria L. Main, *Tobacco Colony, Life in Early Maryland, 1650–1720* (Princeton, N.J., 1982); Menard, "Economy and Society," 241–68; Carr and Menard, "Immigration and Opportunity," especially 210–35; Russell R. Menard, P. M. G. Harris, and Lois Green Carr, "Opportunity and Inequality: The Distribution of Wealth on the Lower Western Shore of Maryland, 1638–1705," *Maryland Historical Magazine*, 69 (1974), 169–84; Walsh, "Charles County," 153–305.

Most colonists still resembled one another in having only minimal education. Illiteracy remained high among immigrants, and few individuals within the colony enjoyed any access to formal education. Tutors and schoolmasters, hired privately, appear occasionally, like Catholic Ralph Crouch, who taught in St. Mary's County in the early 1660s, Robert Douglas, who tutored Governor Charles Calvert's son in 1673, and Quaker Isaac Smith, who instructed Friends' children in the early 1680s. Even these arrangements for the privileged few did not always prove satisfactory.[5] Numerous wills made tentative bequests to encourage the founding of free schools, but little materialized from these efforts. The Catholic mission did establish a school in St. Mary's in 1677, "where humane letters are taught with great fruit," reported one official. Also, some affluent colonists sent their children to schools outside the colony, but individuals with anything but the most rudimentary education remained few in number through most of these years.[6]

During the last third of the century, however, more immigrants arrived with some literary, clerical, or professional skills. Five or six men well trained in the law provided the first community of professional lawyers. A slightly larger number of settlers had acquired extensive education in preparation for the ministry. Others, though lacking university training, possessed clerical and accounting skills in critical demand in this frontier society; such men advanced rapidly, filling positions in the growing political bureaucracy or participating in the burgeoning tobacco trade. The more frequent appearance of sizable libraries in the estates of deceased colonists and the arrival of William Nuthead with the colony's first printing press in 1685 further attest to an improving intellectual climate.[7]

Maryland's population gradually became more heterogeneous as well in its religious affiliations. Charles Calvert reported to the lords of trade and plantations in 1677 that "the greatest part of the Inhabitants of that Province (three of four at least) doe consist of Presbiterians, Independents Anabaptists and Quakers, those of the Church of England as well as

5. *Archives*, 53:13, 14, 251, 599; 54:523, 591; 60:247; Kenneth L. Carroll, *Quakerism on the Eastern Shore* (Baltimore, 1970), 80.
6. *Archives*, 2:262–64; 49:20–21; Wills 6, fols. 62–63, Hall of Records, Annapolis, Md.; Edwin Warfield Beitzell, *The Jesuit Mission of St. Mary's County, Maryland* (privately printed, 1960), 41–42; Geoffrey Holt, ed., *St. Omer's and Bruges Colleges, 1593–1773, A Biographical Dictionary*, Catholic Records Society, LXIX (London, 1979), 48–49, 56, 110; Samuel E. Morison, "Virginians and Marylanders at Harvard College in the Seventeenth Century," *William and Mary Quarterly*, 2nd ser., 13 (1933), 1–9.
7. Alan F. Day, "Lawyers in Colonial Maryland, 1660–1715," *American Journal of Legal History*, 17 (1973), 145–65; Richard Beale Davis, *Intellectual Life in the Colonial South, 1585–1763*, 3 vols. (Knoxville, Tenn., 1978), especially 2:509–10, 596–97; J. A. Leo Lemay, *Men of Letters in Colonial Maryland* (Knoxville, Tenn., 1972), 28–69; Lawrence C. Wroth, *A History of Printing in Colonial Maryland, 1686–1776* (Baltimore, 1922).

those of the Romish being the fewest." Within several years, he could have added the Labadists and some Lutherans to the list. Few places in the English-speaking world contained such a profusion of religious sects.[8]

Actually, amidst this extraordinary religious diversity, most colonists remained unchurched, there being a scarcity of ministers and a vacuum of institutional structures, particularly with respect to the Church of England. A strong local initiative and substantial support from outside the colony enabled the Catholics and the Quakers to establish the strongest and most numerous religious institutions. Building upon the early foundations of the Jesuit mission, new priests arriving after 1660 galvanized the local Catholics; within three decades they had erected nine churches or chapels, primarily on the Lower Western Shore or in Talbot County. Meanwhile, a stream of Quaker missionaries found a receptive audience among the unchurched Protestants. Without dependence on an ordained ministry, the Society of Friends built rapidly on their initial nucleus of converts and by the late 1670s had fourteen active meetings in Maryland.

As officials of the Church of England continued to be remiss in providing trained clergy for the colony, still other dissenting sects threatened to attract those people "who have a long while lived as sheepe without a Shepherd," as one contemporary described them. By the 1680s a thriving fellowship of Presbyterians in Somerset and Dorchester had obtained ministers from Scotland. In the northern region of the colony, the Labadists and the Dutch Reformed Church attracted numerous settlers, and on the Lower Western Shore a small progression of heterodox Church of England clergymen maintained active congregations.[9]

George Alsop in 1666 proclaimed the religious pluralism of Maryland "the Miracle of this Age."[10] Generally, the proprietary policy of toleration for all Christians was a remarkably successful experiment. Only occasionally did religious differences spark much overt intolerance or persecution. At intervals, Quakers suffered for their refusals to swear oaths or to serve in the militia, actions that seemed to threaten the stability of government and allegiance to the proprietor. Authorities actively persecuted Friends in the years from 1658 to 1661, but thereafter it became a more random matter of imposing fines for refusal to perform certain acts, and in 1688 Quakers gained the right to affirm in many instances usually requiring an oath.

8. *Archives*, 5:133–34, 261.
9. David W. Jordan, " 'The Miracle of this Age': Maryland's Experiment in Religious Toleration, 1649–1689," *The Historian*, 47 (1985), 338–59; see also Matthew Hill to Richard Baxter, Apr. 3, 1699, Richard Baxter Letters, Dr. William's Library, London, Vol. 3: fols. 261–62; *Archives*, 5:131; 18:264–66.
10. Alsop, "Character of the Province of Maryland," 349.

Individual homes mirrored the religious diversity and toleration that characterized the larger colony. An interesting pattern of marriages, often compounded by the high death rate, which led surviving spouses to remarry a second, third, or fourth time, created microcosms of the religious heterogeneity Calvert described for all of Maryland. Whether such marriages arose because individuals were less concerned about religious differences than many of their contemporaries outside Maryland or whether a limited choice of potential mates overrode persisting religious ideologies is unclear. Such marriages definitely existed among the more affluent, whose families are easier to trace, and probably existed to some degree as well among the poorer colonists.[11]

The changing economic, social, and religious profile of the settlers greatly influenced the evolving political life of the province. In 1660, the various activities of government still enlisted the participation of the full spectrum of free adult white males, and the extension of settlement multiplied the number of essential offices to be filled. With the creation of new counties, distinctive levels of government became firmly established in the colony. The numerous hundreds remained the political bases for elections and perhaps other local matters; meanwhile, the counties through their own courts, justices, and sheriffs conducted most business at an intermediate level. These local and county governments generally achieved in these years a commendable political stability and produced, on the whole, a responsible and increasingly more experienced body of officeholders. A higher degree of turnover, factionalism, and instability continued to characterize the provincial level of government, where the governor, council, assembly, various executive officers, and an active Provincial Court provided governance on broader issues affecting everyone in Maryland and ruled on controversies appealed from the lower levels of administration. Although few individuals entertained thoughts of serving on the proprietary council, all freemen through the early years of this period remained eligible to vote, and most of them expected at some time in their adult lives to serve as juryman, highway overseer, militiaman, or constable, and a considerable number also sat on the county bench or in the lower house of the assembly.

Men of humble origins and modest means exercised an important influence in both elected and appointed offices, especially in newer counties and in the frontier regions of older areas of settlement. For example, in Charles County, erected in 1658, six of the first twelve justices were former servants, and four others had arrived in Maryland with very little capital. At least one-fourth of the justices in the early years of that county

---

11. Jordan, " 'The Miracle of this Age'," 350–52, explores this phenomenon.

were illiterate, and others possessed little education beyond basic literacy. At their appointments, these men had only modest wealth. They gained access to such positions because few others were appreciably wealthier or better educated. The pattern in Charles was not dissimilar to situations elsewhere in the colony.[12]

Provincial officeholders, although generally more successful than the population at large, did not stand that much above their fellow colonists during the early years of this period. The absence of a greater separation bothered Cecilius Calvert, who proposed some medal or dress to set apart the major officials.[13] Charles Calvert, the resident governor from 1661 to 1675 and proprietor thereafter, regarded dubiously such artificial distinctions and deplored the scarcity of men who might naturally command deference. Lamenting the return to Ireland in 1671 of his cousin William Talbot, Calvert wrote, "I have little comfort or satisfaction in the society of any of the rest of the council here." He worked assiduously in subsequent years to attract into high office men of indisputable wealth and status and often arranged marriages for such individuals to his many stepchildren.[14]

The council by the 1680s had become the prerogative of a small group closely related to the proprietary family, but membership in the elected lower house, like seats on the county bench, belonged as yet to no definite clique. Indeed, few men exercised political influence for any extended period of time, and even fewer individuals managed to transfer their power or position in politics to a relative or friend.

Between the restoration of proprietary authority in 1660 and the Protestant Associators' Revolution of 1689, nine different assemblies met, to which the voters returned a total of 156 men.[15] One-half of the delegates, 77 men, won election or sat for only one assembly, and an additional 27 men served in just two legislatures (see Appendix A). Only 33 of the 137 delegates first elected in these years, or just 24 percent, served in more than two legislatures. An extensive turnover of membership continued to be the norm, despite more frequent elections and larger assemblies. Before 1671 a given legislature usually convened for just one session, and

---

12. Mereness, *Maryland as a Proprietary Province*, discusses extensively the various levels of government. See also Lois Carr's "Sources of Political Stability and Upheaval" and an earlier essay, "The Foundations of Social Order: Local Government in Colonial Maryland," 72–110, in Bruce C. Daniels, ed., *Town and County: Essays in the Structure of Local Government in the American Colonies* (Middletown, Conn., 1978). Walsh, "Charles County," 306–64, especially 342–44, and Menard, "Economy and Society," particularly 266 (quotation), discuss county officeholders.

13. *Archives*, 15:16; Jordan, "Maryland's Privy Council," 67–71.

14. Jordan, "Maryland's Privy Council," 71–76; *Calvert Papers, Number One*, 276 (quotation).

15. Papenfuse et al., eds., *Biographical Dictionary*, 1:23–30.

before 1682 each county had the opportunity to return four representatives. Still, first-term representatives accounted for at least 48 percent or more of the membership of six of these nine assemblies; few of the other delegates could draw on much additional experience. The rare examples of seasoned legislators primarily appear among men first elected in the later years of this period and serving most of their terms after 1689.[16] The Assembly of Maryland closely resembled its counterpart in Virginia in the low incidence of reelection, and both legislatures continued to contrast markedly with the contemporary House of Commons in England, the General Court of Massachusetts, and the Assembly of Barbados, where more frequent reelections, lengthier tenures and a dominant political elite remained characteristic.[17]

A high death rate and an accompanying low life expectancy primarily account for these short legislative careers. Throughout the century, a colonist at age 20 could generally expect to live only to his early 40s, some twenty to thirty years less than his colonial contemporaries in New England.[18] In the decades after midcentury, few men achieved either election or appointment to the assembly while still in their 20s. The average age of delegates in the 1660s ranged from the middle to late 30s, increased slowly thereafter and reached 41.7 for the Assembly of 1682–84 and 44.7 for the legislators elected in 1686. Most men returned to these assemblies were already old by Chesapeake standards, and few survived long enough to make multiple terms, even if desired, a possibility. At least

16. Kenelm Cheseldyne of St. Mary's, first elected in 1676, eventually served in six assemblies, but most of them met after 1689. Nine delegates first elected between 1660 and 1688 accumulated five terms, four sat in four legislatures, and nineteen in three assemblies, but at least half of all these men served mainly after 1689. A few men first elected before 1660 provided some continuity during these years. Richard Preston served eight terms between 1654 and his death in 1669, and Joseph Wickes and Richard Woolman sat in a total of seven and six assemblies, respectively.

17. In Virginia, a high degree of turnover, both voluntary and involuntary, characterized the Long Assembly, which sat from 1662 to 1676. Thereafter, between 1677 and 1706, 45% of the burgesses won election once and 66% to two or fewer assemblies. Only fifteen men, or 5%, served for six or more terms over these thirty years. See Warren Martin Billings, " 'Virginia's Deploured Condition,' 1660–1676: The Coming of Bacon's Rebellion" (Ph.D. diss., Northern Illinois University, 1968), 108–11; Martin H. Quitt, "Virginia House of Burgesses, 1660–1706: The Social, Educational and Economic Basis of Political Power" (Ph.D. diss., Washington University, 1970), 192. In Massachusetts, as a contrast, three men represented Braintree for thirty-four of a possible forty-three terms between 1640 and 1670, and Braintree was not an atypical town (Wall, "Members of the Massachusetts General Court," 19 and *passim*). Continuity characterized membership in Parliament, a decided minority of representatives sitting only one term. See Basil Duke Henning, ed., *The House of Commons 1660–1690*, 3 vols. (London, 1983), especially 1:26–27.

18. Walsh and Menard, "Death in the Chesapeake," 211–27, and Walsh, "Charles County," 51–59.

forty delegates from this period died either during a term in the assembly or before the next election.

Early deaths also greatly limited the ability of males to secure an established place for their families in the political life of the colony. Many men in Maryland never married, or if they did, they frequently died without any surviving children. At least 70 percent and perhaps as many as 80 to 85 percent of the male decedents during the century succumbed without sons or with sons not of age. An unusually low proportion of women in the population, restrictions on the marriages of servants, and other factors accounted for later ages at marriage and a diminished likelihood that parents would see their children enter adulthood. Consequently, it was most difficult for a father's influence to be transmitted to his sons, and access to offices remained unusually open, little significance being attached to one's parentage.[19]

Among the ninety-seven assemblymen serving before 1661, thirty-eight apparently had no surviving sons and another forty-nine left sons who never achieved any office on the provincial level. Only ten delegates and just five other provincial-level officeholders serving before 1661 had sons who subsequently sat in the assembly, and only an additional eighteen men had surviving daughters whose husbands gained the distinction of holding that office.

Between 1661 and 1689, officeholders fared only slightly better in bequeathing political influence. Of the 137 men first elected to serve during these years, 41 left no known surviving sons, and 70 had sons who never won election to the assembly or held a provincial office, although a few of these offspring did serve on the local level, primarily as justices. Only 26 men, most of whom first served after 1675, fathered sons who eventually sat in the assembly, and only 14 more men qualify for possible indirect transfer of political power or status through surviving daughters whose husbands became assemblymen. Among 28 councillors appointed from 1661 to 1689, just 2 had sons who later served in the legislature and through only an additional four men's daughters did families indirectly experience another generation of high officeholding.

Although fathers and sons, brothers and cousins were perpetuating family power in the political life of New England,[20] few officeholders in

19. More than one-fourth of the men who left estates during the second half of the century in southern Maryland died unmarried. The age for men at first marriage was above thirty years at midcentury and fell to about twenty-six in the last quarter of the 1600s. Lorena S. Walsh, " 'Till Death Us Do Part': Marriage and Family in Seventeenth Century Maryland," 126–52, in Tate and Ammerman, eds., *The Chesapeake in the Seventeenth Century.*
20. See, for example, Richard S. Dunn, *Puritans and Yankees: The Winthrop Dynasty of New England, 1630–1717* (Princeton, N.J., 1962); John J. Waters, "Hingham,

the Chesapeake could claim any blood relationship. The exceptions in Lord Baltimore's colony readily stand out. Excluding the Calverts themselves, eight sets of brothers served in the assembly in the first half-century. For various reasons, most of their tenures were brief and not concurrent.[21] Blood relations of differing generations were equally rare, even as late as 1689. Only sixteen assemblymen to that time qualify as the second generation of their families to hold provincial office. Another two individuals were the nephews of earlier officers. Only four of these eighteen men themselves had sons who later achieved provincial office.

Ties through women or steprelatives became slightly more common in these years. At least twenty-five men served in the assembly after marriage to the widow or daughter of a former member. This phenomenon is first noticeable in St. Mary's County in the early 1660s, followed soon after in Anne Arundel and by the 1680s throughout the settled areas of the colony. The most famous example of this pattern is the family of Thomas Gerard; four of his sons-in-law served subsequently in the assembly.[22] Still, the vast majority of assemblymen had no ties, by blood or marriage, with anyone else presently or formerly serving in the government. It would be the achievement of colonists after 1700 to forge the family cliques amd interlocking relationships that characterized the ruling elite of the later colonial period.[23]

Immigrant colonists continued in overwhelming numbers to dominate the membership of the assembly through the end of the century (see Appendix C). A minimum of 84 percent and probably as many as 89 percent of the 150 men first elected or appointed to the assembly between 1661 and 1689 had been born in Europe. The percentage of immigrants increases even more strikingly with the addition of those twenty-five members who had gained their first appointment or election before 1661. An English perspective, and occasionally some experience in another colony, far overshadowed any thoroughgoing local orientation for provincial officeholders through the end of the seventeenth century.

Only a handful of men represented anything at all resembling a native component in the assembly. Just three individuals had definitely spent their entire lives in Maryland – Ignatius Causine, Leonard Greene, and

Massachusetts, 1631–1661: An East Anglican Oligarchy in the New World," *Journal of Social History*, 1 (1968), 351–70; Bruce C. Daniels, "Democracy and Oligarchy in Connecticut Towns: General Assembly Officeholding, 1701–1790," *Social Science Quarterly*, 56 (1975), 460–75.
21. Only four of these seventeen men had sons who later held provincial office.
22. Beitzell, "Thomas Gerard and His Sons-in-Law," 189–206.
23. See Chapter 5 and David W. Jordan, "Political Stability and the Emergence of a Native Elite in Maryland," 243–73, in Tate and Ammerman, eds., *The Chesapeake in the Seventeenth Century*.

Richard Gardiner, all elected from St. Mary's. No native Marylanders gained appointment to the upper house before 1691. The midcentury migrations brought into Maryland at least eight young men, born in Virginia, who subsequently sat in the assembly in this period, and a native New Englander, James Browne, also won election but never actually served. Four other men, possibly natives of Virginia, certainly had spent the majority of their adult lives in the New World. But even generously including all of these individuals, as well as those children or young adults who immigrated with their families directly from England, no more than thirty-one assemblymen before 1689 can possibly qualify for second-generation New World status.

Yet in contrast to assembly members in the first two and a half decades, legislators between 1661 and 1689 were unlikely to be such newcomers to the colony. At no time after 1660 had less than half of any assembly's elected members lived in Maryland fewer than ten years, and the period of prior residency lengthened thereafter (Table 2). By the Assembly of 1676–82, approximately one-half of the delegates had dwelled in the colony more than sixteen years, and in the subsequent assemblies of the 1680s, close to half of the members could look back upon at least twenty years of residency in Maryland. No one elected to the new assembly in 1686 had lived in the colony less than seven years.

Instances of brief residency before one's first election fall primarily into two categories, neither very numerous. Such delegates came from a newly established county, where virtually all eligible voters and candidates were newcomers, or were individuals of exceptional skills, wealth, or status, like the young William Calvert, nephew of the proprietor, and lawyers Thomas Notley, John Morecroft, and Thomas Burford.

In contrast, men of humbler origins now lived in Maryland much longer before winning an election, and the length of that prior residence increased over the course of these three decades. For example, the Assembly of 1661 included three freedmen, each serving his first term; William Leeds, John Brewer, and Henry Adams had been in Maryland for approximately eleven, fourteen, and twenty-two years, respectively. Five freedmen served in the Assembly of 1676–82. Adams, in his fourth term, was now a colonist of thirty-seven years' standing. Newly elected John Edmundson and John Stansby had each been in the colony for eighteen years, and first-termers William Richardson and James Rigby had been transported twenty-one and twenty-two years earlier, respectively.

George Alsop in 1666 described the burgesses of Maryland as "being for the most part good ordinary Householders of the several Counties, which do more by a plain and honest Conscience, than by artificial

Table 2. Years in Maryland at time of election, elected members, 1661–89

Assembly	Total members	1–3 years	4–6 years	7–9 years	10–12 years	13–15 years	16–20 years	21–25 years	More than 25 years
1661	16	5 (37.5)	0	2 (12.5)	4 (25)	2 (12.5)	0	3 (18.8)	0
1662	17	0	4 (23.5)	0	5 (29.4)	3 (17.6)	1 (5.9)	3 (17.6)	1 (5.9)
1663–64	20	3 (15)	4 (20)	1 (5)	2 (10)	8 (40)	0	2 (10)	0
1666	21	2 (9.5)	3[a] (14.3)	3 (14.3)	3 (14.3)	0	9 (42.9)	1 (4.7)	0
1669	27	1 (3.7)	3 (11.1)	4 (14.8)	6 (22.2)	3 (11.1)	10 (37)	0	0
1671–74/75									
Original members	31	2 (6.4)	1 (3.2)	9 (29)	3 (9.7)	3 (9.7)	2 (6.5)	7 (22.6)	4[b] (12.9)
By-elections	14	0	4 (28.6)	4 (28.6)	1 (7.1)	1 (7.1)	2 (14.3)	1 (7.1)	1 (7.1)
1676–82									
Original members	42	1 (2.4)	7 (16.7)	5 (11.9)	7 (16.7)	2 (4.8)	6 (14.3)	6 (14.3)	8 (19)
By-elections	15	0	2 (13.3)	1 (6.7)	3 (20)	1 (6.7)	2 (13.3)	1 (6.7)	5[c] (33.3)
1682–84									
Original members	22	1 (4.5)	1 (4.5)	0	2 (9.1)	4 (18.2)	4 (18.2)	2 (9.1)	8[c] (36.4)
By-elections	1	0	0	0	0	1 (100)	0	0	0
1686–88									
Original members	22[d]	0	0	3 (14.3)	2 (9.5)	2 (9.5)	6 (28.6)	0	8[e] (38.1)
By-elections	5	0	0	0	1 (20)	0	1 (20)	2 (40)	1[f] (20)

Note: Numbers in parentheses represent percentages.

[a] Includes James Neale, who lived briefly in the colony in the first decade, returned to Europe, and then resettled in 1660.

[b] Includes two men who were born in Maryland or moved to the colony as youths.

[c] Includes four men who were born in Maryland or moved to the colony as youths.

[d] The identity of one delegate cannot be determined. Percentages are based on the 21 known members.

[e] Includes three men who were born in Maryland or moved to the colony as youths.

[f] A native-born Marylander.

Syllogisms drest up in gilded orations."[24] Alsop exaggerated, but in the middle decades of the century assemblymen did share a remarkably common profile with the average householder. Most delegates grew tobacco for their livelihood and participated directly, alongside any bound labor, in its cultivation. The estates of the delegates generally ranged in size from 200 to 1,500 acres (Table 3), although most of the acreage was not yet cleared or planted on the larger of these plantations. Thomas Stagwell of Kent County typifies the representatives serving in the early legislatures of this period. Stagwell, who arrived in Maryland in 1659 with no term of deference attached to his name, had accumulated 300 acres by the time of his election. A majority of his assembly colleagues in the 1660s similarly possessed less than 1,000 acres.

Men like Stagwell were less common in the next two decades as the average burgess became a man of greater affluence. A decided majority of the legislators elected in these later years possessed plantations exceeding 1,000 acres, and the proportion of even larger landed estates also grew, with between one-fifth and one-fourth of the delegates now owning more than 2,000 acres. Gradually, representatives came less and less to resemble Alsop's "ordinary Householders," although such men still occasionally won election throughout the period.

The occupations of men serving in the assembly between 1660 and 1689 underscore Alsop's observation and similarly reflect a pattern of homogeneity and general equality gradually giving way later in this period to greater diversity and variation in wealth. The majority of representatives sitting through the 1660s receive in the contemporary records a simple identification as "planter," the same term applied to most ordinary householders. Little in the nature of different economic activities distinguished these delegates from their fellow Marylanders. Occasionally an artisan appears, like Richard Beard, variously called a "planter" and "Boatwright," or in later decades Richard Hall and Thomas Thurston, sometimes termed "carpenter" and "shoemaker," respectively, as well as "planter."

By the 1680s, men engaged in more wide ranging economic activities had clearly supplanted "simple" planters within the legislature. Only three of sixteen delegates to the Assembly of 1661 merited contemporary classification as "merchant" or some comparable term, but that identification soon characterized an increasing number of representatives. Evidence of various entrepreneurial pursuits mounts, especially in the 1670s and 1680s. Another handful of men established lucrative law practices or augmented their income as clerks or placemen. By the end of the century,

24. Alsop, "Character of the Province of Maryland," 351.

Table 3. *Landownership of assembly members, 1661–89*

Assembly	Total members	Unknown	None	1–500 acres	501–1,000 acres	1,001–1,500 acres	1,501–3,000 acres	More than 3,000 acres
1661								
UH	5	0	0	0	0	1	2	2
LH	16	0	0	8	2	3	3	0
1662								
UH	8	1	0	0	0	1	2	5
LH	17	2	0	4	1	6	2	2
1663–64								
UH	8 (2)	0	0	0	0 (1)	1	3	4 (1)
LH	20	1	0	7	3	4	2	3
1666								
UH	8	0	1	0	1	0	4	2
LH	21	0	0	4	3	6	3	5
1669								
UH	6	0	0	0	0	0	3	3
LH	27	0	1	3	10	5	4	4
1671–74/75								
UH	7 (3)	2	0 (1)	0	0	0	2 (1)	3 (1)
LH	31 (14)	1	0	5 (1)	7 (5)	5 (4)	9 (4)	5
1676–82								
UH	6 (8)	0	0	0	0	0 (1)	2 (2)	4 (5)
LH	42 (15)	1 (1)	0	6 (1)	13 (4)	8 (6)	8 (2)	6 (1)
1682–84								
UH	10 (3)	0	0	0	0	1	3 (2)	6 (1)
LH	22 (1)	2	0	2	5	6	4 (1)	3
1686–88								
UH	10 (1)	0	0	0	0	1	4	5 (1)
LH	22 (5)	2	0	2 (1)	4	3 (2)	8 (2)	3

Note: The first figure in each column represents the original members of this assembly; the number in parentheses refers to members appointed or elected during the course of the assembly. UH denotes upper house; LH, lower house.

planters had become as atypical as the entrepreneurial colonists had been at the beginning of the period.[25]

As members of the assembly began to diverge occupationally from ordinary householdership, they also began displaying evidence of greater learning than the average freeman. Illiteracy appears less frequently, and the examples of formal schooling among burgesses become more common (Table 4). Only 9 of the 175 elected delegates of this three-decade period are known to have been illiterate, only 1 or 2 at the most being present in each assembly; as a rule, they were individuals of long standing in the colony.[26] Offsetting the handful of illiterate men was a slightly larger number of delegates with impressive educational credentials.[27] The majority of delegates fell between these two extremes; they were literate, possessed some books, but probably had limited exposure to formal schooling.

Assemblymen, whatever their education, were far more likely after midcentury to bring to their legislative duties a greater experience in government, particularly on the local level, and increasingly in the more important offices. The lengthening period of residence before election afforded a greater opportunity for members to acquire such experience. Again, the pattern of previous officeholding becomes more pronounced with the passage of time. In the first assembly of this period, nine of the sixteen delegates had previously officiated as county commissioners or justices. That proportion increased to twelve of seventeen in 1662, a level at which it generally remained for the next three assemblies. For the two longer serving legislatures of the following decade, the number of individuals of such experience climbed slightly. In both 1682 and 1686, sixteen of the twenty-two representatives had been justices, and 77 and 68 percent of the delegates, respectively, were currently holding commissions for that office.[28]

Over these three decades, the members without previous service of this nature were usually Quakers, who increasingly declined, especially after 1672, to serve as justices and sheriffs because of the necessity of swearing an oath. Other nonjustices practiced law or served as clerks in the various

25. Main, *Tobacco Colony*, especially Chap. 2.
26. Six of the illiterate burgesses were also justices and two served as sheriff.
27. Richard Bennett, Charles Brooke, and Nathaniel Utie had attended Harvard, and John Coode had been at Oxford for two years. Seven men – Robert Carvile, Kenelm Cheseldyne, John Morecroft, Thomas Burford, Henry Jowles, and Christopher and John Rousby – had extensive legal training. William Calvert and others possessed advanced clerical skills.
28. Carr, "Foundations of Social Order," 88, provides data for some of these assemblies. In Virginia, all known burgesses from 1660 to 1676 were also concurrently justices (Billings, " 'Virginia's Deploured Condition,' " 104).

Table 4. *Religion and education of assembly members, 1661–89*

Assembly	Total members	Catholic	Quaker	Other Protestants	Unknown	Well educated	Literate	Illiterate	Unknown
1661									
UH	5	1	0	4	0	1	4	0	0
LH	16	4	2	7	3	1	15	0	0
1662									
UH	8	4	0	4	0	3	5	0	0
LH	17	3	3	8	3	3	12	0	0
1663–64									
UH	8 (2)	4 (1)	0	4 (1)	0	3 (1)	5 (1)	0	0
LH	20	3	6	5	6	4	14	2	0
1666									
UH	8	4	0	4	0	4	4	0	0
LH	21	4	3	8	6	2	17	2	0
1669									
UH	6	4	0	2	0	3	3	0	0
LH	27	1	4	15	7	4	21	2	0
1671–74/75									
UH	7 (3)	5 (1)	1	1 (2)	0	4 (1)	3 (2)	0	0
LH	31 (14)	6 (3)	1 (3)	16 (4)	8 (4)	2 (3)	26 (11)	2	1
1676–82									
UH	6 (8)	4 (3)	1	1 (5)	0	2 (2)	4 (6)	0	0
LH	42 (15)	4 (3)	10 (2)	21 (9)	7 (1)	4 (1)	36 (13)	1 (1)	1
1682–84									
UH	10 (3)	5 (2)	0	5 (1)	0	3 (1)	7 (2)	0	0
LH	22 (1)	4	2	15 (1)	1	3	18 (1)	1	0
1686–88									
UH	10 (1)	5 (1)	0	5	0	2	8 (1)	0	0
LH	22 (5)	2 (1)	2	16 (3)	2 (1)	4 (1)	17 (4)	0	1

Note: The first figure in each column represents the original members of this assembly; the number in parentheses refers to members appointed or elected during the course of the assembly. UH denotes upper house; LH, lower house.

courts and therefore avoided appointments that interfered with their voca-
tions.[29] By the mid-1670s, an extraordinary congruence existed between
membership in the assembly and present or past service on the county
bench.

The assemblymen reflected throughout these decades the heterogeneous religious affiliations of the population at large (see Table 4). Among
elected members, twenty known Catholics served between 1661 and
1689, sitting exclusively from the Lower Western Shore counties of St.
Mary's, Charles, and Calvert. The twenty-three Quakers came from both
sides of the Chesapeake Bay. Seventy-seven other delegates were also
definitely Protestant; of these, at least thirty-one claimed adherence to the
Church of England, perhaps four more were Quakers, and many others
were attracted to the various nonconformist sects or were generally
unchurched, as indeed were many of the professed Anglicans. For thirty-
five burgesses, definite religious affiliation is uncertain, but this group
appears from circumstantial evidence to be predominantly Protestant and
almost certainly included no more than five or six possible Catholics. The
appointed upper house contained thirteen Protestants and nineteen
Catholics over these years. While the number of elected Catholics was
declining to four or fewer of the initial membership of assemblies sitting
after 1676, the upper chamber was steadily becoming more Catholic, as
the proprietor's patronage favored coreligionists. Once again, a religious
discrepancy between the appointed and elected members affected institutional developments and spurred the lower house to assert a stronger
voice in government.

The Calverts influenced relationships within the assembly during these
years in ways extending far beyond the recruitment of Catholics and
relatives for seats in the upper house. A series of political actions in effect
revised the entire electoral process; they altered the size of election districts, introduced new restrictions on the suffrage, formalized the conduct
of elections themselves, and manipulated the membership of the lower
house. The general population often disagreed on the wisdom of these
measures, which prompted many representatives and their constituents to
challenge bitterly proprietary involvement in these areas.

Alterations in the procedures for elections constituted the first of these
important changes. After midcentury, the county replaced the hundred as
the standard electoral district. An act of assembly legislated a similar
change in Virginia in 1661/62, but the transition evolved less precisely in
Maryland. Through the 1660s, elections apparently continued to be con-

29. On Quaker service and oath restrictions generally, see David W. Jordan, " 'Gods
Candle' within Government: Quakers and Politics in Early Colonial Maryland," *William and Mary Quarterly*, 3rd ser., 39 (1982), 628–54.

ducted in most counties by hundreds, as they had been since the first elected assembly. By 1671, however, voting for a particular county was certainly held in one place, although evidence suggests that some unofficial process persisted in several counties whereby various areas continued to have a representative, either by hundred or after 1692 by parish.[30]

Nonetheless, local politics assumed a less personal dimension as changes in representation led to a decline in the intimate atmosphere that had prevailed in the small hundreds. In 1642, for example, eight delegates had been selected to represent five hundreds in St. Mary's County, which contained some 240 taxables and approximately 470 in total population. By 1667, the taxable population of St. Mary's had risen to 688, while the number of elected representatives had declined to four. After 1682, voters chose only two delegates for the entire county to represent a taxable population now exceeding 924. In the 1660s, four delegates from recently established Charles County represented approximately 95 adult freemen in a taxable population of 205, but by the 1680s just two men were representing more than 750 taxables. The ratio of taxable population to elected assemblymen, rarely greater than 30:1 before the late 1650s, climbed to more than 200:1 for most older counties thereafter and at least 75:1 even in newer, sparsely settled counties.[31]

Electoral districts of a larger geographical size and population reduced the likelihood of voters having much direct acquaintance with prospective candidates. The ordinary planter's social world rarely extended much beyond a five-mile radius of his home. With the scattering of settlements in the Chesapeake area, such a neighborhood usually encompassed somewhere between twelve and twenty other families with whom a given colonist might have much intimate familiarity.[32] A voter's limited acquaintance with potential candidates most likely derived from contact during court days several times per year when most residents of a particular county gathered to conduct all sorts of business. It is probably not accidental that burgesses increasingly came from among the current justices of the county court, men appointed by the governor who thus indirectly shaped the pool of likely candidates. Service on the bench both brought

---

30. Jordan, "Elections and Voting," provides the most complete discussion of these changes. On Virginia, see Billings, "The Growth of Political Institutions," 235.
31. These ratios are based upon the reports of taxable population printed in the *Archives* and population estimates established by Russell Menard. The definition of taxables changed slightly during these years, but it generally included free white males sixteen years of age or older, male servants earlier from age ten and after 1676 from age sixteen, and blacks of both sexes, for the same ages. The law excluded ministers and priests as well as poor colonists receiving alms (*Archives*, 2:399, 538–39).
32. Walsh, "Charles County," 291–305, and Daniel Blake Smith, *Inside the Great House: Planter Family Life in Eighteenth Century Chesapeake Society* (Ithaca, N.Y., 1980), 175–230, reconstruct the neighborhoods and "worlds" of several colonists.

men to the attention of the electorate and provided some indication of their abilities.

Most voters elected their "betters" if such men were obviously available, and during these years more men appeared in the various counties with those distinguishing traits of status that had been so rare before the 1670s. Just when that pool was expanding, however, Charles Calvert reduced the size of delegations from four representatives to two per county. Consequently, the electorate during the 1680s made its choices from among more attractive candidates for proportionately fewer seats in the assembly.

The process of voting and the results of elections now assumed a greater potential for divisiveness. Evidence suggests that competition at the polls was heightened considerably over these three decades. A special court evolved for the conduct of elections, and the ceremony became more standardized by various rules and procedures. The formerly simple matter of summoning and convening voters now required a more systematic method of notifying individuals throughout the county, for to ensure fairness, respective candidates and their supporters demanded clearer guidelines for announcing and scheduling elections as well as for conducting the actual polls.[33]

Perhaps no change affected elections as much as the Calverts' new requirements for exercising the franchise. Until 1670, the suffrage remained remarkably liberal, any freeman being eligible to vote. Gradually, however, the distinction between servants and freemen proved less striking to those in authority than the growing differences between landowners and those without property, whether free or under indenture. Actions based on that new perception occurred almost simultaneously in Maryland, Virginia, and Massachusetts with the introduction of property or wealth qualifications for voting. The assemblies in Virginia and Massachusetts took this action, but again Charles Calvert proceeded independently in 1670, without consulting the legislature, to limit the right to vote and to hold office to those freemen within each county with "Visible seated Plantations of fifty Acres of Land at the least or Visible Personal Estates to the Value of forty Pounds Sterling at the least." This proprietary ordinance borrowed more directly from the contemporary English practice than did the new provisions enacted in the two other colonies.[34]

Calvert never explained his reasons for the new restrictions. The burgesses in neighboring Virginia justified their comparable departure with the observation that men recently freed from servitude "having little

33. Jordan, "Elections and Voting," 256–57.
34. Ibid., 247–48. For the ordinance of 1670, *Archives*, 5:77–78.

interest in the county doe oftener make tumults at the election to the disturbance of his majesties peace, then by their discretions in their votes provide for the conservasion thereof." Little evidence exists of widespread disruption by the poor in Maryland or of such pronounced class differences in politics as some have described for Virginia. During the first half of this period at least, the opportunities for freedmen in Maryland remained less limited than they apparently were in Virginia or were to become for Marylanders in another few decades.

Still, Calvert and others doubtless worried about the growing number of landless freemen. In their frustration, these poorer settlers, overwhelmingly Protestant, might become susceptible to demagogic appeals, especially ones directed against a Catholic proprietor claiming regal powers. A particularly combative assembly in 1669 may have shaken the Calverts' confidence in the electorate, although there is no indication that nonfreeholders had affected the membership of that body. The response of proprietary officials in 1676 to popular protests for a reenfranchisement of all freemen does suggest two contemporary justifications for property requirements. The governor and council argued that landowners should not have to "submitt themselves & all that is deare to them to be disposed of by the votes of the freemen that have nothing, & that can as easily carry themselves out of the reach of Lawes by themselves made, to the prejudice of the freeholder as change their Cloaths." Furthermore, the officials noted, the restriction was in "the fittest & most convenient manner, & most aggreeable to the Lawe & Custome of England, For what man in England can be admitted to the Election of Parliament men that hath not a visible Estate in land or Goods."[35]

Although some colonists attacked the new property requirement throughout the 1670s, more resented the proprietor's control over other aspects of the electoral process. Also, alarm over the eruption of Bacon's Rebellion in Virginia in 1676 and the less extensive uprising in Maryland the same year perhaps led many colonists, especially the assemblymen, to attribute some wisdom to the suffrage restriction. After all, the requirements did move the assembly closer to the English model, which most delegates consistently thought it in their best interests to encourage. Certainly, in other respects they appealed repeatedly to parliamentary examples in attempting to gain control of elections and eligibility for membership in the assembly. A comprehensive bill addressing these issues in 1678 explicitly proclaimed that the "Safest and best rule for this Province to follow in Electing such Delegates & representatives is the presidents of the

35. *Archives*, 15:137–39 and 5:149. On Virginia, Morgan, *American Slavery, American Freedom*, especially 238.

Proceedings in Parliament in England as neere as the Constitution of this Province will admitt."[36]

How extensively the new requirements restricted the right to vote is not known. In 1660, according to land records for both St. Mary's and neighboring Charles County, approximately 90 percent of the freemen owned some land. Declining opportunities for economic mobility in the last third of the century, however, meant that a larger number of freemen failed to acquire land and to establish their own independent households. Rent rolls for four counties on the Lower Western Shore for the years from 1704 to 1707 reveal that, even among heads of households, proba- bly just two-thirds to three-fourths owned sufficient land or estate to qualify, as more and more men were tenants with leaseholds. Eligible voters constituted an estimated 65 percent of all adult, free males in Charles County in 1704, or about 40 percent of all adult white males and 10 percent of the county's total population, but Charles at this time had probably the lowest proportion of landless householders on the Lower Western Shore. Across the bay in Talbot, probably 44 percent of the free adult males could vote, a noticeable decline from an estimated 55 percent in the 1680s, and the figure would diminish further to about 33 percent by the 1730s.[37]

How many Marylanders actually voted, from among the males who were eligible at any particular time, is even more difficult to determine. A few surviving returns from before 1650 suggest that half of the adult freemen had actually voted; in the 1690s, authorities frequently ex- pressed concern regarding low turnouts, and again a few surviving vote totals suggest a similarly low percentage. Variations in turnout and often a high rate of apathy parallel the practice of contemporary English voters, who usually participated only occasionally, say in one of four elections, and then in response to the intensity of issues and more vigorous canvass- ing by candidates and their supporters.[38]

Recent studies of Stuart England also describe a well informed elector- ate that increasingly discriminated in its screening of candidates and employment of the vote. The public also actively lobbied elected represen- tatives, who now had to balance more carefully the expectations of the countryside and the demands of the court. In attempting to satisfy both groups, the members of Parliament in the seventeenth century were map-

36. *Archives*, 7:12, 17, 19, 22, 25, 31, 60–63 (act and quotation).
37. Carr, "County Government," Text, 586, 601–56; Carr and Menard, "Immigration and Opportunity," especially 241; Walsh, "Charles County," 22, 314, 399, 415, 500; Clemens, *The Atlantic Economy*, 163–64, 170.
38. Jordan, "Elections and Voting," 257–59; J. H. Plumb, "The Growth of the Electorate in England From 1660 to 1715," *Past and Present*, 45 (1969), 90–116. Only about 15% of the adult males in England qualified for the suffrage in these years.

ping a new terrain somewhere between the independent representative voting in accordance with his own beliefs and the legislator adhering closely to the will of his constituents or his sovereign.[39]

Comparable changes in the evolution of representative government appear throughout England's New World colonies. Residents of Massachusetts, in defining "the character of the good ruler," advocated a greater reliance on the concept of a limited magistracy, or delegated powers as opposed to the discretionary ones championed earlier by John Winthrop and others. This shift placed more emphasis on the role of the elected assembly while also serving to raise the expectations of the voters and to heighten their scrutiny of legislative activity.[40] In Virginia, a gradual change in political style followed Bacon's Rebellion as the leading colonists became more likely to fraternize with the public, to keep them informed, to become their advocates, and to attempt persuasion by treats. The freeholders, in turn, started exercising their franchise in a more discriminating manner and generally made themselves more articulate in the political arena. Again, these trends spurred the lower house to assert a more powerful voice in the colonial polity.[41] Similar shifts appear in Maryland, where colonists demonstrated their own increased awareness, a more vocal presentation of their concerns, and a new sophistication in the use of the ballot. Elected representatives obviously recognized and responded to these new developments.

The fascinating community of Quakers in Maryland illustrates particularly well many of these developments.[42] Indeed, the Friends pioneered in employing several of the important new tactics. From the period of the first conversions to Quakerism in the mid-1650s, Friends constituted an influential presence within the government, an unusually large number serving as justices and delegates. By the 1660s, however, some Quakers' refusal to swear oaths made it virtually impossible for them to testify in court, to administer estates, to serve as guardians for orphans, or to fulfill other obligations. Quakers in the assembly, where no oath was required for sitting, attempted to have the legislature endorse Friends' rights to

39. Hirst, *The Representative of the People?*; Russell, "Parliamentary History in Perspective" and *Parliament and English Politics, 1621–1629.*
40. Timothy H. Breen, *The Character of the Good Ruler* (New Haven, Conn., 1970).
41. John C. Rainbolt, "The Alteration in the Relationship Between Leadership and Constituents in Virginia, 1660 to 1720," *William and Mary Quarterly*, 3rd ser., 27 (1970), 411–34. Jack P. Greene, *The Quest for Power: The Lower House of Assembly in the Southern Royal Colonies, 1689–1776* (Chapel Hill, N.C., 1963), discusses the growing assertiveness thereafter of the elected branch in Virginia, the Carolinas, and Georgia.
42. The following discussion draws upon Jordan, " 'Gods Candle' within Government," 628–45.

affirm, rather than to swear, but throughout the decade they failed in their efforts to pass a law to that effect.

In the 1670s, as Quakers reached a consensus against oath taking, their dilemma became more serious. Friends then inaugurated a sophisticated effort to gain the desired legislation. Quaker meetings in their respective counties carefully selected individuals to stand for election and then subsequently organized the local vote. At the height of that campaign in 1676, at least ten Friends and a number of "fellow travelers" won election and actively pursued Quaker interests within the legislature. The Quaker meetings followed up their electoral strategy with a thoughtful selection of additional individuals to lobby the assembly and to discuss grievances with provincial officials.

In addition to desiring a dispensation from oaths, Quakers wanted to resist wherever possible any war with the Indians of the area, or at least to protect Friends from military obligations. Charles Calvert, generally supportive of the Quakers, became so frustrated by their successful maneuvers and particularly their opposition to his defense proposals at the Assembly of 1681 that he explicitly condemned their political activities, denounced Friends as "Obstinant people," and called upon rational men not to vote in the future for anyone belonging to this faction. Calvert's public statement and appeal attest still further to the arrival in Maryland of a new style of politics.

Quakers were not alone in displaying a heightened interest in elections and in pressuring representatives to promote certain bills and oppose others. The Friends were simply the most organized group and the vanguard in experimenting with the tactics of screening candidates, mobilizing the vote, petitioning, and in various ways pressuring delegates and other provincial officers during meetings of the legislature. Throughout the colony, other freeholders differentiated as well among candidates with respect to their attitudes regarding proprietary prerogatives, defense of the colony, and particularly religious policies. The critical role of such issues in elections became more pronounced after 1689, but the first persuasive evidence of these influences appears in the 1670s and 1680s.

Colonists living in the region known as the Clifts in Calvert County, for example, persistently created trouble for authorities with actual as well as potential resistance to policies of the executive. That resistance frequently came outside the electoral process, but voters in the area clearly expressed their opinions through their suffrage. Similarly, a considerable portion of the electorate in Charles County proved continually ready to follow anyone raising the banner against the Calverts; on at least two occasions in these years, freeholders attempted to elect Josias Fendall, the outspoken former governor, despite his permanent disbarment from every office in the province, and apparently succeeded in garnering a majority of the votes for Fendall in one election.[43]

Even in St. Mary's County, where the Calverts' support was usually the strongest, voters in 1671 declined to return former delegates Thomas Notley and John Morecroft, who had been strong advocates of proprietary policies in the previous assembly. Governor Calvert unilaterally created new borough representation for St. Mary's City, with a limited suffrage he could more easily control, in order to ensure seats for those two men. As Calvert reported to his father, "I durst not putt itt to an Election in the Countyes Butt tooke this way which I Knew would Certainely doe what I desired."[44]

These new delegate-constituent relations began obviously on the local level at the time of elections. George Alsop reported in 1666 the custom for freemen to present their newly elected representatives with an account of local grievances; undoubtedly, private if not public discussion of matters of local concern also preceded elections and probably influenced them. Delegates then carried their constituents' complaints and requests to the assembly. Legislative journals had occasionally mentioned petitions from private individuals on isolated matters, such as requests for naturalization or the statutory settlement of a complicated estate. Such private appeals increased in number in this period, but more significant were the grievances and petitions from groups of individuals that touched concerns affecting more than one person and dealt with long-term issues.[45]

Such grievances often addressed controversial issues, and a tenuous line frequently separated what authorities considered a legitimate complaint from what they might regard as seditious. For example, in 1662, the upper house pronounced a declaration to the burgesses from some residents of Anne Arundel to be "a Libell Conteyning Scandalous and seditious expressions tending to the Utter Subversion and overthrowe of the legislative power of this Province resideing in the Lord Proprietary and both howses of Assembly."[46] Seven years later, the lower house, after considering numerous complaints, decided by a majority vote that seven

43. See, for example, *Archives*, 7:110; 15:137–42; 20:192–93.
44. Ibid., 51:389, 392, 394; *Calvert Papers, Number One*, 265–66. In 1678, St. Mary's City had at most thirty houses with a small resident population, which did not necessarily include all of the town officers who had a vote. See Carr, " 'The Metropolis of Maryland,' " 123–45.
45. Alsop, "Character of the Province of Maryland," 350; *Archives*, 13:354. For examples of earlier private bills, ibid., 1:297–98, 462, 531. Raymond C. Bailey, *Popular Influence Upon Public Policy: Petitioning in Eighteenth Century Virginia* (Westport, Conn., 1979), includes a helpful discussion of seventeenth century developments in Virginia, where the assembly in 1664 described its primary purpose as "making provision for the peoples safety and redresse of their Grievances" (p. 18).
46. *Archives*, 1:427 (quotation), 429–31; 2:86.

issues constituted legitimate grievances. The upper house did not concur and ordered the delegates to "raze the mutinous & seditious Votes contained in the paper Entitled The Public Grievances," because the document unjustly attacked the proprietor's prerogatives. A lengthy argument ensued before the lower house backed down.[47]

The further consideration of complaints in 1669 proceeded through a joint committee of grievances, although it failed to continue as a regular body after this assembly. Probably the delegates preferred not to conduct initial discussions of these grievances in a group containing members of the upper house. For the remainder of the proprietary period, it became the practice for the lower house alone, through its committee of laws, to consider the grievances submitted by delegates and petitioners, and when the members judged it appropriate, to translate these concerns into bills, without any prior involvement by members of the upper house.[48]

In any event, considering the public grievances became commonplace in the last half of the seventeenth century. Lord Baltimore's declaration in 1681 regarding the recent deadlocked legislature pointedly referred to concerned colonists "ready with Petitions at our Doors," in this instance individuals seeking better protection against the Indians and Quakers lobbying for a dispensation from oaths. At a new assembly in 1682, Calvert was immediately informed that "the freemen of this Province . . . have given Instruction to their severall Delegates" on the proprietor's ordinance of the previous year.[49]

In addition to introducing popular grievances, the delegates displayed a new reluctance to act on important issues without first consulting the public. In 1682, for example, when the legislature considered a new proposal for the advancement of trade, the representatives explained to the upper house that "without having first well Considered and Advised upon it in their Counties," they could not take action. Again in 1688, the delegates insisted on a delay until they could "Communicate with those they here Represent." Within nine years, a committee of the lower house was to propose, in response to a governor's request for a new militia act "that a copy of the said proposalls be drawn out for every county of this province, to the end that the Inhabitants of each county may consider of the Same; and give it to their Delegates in charge to the next assembly. It being not usuall for parliaments or assemblyes to enact Lawes altogether new until first acquainting the people therewith and having their sanction."[50]

---

47. Ibid., 2:168–84, especially 177, 181, 183.
48. Ibid., 2:168.
49. Ibid., 17:38 (first quotation); 7:345–46.
50. Ibid., 7:345–46, 369 (quotation); 13:176 (quotation); 19:577 (quotation). See also ibid., 17:408–9; 23:372–73.

Such postponements, whether genuinely intended or simply a stalling tactic, proved decidedly unpopular with the governor and the upper house, but these delays affected relationships less adversely than did outright opposition, which became increasingly common during these years. Disagreements frequently resulted in unresolved battles that prolonged assembly sessions and proved quite costly for the colonists, who wanted a more forceful lower house but also chafed at the tax burden of lengthy meetings. Delegates received no salary, but reimbursements for basic expenses could be considerable. Legislation in 1661 abandoned a set per diem allowance, but costs usually averaged between 1,500 and 2,000 pounds of tobacco per delegate in a typical session. Smaller or poorer counties suffered under this system, which was in effect between 1661 and 1676, especially as the state of the economy worsened and assembly sessions lengthened. In 1669, for example, assessments for the recent assembly constituted 35 percent of the entire county levy for Kent. In these years, newer counties often sought permission to send only a partial delegation in order to reduce the tax burden.[51]

In light of the public outcry over levies, delegates had to think carefully about actions that would prolong the meetings. Charles Calvert had his own solution to these costs, and probably to the growing contentiousness of some delegates. In 1676, he actually summoned only two delegates per county, from among the elected four, to the first session of the new assembly. He later explained that he was responding to the financial plight of the taxpayers. Suspicious delegates feared some nefarious plot to deny full representation and to summon only the more compliant members. This issue itself became a major grievance that prolonged two successive sessions of this assembly.[52] Since some counties had three times as many taxables as others, the delegates suggested a more equitable alternative and successfully enacted a bill to levy the expenses of assemblies on a provincewide rather than countywide basis.[53]

Expenses persisted as a nettlesome issue. The controversy reached a peak at the new Assembly of 1682. Lord Baltimore had officially reduced representation to two delegates per county in the previous year, a step taken, he argued, to reduce the public levy. Noting the proprietor's pro-

---

51. Ibid., 1:237, 440, 505, 540; 2:234, 241; 7:110; 53:174; 54:274. Assembly sessions averaged fifteen days in length in the early 1660s, but after 1664 only five of the subsequent sessions met fewer than twenty-three days and three went over a month.
52. *Archives*, 5:137–38; 2:507–8; 7:17. Calvert agreed to summon all delegates in the future if the representatives would take an oath of fidelity to him and his heirs. They would not so agree.
53. For unexplained reasons, the next session reverted to having each county pay for its own delegates, but in 1682 the legislature returned to the practice of a provincewide levy (*Archives*, 2:509, 511, 514, 554–55; 7:13, 31, 81).

fessed dedication to relieving taxpayers, the delegates opposed the public's even having to pay the charges of the upper house. The elected members resolved "Nemine Contradicente That the Deputies and Delegates chosen by the freemen of this province in a Generall Assembly Assembled, are the onely Representative body of the freemen of this province." The members of the upper house did not even deign to respond.[54]

The lower house boldly asserted such claims in the 1680s but could rarely back up its language with true power. Many colonists had certainly hoped that the division of the assembly into two houses would bestow greater strength on the elective voice in promoting the interests of the majority of the population and in defending them against arbitrary measures. Indeed, the lower house did possess, at the minimum, a veto in the legislative process. The executive, however, retained considerable influence within the lower house and often had his way there as well as in the upper chamber. In the last analysis, he could always resort to a veto of undesired legislation or attain his objectives through executive ordinances.[55]

The delegates had to invest their separate chamber with sufficient protection to hold their own against the governor and councillors. First, the representatives needed security to speak more frankly and critically in their own deliberations without fear of reprisals. Philip Calvert assured the anxious delegates in 1661 that they had "as much liberty as any Burgesses had or have in the Parliament of England" and that no special legislation for freedom of speech within the assembly was necessary. Still, the routine guarantees of freedom of speech regularly granted at each new session and the careful swearing of clerks to secrecy provided only minimum protection; wary delegates still hesitated to speak forthrightly or to have the journal of the lower house record precisely what was said and by whom.[56] They struggled, usually unsuccessfully, to avoid direct debates with the governor and upper house, to communicate only through written messages, and in other ways to combat Charles Calvert's uncanny facility for discovering opposition among the elected members and then effectively silencing or containing it. One discontented colonist complained as late as 1683/84 that "my Lord did wyerdraw the Assembly," and rebels in 1689 railed specifically against Calvert's ability to "craftily" obtain his way with "unwary Representatives."[57]

54. Ibid., 7:334, 373, 419 (quotation).
55. For example, Calvert vetoed eight acts from the Assembly of 1663–64 (*Archives*, 2:157–58) and almost all legislation from the session of 1678, passed when he was away from Maryland (ibid., 17:253–54).
56. Ibid., 1:398 (quotation), 429–30; 7:261, 262, 335.
57. Ibid., 2:41, 42–43, 179, 180, 432, 454, 455; 8:216 (quotation); 17:182 (quotation). On Calvert's adroit interaction with delegates, see also *Calvert Papers, Number One*, 256–57, 264–65, 295.

Another goal became development of the speakership into a more independent position. The representatives took seriously the governor's request at the opening of each assembly "to chose their Speaker." In fashioning this office, they followed as closely as possible the example of the House of Commons, even borrowing directly the elaborate "disabling" ceremony, fully described in contemporary literature on Parliament.[58]

How independently the lower house exercised its choice remains uncertain. The first five speakers were Protestants with strong support in the nonconformist community and men outside the proprietary circle. Through the 1660s, little continuity prevailed since men usually served in the position for only one assembly, although these individuals were often returned to the next legislature. No incumbent accrued substantial power given the turnover in office, but none of these early speakers seems to have been the agent of the Calverts either.

If the governor had not initially influenced the choice of speakers, by the 1670s Charles Calvert was certainly doing so. Copying the English model himself, for the Crown greatly influenced the selection of a speaker for the House of Commons, Calvert in 1672 boasted of securing the post for proprietary stalwart Thomas Notley and indicated that this gentleman would remain speaker as long as the partnership worked well. Calvert had also amply rewarded Notley's predecessor Thomas Taillor for his cooperation, and this became a common strategy for maintaining cordial relations with any speaker. Taillor, Notley, and their two successors, Philemon Lloyd and Kenelm Cheseldyne, were all able men; each was a logical choice, whatever the degree of influence exerted by Calvert in the process of selection. Lloyd and Cheseldyne, both chosen during a period of Calvert's absence from the province, probably reflected again a more independent selection by the delegates.[59]

Speakers gradually accumulated more power, especially as they began to preside through several sessions. The speaker determined who drafted official statements, who served as messengers to the upper house, and most important who served on the committees, which began to evolve in a more regular fashion during these years. Earlier, an erratic series of ad hoc committees had handled any special tasks arising in the assembly,

58. *Archives*, 1:397, 426, 460; 2:10, 150, 239, 312; 7:3, are examples of elections of speakers and the subsequent "disabling" ceremonies. For English practices, see Henry Scobell, *Memorials of the Method and Manner of Proceedings in Parliament in Passing Bills* (London, 1670), 4, and Henry Elsynge, Esq., *The Ancient Method and Manner of Holding Parliaments in England* (London, 1675), 151–57.
59. *Calvert Papers, Number One*, 264–65; *Archives*, 5:141. Similarly, the lower house seems to have chosen its own clerk until 1671, but thereafter until 1689 the governor made the selection. See Mereness, *Maryland as a Proprietary Province*, 219–20; *Archives*, 5:505–06; 7:3, 260–62, 335, 447.

and the responsibilities usually did not extend beyond one particular assignment. Speakers began to delegate routine tasks to a subgroup of the membership; in the process, the lower house came to rely more consistently on a few influential delegates to consider critical issues, to draft bills or review past legislation, and to make recommendations on special matters to the full body. The delegation of these responsibilities became critical as the chamber assumed a greater initiative in the legislative process. In the Assembly of 1676–82, for example, the speaker appointed five such committees to examine public accounts, review elections and privileges, draft and revise laws, and consider issues involving trade and defense. Comparable committees appeared in most assemblies during the last decade of the period, but not until 1692 did a full committee structure become a permanent feature of the lower house's organization.[60]

Working collectively as well as through committees, the delegates particularly attempted to acquire greater control over their own membership. Debates raged almost continuously over efforts to maintain a full house on all occasions, to have the speaker rather than the governor issue writs for by-elections, to determine procedures and eligibility for elections, and in other ways to terminate or limit proprietary jurisdiction in these areas.[61] Attempts to obtain satisfactory legislation addressing any electoral matters encountered repeated failure. The delegates managed to pass their comprehensive act in 1678, no doubt because of Calvert's temporary absence from the province, but frustration mounted upon its veto three years later. The lower house throughout the 1680s influenced only slightly proprietary ordinances regarding elections. Typical of Charles Calvert's responses was an exchange over who should issue warrants to fill vacancies. He sharply disputed the delegates' analogies to the House of Commons' procedure and noted that the speaker's issuance of writs was not a right practiced "in Virginia, Barbadoes or any other of his Majesties Plantations;" the proprietor haughtily instructed the representatives to "Amuse not themselves with things they understand perhaps as little as we and Serve only to foreslow Business and Ruine the Publick."[62]

---

60. Papenfuse et al., eds., *Biographical Dictionary*, 1:15–31, lists committees and their members for all assemblies from 1635 through 1688. Appointed men tended to be the better educated members or occasionally the rare delegate like Richard Beard or Joseph Wickes whose service in previous assemblies provided a valuable perspective. Membership frequently overlapped from one committee to another during a given session; for example, Kenelm Cheseldyne, Robert Carvile, John Coode, and Christopher Rousby, indisputably the best educated members of the Assembly of 1676–82, served on two or three committees each; the majority of delegates never received an assignment.

61. Jordan, "Elections and Voting," 243–49.

62. *Archives*, 7:123–24, 127. See also, Scobell, *Memorials of Proceedings in Parliament*, 20.

The delegates, nonetheless, clearly understood that any additional power did depend upon a firmer control over who sat in the assembly and under what conditions. The lower house enjoyed somewhat more success in other tactics than in its futile attempts to legislate in these matters. Delegates ventured tentatively in 1669 to discipline sheriffs for improper conduct of elections and in 1671 actually fined one member, James Browne, for contempt in not honoring the writ to appear for the current session. In the latter instance, cautious burgesses determined that it was necessary to obtain the concurrence of the governor and upper house, but by 1678 the delegates proceeded confidently and independently in fining representatives not in attendance and without acceptable excuses.[63]

An effort of the house in 1669 to impeach delegate John Morecroft, a proprietary protégé accused of misconduct in his legal practice, failed and elicited an angry rebuke from the upper house.[64] Twelve years later, however, the delegates defeated a similar effort by Calvert and the councillors to force the expulsion of representative John Coode, accused but not yet convicted of a breach of peace. The lower house resisted intimidating threats and boldly asserted after "a Diligent Search of Such Records and Authorities as might best inform us of the Rights and Priviledges" of this house that a breach of peace, much less only an accusation, should not divest a member of his right to sit. With this parliamentary precedent, the delegates made their point. The episode reflected a growth in maturity and sophistication since 1669.[65]

Slight gains accumulated as well in curtailing proprietary influence in the assembly. In 1678, the Committee of Elections and Privileges questioned the right of sheriffs to sit concurrently as burgesses; three men were then serving in that dual capacity. The proprietor's patronage constituted a powerful weapon for influencing ambitious delegates. Calvert vetoed the act from this session that explicitly excluded sheriffs and undersheriffs from eligibility, but the delegates continued to claim that English practice "incapacitated" sheriffs and that the same should apply in Maryland. Their reasoning lacked official sanction until Calvert incorporated the exclusion of sheriffs in his ordinance of 1681; he conceded on this limited point while preserving the larger principle of no legislation on this subject.[66]

63. *Archives*, 2:187–88, 243, 244; 7:6, 9, 10.
64. Ibid., 2:166–67, 172–73.
65. Ibid., 7:112, 113, 115, 116, 119, 135 (quotation), 136, 137, 138, 139; David W. Jordan, "John Coode, Perennial Rebel," *Maryland Historical Magazine*, 70 (1970), 9–13; and on English proceedings in such cases, Paul R. Ward., ed., *William Lambarde's Notes on the Procedures and Privileges of the House of Commons (1584)*, House of Commons Library Document No. 10 (London, 1977), 59.
66. *Archives*, 7:17, 19, 39, 68–70, 114, 134, 216, 247, 329, 451, 531; 17:16. Sheriffs, of course, could not sit in Parliament (Elsynge, *Method of Holding Parliaments*, 71).

The slow course of legislative gains in these critical areas, and frequent failure to achieve popular objectives, disappointed the electorate. Like the Calverts, the public was not always patient and understanding, and its pressures usually pushed the representatives in an opposite direction from the proprietor's demands. At the height of the contretemps in 1669, frustrated delegates remarked to the upper house, "We should readily and willingly Embrace any way to peace whereby We may not be found to betray our Trust reposed in Us & to violate the Dictates of our own Conscience."[67]

Elected members caught between these conflicting interests, like contemporary members of Parliament, tried to balance demands. Facing this difficult dilemma, delegates sometimes found their personal positions more in harmony with the policies of the Calverts and sometimes more with complaints arising from constituents. There were advantages and costs to be weighed continuously in deciding any position, and the problems involving the economy, defense, or the powers of the proprietor were not simple issues, although some individuals always tried to present them as such. Furthermore, the representatives never knew in advance on which issues the Calverts might be willing to compromise or how firmly the lower house might wisely persist in adhering to a controversial position.[68]

Several episodes suggest the growing importance of an impatient public in this delicate situation. Charles Nicholett, a nonconformist minister, in a sermon before the lower house in 1669 admonished the delegates that they "were now chosen or Elected both by God & man & have a power putt into their hands. The Country has often had an Assembly, but never an assembly that soe greate expectacons were as from this." Nicholett urged them to follow more closely the model of the House of Commons, to be considerate of the burdens of the people, and "to goe with Courage for that you have a power of your selves & Equall to the rest of that the people & a Liberty equal to the people of England." The sermon drew immediate censure from the upper house, and Nicholett subsequently confessed that some delegates had urged him "to stir up the Lower house

67. *Archives*, 2:180.
68. Conrad Russell has written that "Parliament was not the champion of one side; it was a collection of those whose interests did not permit them to let two sides develop. The conflict between the central government and the county communities was one in which almost every member of Parliament had divided loyalties. The conflict between these divided loyalties was one of the most important reasons for their powerlessness. The conflict between 'court' and 'country' was not fought out between members of Parliament and the King; it was fought out within the members' own minds." ("Parliamentary History in Perspective," 26–27).

to do their Duty." He was fined and forced to acknowledge his error publicly.[69]

Disputes raged over what should constitute the "Duty" of elected representatives. Verbal and physical assaults on assemblymen attest further to the high expectations and the changing mood of the electorate. Before the 1660s, legislators rarely suffered such abuse. Now, many officials worried about acts of insolence deliberately committed against delegates and councillors. Anyone openly disparaging officials was charged and, if convicted, sentenced and fined in an attempt to contain these differences. In 1666, for example, Edward Erberry was sentenced to be whipped with thirty-nine lashes in view of the assembly for having verbally assaulted several members. Erberry had called the men "a Turdy shitten assembly" and a "Company of pittiful Rogues, & puppyes" who were "ashamed of the place from whence wee came."[70]

Such attacks became more frequent as elected delegates failed to make sufficient progress in their battles with the proprietor. A "Complaint from Heaven with a Huy and crye," issued in 1676, provided the most colorful indictment. The representatives, the statement bitingly noted, "are called Deligates, but the Country calls them Delicats, for thy gladly com to sutch Christenings at St. Mary's where there is good cheere made, and the poore Country payes every time, one two or more hundred thousand pounds of tobacco for it." The upper house dictated what the lower house was to do, the protest continued, and if there were "any grummels at, then perswadinge spirits goe forth, and if any stands out or up for the common good, frowns and threatnings scares them to be quieth right or wrong: and this thy call Acts of Assembly, but the Country calles them, dissemblings, and abreptive procured Acts." The document attacked several men by name for doing the bidding of the Calverts and then, addressing the larger body, beseeched, "O yee Assembly men, why are yee so meal mouthed and affraighted to speke the truth and for the people's comon good and the publick welfare of the Country?"[71]

Several burgesses did become significantly less "meal mouthed and affrighted" in the assemblies of the 1680s. Neither Charles Calvert nor any freeholders could consider Robert Carvile, John Coode, or Christo-

69. *Archives*, 2:159–60 (quotation), 162 (quotation), 163. Ministers preached before the assembly on various occasions, but the journals fail to disclose the contents of sermons. However, delegates did balk in 1683 at the upper chamber's request of a gift to the Rev. Duell Read for his recent sermon before both houses (ibid., 7:478, 570). In 1696, Governor Francis Nicholson, at odds with the assembly, sent the delegates a sermon by the archbishop of Canterbury "of doing good to Posterity" (ibid., 19:307–8).
70. Ibid., 2:55–57.
71. Ibid., 5:134–49, especially 137–38 and 146 for quoted passages.

pher Rousby "Delicats." They were recklessly outspoken in their attacks on the proprietary circle and its policies; the subsequent loss of numerous positions at Calvert's behest made these men even more assertive and vindictive. An incipient revolt in 1681 and an actual rebellion in 1689 built upon public grievances and depended on the leadership of a few individuals, like these men, who declined to back down but who were also not above employing such issues upon occasion to promote less altruistic interests as well.[72]

Unfortunately, no latter-day George Alsop recorded his observations of the assembly and its members in the late 1680s. Such perceptions, had they been written and preserved, would certainly contrast considerably with Alsop's account of 1666. An astute observer near the end of the century would have described more extraordinary householders among the burgesses and acknowledged a greater complexity in the organization of the assembly and in the way representatives performed their tasks. Any commentary would also have emphasized greater contention within the legislature and between the delegates and "those they here Represent." In the absence of such a report, other evidence does establish these developments. The proponents of a more representative government may have realized only limited gains in these thirty years, but they laid the foundation for more substantial victories eventually achieved during the royal period.

72. See, for example, ibid., 5:274–76, 278–80, 286–308; 17:181–86, 244–45; and Jordan, "John Coode, Perennial Rebel," 1–28.

4

"To Liken Us to a Conquered People"

They [the lower house] are not to Conceive that their privileges run paralell to the Commons in the Parliament of England, for that they have no power to meet but by Virtue of my Lords Charter, so that if they in any way infringe that they destroy themselves; for if no Charter, there is no Assembly, No Assembly no Privileges. Their power is but like the common Council of the City of London which if they act Contrary or to the overthrow of the Charter of the City run into Sedition & the Person Questionable.

Chancellor Phillip Calvert to lower house, April 24, 1669

Forasmuch as the Cheifest and onely foundation & support of any kingdome State or Commonwealth is the provideing enacting & establishing good and wholesome lawes for the well Ruleing & Government thereof & allsoe upon any necessary & imergent occasions to Raise & leavy money for the defraying the Charges of the said Government & defence thereof neither of which according to the Constitutions of this Province can be made ordeined established Leavyed or raysed but by & with the Consent of the freemen of this Province by their severall delegates and representatives by them freely nominated chosen & Elected to serve for their severall Cittyes & Countyes in a Generall Assembly and for as much as the Safest & best rule for this Province to follow in Electing such Delegates & representatives is the presidents of the Proceedings in Parliament in England as neere as the Constitution of this Province will admitt the Delegates of this present Generall Assembly doe humbly pray That itt may be Enacted.

Preamble to An Act directing the manner of
Ellecting and Summoning Delegates and Representatives
to serve in succeeding Assemblyes, 1678
(vetoed by Charles Calvert, third Lord Baltimore, 1681)

With the restoration of proprietary authority in Maryland in 1660 and the concurrent accession of Charles II to the throne of England, Cecilius Calvert anticipated at long last a less troubled enjoyment of his own "Monarchical Government" in the province. It had required unceasing vigilance, adroit maneuvering, and considerable effort and expense over recent decades to maintain the colony and to preserve the Calverts' rule there. Now, the future of the province seemed more secure. The population was finally growing, the economy was flourishing, and Lord Baltimore welcomed a period of relative peace in which to establish more firmly his supreme authority in Maryland, as promised by the charter of 1632.

The proprietor's prospects in 1660 for achieving this elusive goal were by no means ensured. Since the death of Leonard Calvert in 1648, three different men had officiated as Lord Baltimore's resident governor in Maryland, and all three had bitterly disappointed him. Furthermore, colonists had repeatedly demonstrated their growing uneasiness with the Calverts' vaunted claims to regal authority. Many freemen refused to heed just any proprietary deputy or to obey just any dictate. As the two briefly successful rebellions of the last decade amply attested, not even the assembly's obliging enactment of Lord Baltimore's cherished legislative code could guarantee the obedient submission of all colonists to an unchecked proprietary rule in the province.

Lord Baltimore perceived that the characteristics of leadership essential for sustaining the Calverts' design of government dictated a return of trusted family members to the most critical posts in the colony. Moreover, he finally felt secure again in appointing Catholics to the principal offices. For the first time since Leonard Calvert's death, the proprietor also had suitable relatives of talent and diplomacy whom he could dispatch to Maryland.

Philip Calvert, a younger half-brother, had arrived in Maryland in 1656 as secretary of the colony. He vindicated the proprietor's trust by loyal resistance to Fendall and other rebels in the Assembly of 1659/60 and by a capable assumption of the reins of responsibility as chief executive after defeating these men in late 1660. Calvert presided as governor for approximately another year before stepping aside in favor of Lord Baltimore's son, Charles Calvert. Thereafter, the uncle served as chancellor, councillor, and a valuable senior adviser until his death in 1682.

Charles Calvert was only twenty-four years of age when he arrived in Maryland in 1661, but few colonists could question the legitimacy of his claim to leadership. Equally important, he proved generally to be an astute judge of men and a crafty employer of the disputed proprietary powers. First as governor until 1675 and then upon his father's death as the resident proprietor for another decade, Charles Calvert skillfully directed the provincial government of Maryland. Not until circumstances required his return to England in 1684 to defend the colony's charter did the third Lord Baltimore cease to exercise an extremely effective supervision over all political affairs in the colony. His lengthy absence from Maryland in the latter half of the 1680s, coupled with the death of Philip Calvert, created once more a vacuum in leadership, and only then, in

1689, did dissident colonists, effectively restrained for almost three decades, again successfully challenge proprietary authority and overthrow the government.

For almost three decades, however, Charles Calvert delayed in numerous ways the progress of the assembly toward acquiring a stronger voice in the colony's governance. To an extent unmatched certainly by Leonard Calvert and other provincial executives, Lord Baltimore's son masterminded the business of the assembly and generally prevented the passage or implementation of any legislation that infringed upon proprietary prerogatives. Charles Calvert's very success in these endeavors provided in time additional force to the demands for a greater popular role in decision making. As long as Calvert remained in the colony, such demands met with little success.[1]

In 1661, the young governor's initial task was to quell any dissent in the aftermath of the recent rebellion. Fortunately for Calvert, many of the most outspoken opponents of the government were barred during the 1660s from serving in the assembly, and other dissidents had left Maryland. Consequently, the governor could focus his attention and patronage on a more malleable body of men. He established generally cooperative relations with most members of the legislature. The governor actually sat as a member of the upper house before 1665; thereafter, he was excluded by proprietary order from any official membership in the assembly, but Calvert still frequently joined the councillors for much of their deliberations and always addressed both houses at the beginning and end of each session.[2]

Improved relations, at least for the time being, enabled the legislature to dispatch its business rather expeditiously in sessions that usually lasted just two weeks. With a basic legal code in place, the assembly began to address an increasing number of new concerns pressing upon the expanding Chesapeake society and economy. As in contemporary Parliaments, the majority of laws were phrased to last for a short period, generally for three years or until the next meeting of the assembly, if that occurred sooner. There seemed little disposition to enact permanent legislation in most areas; members preferred to test legislative solutions cautiously and

---

1. On Charles and Philip Calvert, see Papenfuse et al., eds., *Biographical Dictionary*; Hall, *The Lords Baltimore*, 99–137; Nicklin, "The Calvert Family;" and *Calvert Papers, Number One*, 251. Lois Green Carr and David William Jordan, *Maryland's Revolution of Government, 1689–1692* (Ithaca, N.Y., 1974), 1–45, and Andrews, *Colonial Period*, 2:325–79, ably survey the years between 1660 and 1689.
2. *Archives*, 15:10, documents the official change in the governor's status as a member of the assembly. After 1692, royal governors again sat regularly with the upper house.

through temporary laws to gain as much advantage as possible in strengthening the hand of the elected lower house.[3]

Throughout the 1660s, members of the upper house usually proposed the new laws and considered which statutes from previous assemblies merited revival, although bills might originate in either chamber. The governor himself largely shaped the business of a particular session by preparing for both houses a list of measures requiring action. Calvert had drafts of bills ready for submission to the councillors. The delegates, most of whom were inexperienced in the framing of the laws, generally looked unapologetically to the governor and upper house for direction in conducting unfamiliar business. For example, the burgesses asked the upper house in 1664 to draw up a law "obligeing negros to serve durante vita" and addressing the claims of some slaves "pretending to be Christned And soe pleade the lawe of England."[4] Occasionally the two houses met in joint conference to explore a critical issue, as in 1661 when they came together to discuss Indian relations. As a rule, however, they sat separately, and by 1666, the delegates were displaying less willingness to combine the two houses for any business. About this same time, the representatives became less disposed as well to wait for the upper house to forward its version of proposed legislation and less happy with the Calverts' resistance to any laws addressing certain sensitive issues.[5]

Despite the increasing influence of the provincial government and particularly the assembly, much ignorance and confusion persisted throughout the colony as to just what were the laws of Maryland, both the recent statutes and legislation that predated the immigration of most residents. Some colonists also worried about those subjects on which the province's laws remained silent and the degree of application, desired or not, of English statutes. On this controversial issue not even the assembly members could reach any definitive resolution. The government generally adhered to an agreement of 1662 that in civil proceedings the justices of the various courts in the colony should base their decisions on English law and precedent if no provincial statute pertained. This temporary accommodation completely pleased no one and ignored the reality that justices often had differing degrees of knowledge themselves about English law, not to mention their occasional ignorance of provincial legislation. By 1666, the body of both permanent and temporary laws passed by the Assembly of Maryland had become sufficiently large and uncertainty so great regarding what statutes had expired, been repealed, vetoed, or

---

3. No lower house journal survives from the early 1660s, but the records of the upper house for these years reveal little evidence of acrimony.
4. See, especially, *Archives*, 1:402, 428, 461, 526 (quotation); 15:9.
5. Ibid., 1:400; 2:68, 78, 106.

amended that the legislature ordered all acts to be transcribed on parchment and carefully published or proclaimed at convenient places in each county.[6]

Indicative of new areas into which the assembly was now moving, the gradual way it tended to proceed, and the confusion that remained was the body's attention to the subject of slavery. Although earlier assemblies had indirectly acknowledged its existence, in neither Maryland nor nearby Virginia had there been any haste to legislate extensively in this area. Both colonies wrestled gradually with the presence and condition of Africans in their populations; laws followed many years after the evolution of a distinctive slave system.[7]

Before the 1660s, no more than 100 Negroes lived on the Lower Western Shore of Maryland, constituting just 3 percent of the colony's total population. Most blacks had come from the West Indies and were already substantially acculturated to European ways. Society responded to them generally as a subcategory of the larger world of servants. Not until the 1690s were local planters to turn to Negro slaves as a primary source of labor.[8]

Still, the number of Negroes did increase during the second half of the century, and the status of black laborers clearly differed from that of white servants. Those differences increasingly appeared in the prices paid for their respective services, in inventory appraisals, and finally, in the colony's legislation, at first almost as afterthoughts or statements of a common understanding and then gradually as a more explicit legal recognition of the pronounced difference. As early as 1639, members of the assembly argued that all Christian inhabitants, "Slaves excepted" should enjoy the rights of Englishmen. Subsequent incremental acknowledgments of slavery came primarily in statutes dealing with servants, a com-

6. Ibid., 1:448, 504: 2:133, 347–48. On the issue of English law in the colony, consult Joseph H. Smith, "The Foundations of Law in Maryland, 1634–1715," 92–115, in George Billias, ed., *Selected Essays: Law and Authority in Colonial America* (Barre, Mass., 1965); Souissat, *The English Statutes in Maryland*; and Carr, "Extension of Empire."

7. *Archives*, 1:533–34 (act of 1664). See also Jonathan L. Alpert, "The Origins of Slavery in the United States: The Maryland Precedent," *American Journal of Legal History*, 14 (1970), 189–221, and Winthrop D. Jordan, *White Over Black: American Attitudes Toward the Negro, 1550–1812* (Chapel Hill, N.C., 1968), especially 71–82.

8. Russell R. Menard, "From Servants to Slaves: The Transformation of the Chesapeake Labor System," *Southern Studies*, 16 (1977), 355–90, and Menard, "The Maryland Slave Population, 1658 to 1730: A Demographic Profile of Blacks in Four Counties," *William and Mary Quarterly*, 3rd ser., 32 (1975), 29–54. Other informative studies include Main, *Tobacco Colony*, 129–39; Whittington B. Johnson, "The Origins and Nature of African Slavery in Seventeenth Century Maryland," *Maryland Historical Magazine*, 73 (1978), 236–48; and Ross M. Kimmel, "Free Blacks in Seventeenth Century Maryland," ibid., 71 (1976), 19–25.

mon subject of early legislation. For example, an act of 1663 regarding the punishment for runaway servants noted that Negroes and other slaves were "incapeable of makeing Satisfaccon by Addicon of Tyme."[9]

Some delegates determined in 1664 that it was at last necessary to resolve some troublesome questions about slavery. Thomas Notley, one of the early major slaveholders in the province, a recent immigrant from Barbados, and currently the speaker of the house, was undoubtedly familiar with the extensive legislation of the Barbados assembly on slavery and may well have originated the request for a bill to be drafted. By 1659, the legislature in his former colony had already passed twelve acts addressing this subject and in the Governing Act of 1661 had legislated its own comprehensive statute. Notley had left the island colony the following year.[10]

The Maryland act of 1664 remained more general than the detailed Barbados statute. One paragraph in length, the new law succinctly established slavery as a lifetime and hereditary condition for imported Negroes. Furthermore, "freeborn English women" who married slaves after 1664 were themselves to become slaves for the life of the husband and any offspring became slaves; the children of such women who had married before 1664 were to serve as slaves only until the age of thirty. The statute failed to treat the consequences of a slave's conversion to Christianity. The framers probably intended that religious conversion not affect the condition of slavery, but questions persisted nonetheless. As slave owners voiced their uneasiness regarding obligations to proselytize, the assembly subsequently legislated in 1671 that conversion and baptism did not manumit slaves or discharge them in any way from their servitude. As with other issues receiving legislative attention, slavery continued to be addressed through various revisions and extensions of these early laws. The journals of the assembly record no extensive debates about slavery, and members apparently had little difficulty in reaching agreement during these years on the provisions of their laws affecting Negroes.[11]

Requiring increasingly more attention at legislative gatherings were the issues of Indian relations, the defense of the colony, the condition of the economy, and the proprietor's right to control the process of representative government itself. Such topics dominated discussion by the late

9. *Archives*, 1:41, 489, for the two quoted passages.
10. Notley, elected to the assembly within a year of his arrival, owned twenty-nine slaves at his death in 1679. On Barbados, see Steven Joseph Ross, "Slavery, Law and Society in 17th Century Barbados" (thesis, New College, Oxford, 1973); and Dunn, *Sugar and Slaves*, 224–62.
11. *Archives*, 1:533–34; 2:272 (act of 1671); also 5:267, for Charles Calvert's comments in 1678 on the persistence of these concerns about Christianizing the slaves.

1660s and thereafter repeatedly aroused tensions. Of course, previous legislatures had also considered these subjects, often quite acrimoniously, but the intensity of feeling displayed in the Assembly of 1666 and later meetings was new to Charles Calvert's tenure.

A few discontented delegates usually pushed the legislature's consideration of these sensitive subjects, but in 1666 Calvert himself encouraged the debate of issues he knew to be divisive. The governor approached the delegates warily that session, for he recognized the lower house's jealous protection of its power to tax and to approve any military expedition. Nonetheless, the recent activities of some wandering Indians, members of a tribe that usually remained well outside the boundaries claimed by Maryland, greatly worried the governor. The previous assembly in 1664 had explicitly denied Calvert both the requisite authority and revenue to conduct the military expedition he had proposed at that time, but in the subsequent months complaints had mounted from colonists suffering from a series of Indian raids. Residents on the highly exposed northern frontier were protesting that they bore an inequitable burden of the colony's defense. Some legislative response seemed called for in Calvert's estimation; at the least, he wanted the assembly to receive the blame for inaction if approval for a military expedition were still not forthcoming.

Initially, a group of delegates opposed any measure that might enable Calvert to muster the militia. It is uncertain whether they dismissed the seriousness of any threat, opposed waging a war beyond their actual boundaries, distrusted Calvert's discretion in the possible use of troops, or simply feared any increase in the tax burden during these depressed times. While they argued, the governor perhaps encouraged a greater confidence in his own leadership by successfully concluding articles of peace with several other tribes. The assembly eventually empowered Calvert and the council to raise men and secure arms as necessary for a possible war or negotiation of peace "with any Indian Enemy without the bounds of this Province for the Space of two yeares only and no longer," with expenses to be levied equitably on all taxpayers.[12]

Greater disagreement attended discussion at this assembly on the state of the economy. The upper house, noting "the present deplorable State of the Province reduced to almost extreme Poverty," proposed a cessation of the planting of tobacco, the solution most favored by Charles Calvert. The representatives strongly disagreed, preferring that "every man be left to his Liberty" to plant whatever he wished. The delegates feared a depopulation of the province if any cessation were legislated, and

---

12. Ibid., 2:11, 14–17, 19–20, 25–27, 136 (quotation). Francis Jennings, "Indians and Frontiers in Seventeenth Century Maryland," 216–41, in Quinn, ed., *Early Maryland in a Wider World*, insightfully discusses Indian relations.

shrewdly it was they who first expressed concern about a possible diminution of proprietary income as another consequence. In the ensuing debate, irritated councillors voiced suspicions that the business of the lower house was being "Managed by the Artifice of a few." If Charles Calvert wanted a cessation, the members of the upper chamber caustically remarked, then the delegates should not presume that they knew better Lord Baltimore's interests and wishes on this matter than did his own son. For two days, the delegates angrily avoided any joint meeting while the upper house argued that the recently passed act for support of a war against the Indians would be meaningless if tobacco became worthless and no arms could be purchased. Should enemies successfully invade because the colony had insufficient weapons owing to the declining value of tobacco, the appointed members haughtily lectured the delegates, then "the Guilt lyes at your Doors." With this threat, the councillors forwarded two bills on the economy to the lower house.[13]

The delegates proceeded to itemize their objections. They feared the proposed cessation would be ineffective, that merchants would send fewer ships to the colony, and that "young Freemen being the greatest Strength of this Province" would leave Maryland. Finally, they argued that the quantity of tobacco affected the price less than did the scarcity of ships to transport it. The upper house tried to refute each objection and particularly commented that freeholders, not freemen, were the colony's special strength and that the departure of poor freemen might even be an advantageous consequence. At length, the delegates reluctantly agreed to a cessation, but only if provisions were made for the satisfaction of debts and if the assemblies of Virginia and the Carolinas complied with similar legislation. The eventual statute also called for a delegate from each house to meet with commissioners from the other colonies.[14]

The governments of Virginia and the Carolinas subsequently concurred in this response to the economic situation, and the Maryland council issued in October of 1666 a proclamation for a cessation of the planting of tobacco during the next year.[15] By January, however, word had reached the colony of Lord Baltimore's opposition. On the basis of "great Inconvenience . . . not only to the Poorer Sort of Planters," but also to the king with respect to customs duties, Cecilius Calvert had disallowed the Maryland statute. As the governor and council of Virginia remarked later, the news from Lord Baltimore "overtook us like a Storme," leaving the other participants in this collective enterprise like "distressed Mariners." The proprietor's action no doubt stunned his son

13. *Archives*, 2:35–43.
14. Ibid., 43–49, 143–44 (act), 149–50; 5:18.
15. Ibid., 3:547–48, 550–52, 558–60.

as well and emboldened many delegates to assert themselves against the governor and council. The burgesses could apparently be as legitimate interpreters of the proprietor's will and interests as members of the upper house or even the governor, and the delegates already considered themselves the only appropriate representatives of the public's needs and concerns.[16]

In this instance, the proprietor's veto of an act upheld the position of most delegates. More often, a rejection of legislation frustrated the wishes of the lower house. Increasingly, the delegates objected to this proprietary prerogative, as they were vehemently to do in 1669. The governor had summoned a new assembly, because all temporary legislation was to expire soon. When the representatives gathered in St. Mary's City, they learned that Lord Baltimore had vetoed eight acts passed by the Assembly of 1663–64. The news forcefully reminded them that the proprietor always possessed the final word on legislation and that he might allow years to elapse before signifying his rejection of statutes.[17]

This unsettling news of disallowed legislation, combined with worsening conditions in the province and popular unrest, made the Assembly of 1669 a particularly argumentative legislature. Calvert had the formidable task of winning over a majority of the twenty-seven delegates who gathered for this meeting. Thirteen individuals were serving for the first time, and only eight men had been members of the previous assembly. Other representatives included Joseph Wickes, elected once again after the long period of ineligibility imposed following his earlier opposition to the proprietor, and several other men formerly active under the parliamentary commissioners. Only one definitely identifiable Catholic won election. Thomas Manning, a fiery Protestant and veteran of two earlier terms, became the speaker of this decidedly unfriendly lower house. A proprietary appointee as attorney general from 1660/61 to 1666, he had been discharged to make room for William Calvert, the young nephew of Lord Baltimore, and in 1669 the governor also dropped Manning from the Calvert County judicial commission for having struck the sheriff. The new speaker had earned a reputation in proprietary circles as "a fighter a sower of strifes and discord amongst his neighbours."[18]

Before the two houses had even undertaken any substantive business, they quarreled over the Reverend Charles Nicholett's inflammatory sermon that challenged the delegates to a more forceful representation of

16. Ibid., 561 (quotation); 5:5–9 (quotation), 15–19.
17. Ibid., 2:157–58, 161.
18. Owings, *His Lordship's Patronage*, 132; *Archives*, 51:332–33; 55:244; 57:607. Proprietary officials soon prosecuted Manning for common barratry, a legal term for "troublemakers who were repeated offenders" (ibid., xxxii).

popular grievances. Disputes also arose over the lower house's attempt to transfer its place of meeting to a nearby building, presumably for greater privacy. Thomas Notley and John Morecroft, objecting to this move, reported it to the upper house, which in turn insisted that the governor's permission was necessary before the delegates could relocate. Soon after, members of the lower house compounded the rising ill feelings by instituting impeachment proceedings against Morecroft on the charge of extortion.[19]

The delegates had come armed with numerous petitions and grievances from their constituents. The lower house eventually distilled these complaints to seven major items. Heading the list was the absence of anyone in Maryland with full authority to confirm laws, an understandable protest in light of the recently announced vetoes. The delegates wanted the governor to possess a final voice, without having to await further word from England. Angry protests had also arisen regarding the previous year's levy for defense measures. People further objected to Charles Calvert's efforts to obtain a more professional bar through the licensing of attorneys and by restricting to a select few the privilege of practicing in certain provincial courts. Sheriffs had allegedly seized tobacco illegally, and as usual there were a host of complaints about other officers and their fees. Finally, the representatives endorsed protests that "vexatious Informers" were communicating falsely to proprietary authorities about some colonists' allegedly "mutinous & seditious Speeches."[20]

The members of the upper house responded promptly and negatively to all of these grievances. The first few items, they observed, touched matters of proprietary powers indisputably granted by the charter, and therefore they could never be legitimate complaints. Moreover, any vote on the record of the journal of the lower house declaring such actions as grievances was itself seditious. The councillors lectured the delegates that their privileges did not run "paralell to the Commons in the Parliament of England, for that they have no power to meet but by Virtue of my Lords Charter, so that if they in any way infringe that they destroy themselves; for if no Charter, there is no Assembly, no Assembly no Privileges." The ultimate affront, directly challenging the elected house's growing perception of its own role, was the assertion that "their power is but like the common Council of the City of London which if they act Contrary or to the overthrow of the Charter of the City run into Sedition & the Person Questionable."[21]

19. *Archives*, 2:158–59, 159–62, 165–67, 169–73. The upper house acquitted Morecroft.
20. Ibid., 168–69; 57:xvii (on the new licensing of attorneys).
21. Ibid., 2:173–78.

Insulted by these remarks, the delegates refused to erase their journal as the upper house had requested, at least not until the grievances had been sincerely addressed. The governor threatened to dissolve this assembly, but astute delegates realized that such an action would automatically terminate all temporary legislation, and without statutory law in several important areas, the colony would be thrown into a crisis. Calvert, hesitating to precipitate that crisis, instead exerted pressure on the recalcitrant delegates during an ensuing three days of stalemate. His arm-twisting succeeded, for a majority eventually agreed to obliterate the first three grievances from their journal.[22]

Not until fifteen days into the session did the membership begin discussion of several proposed bills. The two houses' disagreements carried over into their consideration of this pending legislation. The upper house defeated two bills, one concerning the gauge of tobacco hogsheads and another appointing certain officers, both of which had been temporary laws the lower house wished to revive. In turn, the burgesses initially refused to approve the Act of Gratitude for the Lieutenant General, a traditional temporary statute that reimbursed the governor for his duties. The upper house requested a conference, but the delegates resolutely declined to meet or to give reasons for their opposition to the bill. Meanwhile, the lower house amended several temporary laws and failed to forward for revival eleven other statutes. In addition, the delegates pursued efforts to attain greater precision in the proprietary bill for the levying of war, in order to correct what many obviously considered to be abuses committed under the act of 1666.[23]

The two houses eventually joined in conference after the delegates established the procedural rule that no bill "already quashed & laid aside" was to be discussed. The meeting resolved some differences but could not agree on the proposed statute for defending the province. A compromise act of gratitude did give Charles Calvert a six pence per hogshead duty on exported tobacco, but for one year only. The governor had been accustomed to receiving twenty-five pounds of tobacco annually per taxable, and these former laws had generally been in effect for three years or until the next assembly. Delegates shrewdly guaranteed that Calvert would not again wait three years before summoning the next assembly.[24]

The legislature had sat for almost a month, had cost the colony at least 68,752 pounds of tobacco in members' expenses, and had still failed to enact the legislation the governor most desired. Some delegates had become openly insubordinate. No previous elected chamber had been so

22. Ibid., 178–84.
23. Ibid., 186, 189–91.
24. Ibid., 1:491; 2:193 (quotation), 217–18.

feisty and so disinclined to follow the leadership of the upper house. Calvert undoubtedly discussed this situation at length with his closest associates in the colony and with his father during a trip to England that year.[25]

The governor returned to the province by early November of 1670. As he began his second decade of residence in Maryland, Calvert determinedly pursued a more aggressive course to regain the ascendancy. His own experiences through the 1660s, counsel from his father, and the contemporary models of Charles II in England and Governor William Berkeley in neighboring Virginia probably all influenced the steps he now undertook. The governor drew encouragement from the somewhat more congenial company of advisers with whom he increasingly surrounded himself. A favorite cousin, William Talbot, had returned with Calvert to serve as secretary and joined Philip Calvert and another cousin William Calvert in forming the nucleus of the council. Charles Calvert now employed his powers of patronage more decisively. In making appointments to lesser positions, especially the shrievalty, he abandoned his earlier practice of having a frequent turnover of incumbents and began to renew commissions for extended periods, generally for as long as the officeholders performed their duties to his satisfaction. For example, Benjamin Rozer and William Chandler, each of whom married a Calvert stepdaughter, dominated the shrievalty of Charles County for twelve of the next fourteen years. A more permanent bureaucracy of a tightly knit character was emerging under Calvert's direction.[26]

Concurrently, the governor directed additional changes toward the assembly itself. First, he announced the new restrictions on the suffrage that excluded nonpropertied freemen from voting. Second, as with sheriffs and other officers, he decided to extend the life of any satisfactory assembly. This would afford him a better opportunity to win over delegates and then to enjoy the fruits of his labors. After the first meeting of a new legislature in 1671, Calvert reported to his father that "as long as I find them psons soe well tempered and disposed, I shall not Change for new faces." He was to continue this same body for four sessions over the next five years, a longer life than any previous assembly had attained in Maryland.[27]

Just why these representatives proved "soe well tempered and dis-

---

25. Ibid., 2:234. Calvert left soon after adjournment and denied his deputies the power to call an assembly in his absence (ibid., 5:52, 69).

26. Ibid., 2:435; 5:72: 51:174–75; *Calvert Papers, Number One*, 291, 297; Jordan, "Maryland's Privy Council," 72–75.

27. *Archives*, 2:435; 5:77–78; 51:174–75; *Calvert Papers, Number One*, 261 (quotation).

posed" is unclear. Nineteen delegates did not return from the previous legislature, but their absence does not necessarily imply that the voters were now more favorably disposed toward the proprietor. Speaker Thomas Manning and three other incumbents had died since the last assembly, and two other members were probably in ill health. If anything the electorate declined to return those men closest to the proprietary circle. In St. Mary's County, where the Calverts' influence was usually the strongest, Notley and Morecroft, two known favorites of the governor, did not return to the assembly, nor did Nathaniel Utie of Baltimore County; Calvert soon made a place for this important manor lord on the council. Joining Utie in the upper house at later sessions of this legislature was William Stevens of Somerset, a dependable proprietary supporter, also not a carryover in the lower house. Finally, Robert Dunn of Kent, a less affluent man, was also missing from the new assembly; the governor appointed Dunn sheriff of his county by 1673.

Ten of the nineteen newcomers had never received even a proprietary commission to serve as justices of the peace. Two other new delegates were not currently sitting on their respective county benches. This exclusion from patronage is understandable only for Daniel Jenifer, an active attorney, and for Ambrose Dixon, a Quaker. Collectively, the full returns of the new assembly suggest a continuing disinclination to reelect any incumbents, a tendency to shun proprietary adherents more often than to favor them, and a predisposition in most areas to elect new men not currently enjoying the governor's favor.

Changes in the pressing issues before the assembly and somewhat improved economic conditions in the province perhaps better account for the smoother relations that prevailed when this legislature convened. Certainly, these men focused less intensely on concerns of the economy and defense of the province than had been the case in 1666 and 1669. The points of disagreement concentrated instead on the proprietary control of election procedures and membership in the assembly. For example, the delegates, sensitive to any possible misuse of power by the Calverts, immediately questioned in 1671 the absence of full delegations from Kent, Somerset, and Dorchester counties. Only when the lower house learned that these more sparsely populated areas had requested partial representation in order to limit the local tax burdens did the delegates turn to other business. With lingering suspicions of Calvert's motives, however, they remained attentive to any suggestion of proprietary manipulation of their membership.[28]

Discussion at this first session centered on routine business, the reviv-

28. *Archives*, 2:237–308, particularly 240–41 on the issue of full delegations.

ing of satisfactory laws, and the drafting of several new statutes, such as further legislation to alleviate the concerns of some planters that the baptism of slaves might lead to their manumission. The two houses reached a seemingly easy agreement on a new Act for Quietting Possessions to replace an important statute vetoed by Lord Baltimore two years earlier; this legislation extended protection to colonists whose titles to property were in dispute, if those people could provide a witness to the sale or transfer of ownership whereby they had acquired the land in question. The lower house surprisingly initiated action and gained passage of An Act for Advancement of Foreign Coynes, An Act Against Divulgers of False News and An Act Prohibiting Importation of Horses, measures previous delegates were not usually inclined to support. Burgesses attempted less successfully to limit the appeal of cases from county courts to the Provincial Court when less than 1,500 pounds of tobacco was involved; struggles over the jurisdiction of courts were to become more pronounced in later years. Religious differences probably account for the defeat of a bill for erecting schools or a college in the province.

The upper house focused on the passage of An Act for the Rayseing and Provideing a Support for his Lordship. The delegates introduced some important amendments, but the bill's ultimate passage testifies quite clearly to Calvert's improved relations with the assembly. Any previous "acts of gratitude" passed only for a temporary period, and the lower house had been particularly hard-nosed on this point in 1669. Now, however, the delegates gave Cecilius Calvert a duty of two shillings per hogshead on all exported tobacco for the remainder of his life to defray "the many great and Necessary Expenses of Government."

The explanation for this extraordinary legislation lies unquestionably in the important concessions extracted by the lower house in exchange for its support. First, although the revenue was to provide for "Competent Sallaries and Encouragement" to the governor and council, one-half of the money had to be employed toward maintaining a magazine of arms and ammunition for the purposes of defense and thereby reduce the heavy burden taxpayers were currently carrying for these needs. Furthermore, the act, in amending a taxing clause of the permanent statute of 1650 on the levying of war, restated the necessity of the explicit consent of the assembly before any future public levy could be raised for defense purposes, and the new law also abolished the customary mustermaster's fee. Finally, in probably the crucial compromise, the proprietor agreed to accept tobacco in payment of fines or quit rents at the rate of two pence per pound, almost double the current price. With specie scarce, tobacco prices continuing to fall, and rents recently doubled, this concession provided a considerable advantage for the landholders.[29]

This legislation had attractions for the proprietor as well. It assured the government, at least through the life of Cecilius Calvert, of a much appreciated means of support for officials without having to worry about the good will of each individual assembly and without having to bargain so frequently, as the act of support in 1669 had threatened. Acknowledging the mutual advantages of the statute, assemblymen three years later gladly extended its provisions through the life of Charles Calvert, with some slight amendments addressing the problems of tobacco lost in shipwrecks or through seizure of cargoes. The representative branch was learning to balance the advantages and disadvantages of certain bills, to negotiate more astutely, and to perceive the cleverness of Charles Calvert as their antagonist.[30]

Six months after adjourning the first session of this assembly, Calvert reconvened its members. He had by this time furthered his influence in the lower house through the new representation given St. Mary's City and his success in having its burgess Thomas Notley placed in the speaker's chair.[31] Even so, the governor could not completely have his way with the elected membership. Preparing for another military expedition against threatening Indians, Calvert wanted an alteration of a "prejudicial restriction in the Act for Support," presumably the clause prohibiting any charge to the public without the explicit consent of the assembly. The legislature, more specifically the lower house, declined to make the change. The delegates realized that their power to tax and thereby control the government's ability to wage war constituted their greatest strength at this point, and they intended to employ this advantage for bargaining on other issues. The representatives had reached preliminary agreement on a pay table for militia officers but had passed no law to make the table official when the news of the death of the governor's sister interrupted the session; Calvert abruptly concluded the meeting after only ten days of business.[32]

When the threat from unfriendly Indians temporarily subsided, Calvert proved in no hurry to involve the assembly again in governmental affairs. Another session was not essential for almost three years. Calvert finally summoned the members to gather again in May of 1674 and issued writs

29. Ibid., 249, 255, 256, 257–58, 284–86 (act); 5:141. The mustermaster fee had been four pounds of tobacco per taxable.
30. Ibid., 2:381–82, 386–89 (act).
31. *Calvert Papers, Number One*, 264–65.
32. Ibid., 253, 265; *Archives*, 2:314, 321.

for filling the numerous vacancies. The replacements included three Catholics, two Quakers, and one adherent of the Church of England. The Quakers, Richard Hall and William Berry, were the vanguard of the growing number of Friends being carefully promoted at the polls, but the most important new member was Robert Carvile, a Catholic, who had served as clerk of the lower house in 1669 and at the first session of the current legislature. A well-trained lawyer and active practitioner in the colony's courts, Carvile brought to the assembly a knowledge of English law and parliamentary procedure and a detailed familiarity with the province's own statutes. He immediately assumed an important place on the joint committee of laws.[33]

Carville and his colleagues initiated a valuable review of the colony's entire legislation and codified those acts of Parliament that the assembly thought it essential for judges of the Provincial Court to know. A careful scrutiny by the lower house revealed numerous duplications in laws passed by previous assemblies, as well as some incomplete coverage of important matters; the delegates accordingly proposed the repealing of some acts and revision of others as required. The upper house concurred, and through this review the legislature reduced from forty-one to twenty-four the number of temporary laws. In the process, the representatives exhibited a greater skill than before in preparing statutes. The delegates desired that in the future all instructions from the proprietor to the governor concerning land be published, and they requested clearer communication to the legislature regarding the status of laws passed but still pending approval by Lord Baltimore. Differences over the question of allegedly deserted plantations and the proprietor's reclaiming of certain land briefly threatened to disrupt the meeting; in these economically difficult times, the delegates protested Lord Baltimore's quick escheating of plantations for which rents had not been paid. The representatives also objected to the governor's proposed bill authorizing a military expedition "without the province." These disagreements never reached the stage of overt hostility, however. Members finally compromised on the defense question and approved a special levy of 50,000 pounds of tobacco if needed in resisting the Indians. The delegates departed from the capital having shown little evidence of any serious rancor against the Calverts.[34]

The colony at large, however, already displayed signs of serious problems ahead. A periodic downturn in the state of the tobacco economy had renewed the straitened conditions of the previous decade. Simultaneously, deteriorating relations with several Indian tribes promised to

33. *Archives,* 5:124; Papenfuse et al., eds., *Biographical Dictionary*; Jordan, " 'Gods Candle' within Government," 638–41.
34. *Archives,* 2:243–417.

raise still further the costs of defense and the already burdensome levies. The immediate prospect of an extended war with the Indians persuaded Calvert to convene a fourth session early, during the following winter. The northward expansion of the colony had carried settlers into land previously occupied by natives less friendly than the Piscataways, Matta-womans and other tribes that had reached an accommodation years before with the English. Conflicts still farther north among the Indians of the Five Nations were also disrupting the usual territorial claims and forcing some relocation of natives along the eastern seaboard. The Sene-cas, or Northern Indians as the Marylanders often labeled these Indians collectively, were pressing hard upon the Susquehannahs, now quite numerous in those very areas where Lord Baltimore's colonists were establishing their new plantations. Delegates feared that the presence of the Susquehannahs as far south as the Patuxent River "may corrupt our Indians" and "be of Dangerous Consequence to the Province in Gen-eral." The legislature desired a peace treaty with the Senecas, but many members also feared that such a settlement might further alienate the Susquehannahs. Although the governor had not yet expended the spe-cial levy of the previous year, worried assemblymen now authorized for one year any charges necessarily incurred in "making warr or peace with the Indians." Besides reviving the necessary temporary laws, this session conducted little additional business.[35]

Anxiety mounted over the next few months, as hostilities between various Indians and colonists erupted all along the extended frontier. In July of 1675, skirmishes in northern Virginia seriously alienated what had formerly been the peaceful Doeg Indians and kindled new fears. A group of Virginians had ventured into Maryland and killed some inno-cent Indians in retaliation for damages inflicted by unknown attackers. Alarm thus spread from the northern frontier, already on full alert, to the more established areas of the province, where residents worried about a possible response from the angry Doegs.

Calvert activated the militias of Anne Arundel and Baltimore counties and placed in readiness 200 men from St. Mary's and Charles for service with other troops being raised in Virginia. On September 26, soldiers from the two colonies surrounded a fort of some Susquehannah Indians suspected of collaborating with the Doegs and terrorizing the frontier. Under the command of Major Thomas Trueman, a member of the Mary-land council, these forces demanded satisfaction from the Indians, who

35. Ibid., 419–70, especially 428–29 (quotation) and 463–64 (act). See also Jennings, "Indians and Frontiers," and his "Jacob Young: Indian Trader and Interpretor," 347–61, in David G. Sweet and Gary B. Nash, eds., *Struggle and Survival in Colonial America* (Berkeley and Los Angeles, 1981).

denied any responsibility for the recent attacks. Negotiations broke down, and despite the presentation by the chiefs of a medal given them by Calvert as a pledge of peace and protection, the colonial troops brutally murdered five of the Indians participating in the conference. A full-scale siege of the fort ensued, but most of the Indians eventually eluded the militia and in the next few months attacked exposed settlements in Maryland and Virginia to exact revenge.[36]

The military expedition, concluded in November, proved costly in several regards. It failed to achieve its aim and left the security of the province even more seriously threatened, for the actions of the troops had gravely impaired the confidence of otherwise friendly Indians that the government of Maryland would honor its treaties and carefully differentiate between peaceful and hostile natives. Moreover, these futile efforts to defend the province had placed an exceedingly heavy burden on the public treasury. Within six months, the council had to order an additional levy of eighty-five pounds of tobacco per poll beyond the earlier assessment of eighty pounds. Planters suffering from a worsening economy voiced acute distress and forced Calvert to rule that public obligations in this time of crisis assumed a primacy over any private debts.[37]

The one-year authorization for defense of the colony was about to expire. Before Calvert could convene another assembly, he learned of the death of his father. In keeping with the English practice of dissolving a current Parliament immediately upon the death of the monarch, Calvert terminated the present assembly. Then, in April of 1676, the third Lord Baltimore, now proprietor in residence, summoned freeholders to choose new representatives. Rumors of alleged Indian attacks against the settlers abounded throughout the Chesapeake. News of the disastrous King Philip's War in New England was circulating, and many Marylanders undoubtedly knew as well of the tense situation in nearby Virginia, where an assembly in March had aired fierce differences over the best strategy to pursue with respect to the Indians.[38]

The voters in Maryland once more returned a substantially different membership to the lower house, but again no obvious pattern of alignment emerges in the low incidence of carryover. Only thirteen delegates from the previous assembly won reelection. Death or known absence from the province accounts for only six of the remaining twenty-four representatives sitting in the most recent session. Sixty percent of the men chosen at the April election courts were first-term delegates. Former as-

36. *Archives*, 15:47–49, 136; Wilcomb E. Washburn, *The Governor and the Rebel, A History of Bacon's Rebellion in Virginia* (Chapel Hill, N.C., 1957), 19–25.
37. *Archives*, 15:50, 57–59, 62.
38. Ibid., 51:174–75; 2:435; 15:65; Washburn, *The Governor and the Rebel*, 25–32.

semblymen returned to the legislature included a combination of proprietary and antiproprietary figures. The new membership included only four Catholics, a notable decline from the last legislature, but at least ten Quakers, in striking testimony to the Friends' growing success in their electoral tactics.[39]

Calvert surprised the delegates, and the colony at large, by inviting only two of the four elected representatives from each county and just one burgess from St. Mary's City to convene with members of the upper chamber on May 15. Attendance at any assembly still required a specific writ of summons, and uninvited members could not participate. The journal of the lower house does not survive from this first session, and the records of the upper chamber identify in passing only fourteen of the delegates who received a writ of summons and were present. All but four of these individuals had served in the previous assembly, but that may have been coincidental rather than intentional on Calvert's part. In any event, the partial membership, as a first order of business, noted the absence of full delegations and specifically requested that Calvert call at least one of the missing delegates, the invaluable Robert Carvile. The proprietor complied with this request but declined to summon anyone else.

Calvert justified these partial delegations as a measure of economy to relieve taxpayers, but he probably wished as well to avoid confronting those individuals from whom he anticipated the greatest opposition. The announcement of a special oath of fidelity to be required at any future meeting of this legislature specifically from those members not present at the first session suggests Calvert's uneasiness regarding their allegiance and cooperation. More telling are the initial absence of Carvile and the apparent exclusion of most of the recently elected Quakers. Only one Friend is known to have served in the lower house during this first session, and the future imposition of any oath would likely discourage still further any later involvement by these missing Quakers. Calvert was well aware that the Friends particularly resisted service in the militia and opposed taxes raised for the purposes of defense.[40]

Perhaps because of the unusual circumstances of membership, the lower house cooperated more congenially at this first session than at any subsequent meeting. The external crisis spurred cooperation, as did a general desire to establish favorable relations with Calvert in his new

39. Jordan, " 'Gods Candle' within Government," 641–42.
40. *Archives*, 2:474, 507–08; 5:137; 8:225. Papenfuse et al., eds., *Biographical Dictionary*, 1:28, provides the most authoritative list of those members present at the first session.

capacity as proprietor. In turn, he was anxious to avoid needless disagreements and to accomplish a wide range of objectives at this meeting. Planning soon to depart for England on business regarding his father's estate, the new proprietor wished to leave the province in as secure and stable a condition as possible. The lower house advanced the likelihood of cooperation by reelecting Notley, the proprietor's choice, to serve as speaker.[41]

Discussion of Indian relations dominated the month-long session. The assembly particularly investigated, at Calvert's behest, Thomas Trueman's role in the controversial expedition of the previous winter with its "barbarous and inhumane Murder [of] five Susquehannough Indians." In impeachment proceedings, the delegates concluded that Trueman bore primary responsibility for those deaths, which had endangered the security of the province. The upper house subsequently found Trueman guilty as charged in the impeachment, but the representatives declined to support the death penalty urged in some quarters and argued that extenuating circumstances warranted a lesser punishment. Dissidents were later to assert that Lord Baltimore deliberately tried in this assembly to shift blame for the incident to Truman when Calvert himself bore most of the responsibility.[42]

The lower house also questioned the government's supplying of arms and ammunition to any Indians, even those friendly to the colony. The representatives further asserted that in the future neither Calvert nor his deputies should proceed independently of the lower house in assessing any levies for defense costs or in calling out the militia. This house obviously thought the previous assembly's authorization afforded Calvert too much leeway. A new act of three years' maximum duration carefully stipulated that at least one delegate from each county be present when any levy for defense purposes was assessed on the taxpayers. Delegates further reminded the proprietor that public levies did not absolve him of the responsibility to provide arms and ammunition as required by the act bestowing on him the two-shilling duty on exported tobacco.[43]

At this first meeting, the legislature also continued the efforts of the previous assembly to clarify the existing laws of the colony. The members passed a statute explicitly detailing those earlier acts that were no longer in force and ratifying anew those acts that were. New legislation restricted certain activities of servants, particularly travel, established a table of fees for various offices, and addressed some aspects of the tobacco economy, notably the seizure of tobacco by sheriffs to satisfy debts.

41. *Archives*, 2:470–515; 5:141.
42. Ibid., 2:475–78 (quotation, 475–76), 485–86, 494; 5:134–35; 15:182–83.
43. Ibid., 2:492, 493, 504, 557–60 (act).

To show support for the new proprietor and to continue the favorable conditions for payment of quit rent and fines, the assembly extended the two shillings per hogshead duty through the life of the young Cecilius Calvert, Lord Baltimore's son and heir.[44]

The proprietor left Maryland in late June. In preparation for his absence, he established articles of war to govern any possible military activity and devised an oath of fidelity to be sworn by all soldiers. Disregarding the sentiments of the lower house, Calvert supplied arms in early summer to friendly Indians and enlisted their cooperation in any eventual conflict. In a surprising move, the proprietor also commissioned his son-in-law Jesse Wharton to serve as governor, an appointment that bypassed four more senior councillors including the venerable chancellor Philip Calvert. Wharton was much less well known to most colonists than others Calvert might have named.[45]

Why Calvert commissioned Wharton remains unknown, since the new Lord Baltimore surely realized it was not an auspicious time to leave the province in untested hands. In neighboring Virginia, the highly experienced Governor Berkeley was desperately struggling to maintain his authority and a policy toward the Indians quite similar to the one Calvert himself was fostering. Through the spring and early summer, an assertive Nathaniel Bacon had challenged Berkeley's leadership and marshaled frightened colonists for an unbridled attack on the Susquehannahs and other Indians. Discontent was so rife in Virginia that Berkeley even suspended the usual suffrage requirements and allowed all freemen to vote in elections held that June for a new assembly. That momentous legislature set in motion what has become known as Bacon's Rebellion. Berkeley's administration toppled to the headstrong rebel in late July amid widespread public clamoring for better protection against the Indians and relief from economic problems plaguing the colony. Such trouble could easily spread into Maryland.[46]

Through the summer, the proprietor's deputy government anxiously watched the successive stages of this rebellion in Virginia while their own colonists nervously awaited further signs of any hostile intentions toward

44. Ibid., 515–64.
45. Ibid., 15:80–90, 90–91, 93, 98, 105–8.
46. Washburn, *The Governor and the Rebel*, 32–76. The literature on Bacon's Rebellion is quite extensive, but particularly important treatments also include Morgan, *American Slavery, American Freedom*, 250–70; Craven, *Southern Colonies in the Seventeenth Century*, 360–93; and Thomas Jefferson Wertenbaker, *Torchbearer of the Revolution: The Story of Bacon's Rebellion and Its Leader* (Princeton, N.J., 1940). Stephen Saunders Webb examines these Maryland and Virginia events in an even broader continental context in *1676: The End of American Independence* (New York, 1984).

Maryland by the Indians. By July 13, the council issued orders for all inhabitants of the Western Shore "to infort themselves in their houses" and to establish a strong defense. Before any further developments ensued, however, the colony experienced unexpected change in leadership. Wharton fell ill and died within a few days. Calvert had wisely left a second commission that instructed a transfer of authority to Speaker Thomas Notley in the event of Wharton's death. This appointment, bypassing Catholic relatives and councillors in favor of an elected Protestant representative, at once a dependable proprietary ally and a respected figure in the broader community, probably saved the province in subsequent months from a fate similar to Bacon's Rebellion.[47]

Fear of the Indians and the serious state of the economy indeed propelled Maryland into domestic turmoil during the next few weeks, but the challengers of Lord Baltimore's government proved less successful and disruptive than Nathaniel Bacon and his followers in Virginia. No one was confident of this outcome in late summer, however, as Maryland entered a period Notley was to call "these dangerous & Rebellious tymes." He reported to Charles Calvert in December that "never Body was more repleat with Malignancy and Frenzy then our people were about August last, and they wanted but a monstrous head to their monstrous body." Maryland's discontented populace failed to find a charismatic Bacon to lead them, Notley observed to his superior. The governor might also have noted that he did not play so easily into the hands of the opposition as did Berkeley in Virginia.[48]

Immediately upon assuming authority, Notley prepared for a possible attack on his government by Englishmen as well as Indians. He expected Bacon, now in ascendancy in Virginia, to embroil Maryland in his war against all Indians in the Chesapeake area. The Virginian was reputedly stirring up "all the needy and desperate persons" around Piscataway River and threatening to cross over into Maryland to lead a rebellion there as well. In a hurried letter to Calvert, Notley and the council appealed for additional arms and ammunition to defend the colony. Meanwhile, at home they placed the province on full alert, carefully addressed domestic problems, and avoided any action that might provide Bacon's forces, poised on the southern border, with an excuse to enter Maryland.[49]

Serious trouble erupted in Calvert County in late August. Numerous residents refused to pay the levy for 1676, arguing that it had not been laid by their full delegation of legal representatives. This resistance escalated under the leadership of William Daveys, John Pate, Giles Haselham, and

47. *Archives*, 15:97–102 (quotation, 100), 111–18.
48. Ibid., 15:136 (first quotation); 5:153 (second quotation).
49. Ibid., 15:118–19, 120–27 (quotation, 124).

"divers others," all unfamiliar figures about whom almost nothing further is known. These individuals gathered support among people overburdened by a new levy of 297 pounds of tobacco per taxable, an amount that surpassed the already abnormally high assessment of 1675. Colonists questioned how this money was being spent and demanded an accounting of the revenue from the two-shilling duty that was supposed to provide arms. Additional grievances attacked the property requirement for the vote and the uniform poll tax; sentiment existed for wealthier colonists to be taxed at a higher rate. According to later accounts, sixty of these discontented men assembled on September 3 "with force & Terror of Armes," issued their demands of the government, and with cocked guns threatened the uncooperative officeholders of Calvert County. Notley, reasoning that most of these people had been "seduced in a mutinous & Seditious manner," promised a pardon to everyone but Daveys if the protestors would lay down their arms, and he guaranteed a trial to the ringleader. When the rebels declined these offers, the authorities aggressively pursued their opponents, who quickly dispersed. Proprietary agents eventually captured Daveys and Pate at New Castle, and following a hasty trial and conviction, the two men were executed as a dramatic warning to others. This quick and forceful response effectively squelched the "insurrection at the Clifts."[50]

Notley and the council tried to quell just as quickly any likelihood that other "ill affected persons" might capitalize on the fundamental concerns of so many colonists. The authorities issued a public "Remonstrance of the True State of the Province." The document explained the need for the high taxes, noted that only the assembly could change some of the matters protested by the freemen, and promised to carry the heated grievances about taxes and the suffrage to the next legislature. The response apparently mollified most colonists, for active resistance largely subsided for the time being. Notley continued to worry, however, that "the common people will never be brought to understand the just reason of a publicke charge, nor will they ever believe that the expences [are] for their own preservation, although never so apparent."[51]

The colony's troubles were, indeed, by no means completely over. Skirmishes with various Indians continued to punctuate life in Maryland, and authorities had to maintain their vigilant alert to keep Virginia's rebels out of the province. The latter threat diminished with the death of Bacon on October 26 and the apprehension in subsequent days of the remainder of his major followers. Soon after Virginia's "Intestine Warre"

50. Ibid., 127–31, 136–42, 344; 5:143, 153; 8:225; 67:248.
51. Ibid., 15:137–40; 5:153 (quotation).

had been concluded, however, a renewed prospect of domestic upheaval confronted Notley. A "Complaint from Heaven with a Hue and crye," written probably in late fall, colorfully rehearsed the full range of local grievances. Composed skillfully with an eye toward enlisting support in England against the proprietary government, the document catalogued wrongdoings on the part of Calvert and his deputies and particularly attacked their growing favoritism toward a narrow, select circle in the colony. The complaint also denounced the allegedly heavy-handed response of authorities to the protests raised in Calvert and the execution of Daveys and Pate. Josias Fendall, the former governor who had led the rebellion in 1659/60 against the Calverts, probably authored the document and certainly supported its contents. Fendall boasted in the aftermath of these tense months that he could have successfully overthrown Wharton and presumably any other proprietary relation; Notley, however, proved too formidable a head of government in Calvert's absence. This time, the "monstrous head" as represented by the author of the "Complaint from Heaven," failed to mobilize the "monstrous body" of discontented Marylanders whom Notley had readily acknowledged were present in the province in the late summer of 1676. No widespread armed resistance ever materialized as in Virginia, and the proprietary government successfully weathered the abortive attempts to rally colonists against it.[52]

During these troubled times, Notley shrewdly postponed convening the assembly. He realized that a meeting of the legislature in Virginia had afforded Bacon the opportunity to rouse his supporters against Berkeley. Besides, Notley had instructions from Calvert to delay, if possible, any new session until the proprietor's return. Proceeding without any assembly's sanction, Notley and the council deployed the militia as necessary and negotiated with various Indian tribes. The governor dispatched Henry Coursey as an envoy to New York in April of 1677, and meetings ensued throughout the early summer with representatives of six or seven tribes of that region. On October 5, Notley announced with considerable relief satisfactory treaties of peace with the Northern Indians. Meanwhile, provincial authorities had improved relations with those tribes resident in the Chesapeake area as well, and for the time being, the worst of the fears of war with the Indians abated.[53]

Repeated delays in the proprietor's departure from England and press-

52. Ibid., 15:140 (first quotation); 5:134–49 ("Complaint from Heaven"), 152–54. On Fendall's probable role in 1676, ibid., 5:281; 15:246–47, and marginal note, "Capt. Fendall & others can give a larger acct iff sent for," on the manuscript copy of "Complaint from Heaven," CO 1/36 Public Record Office, London.
53. *Archives*, 15:148–53, 157–89; 5:243–52, 254–60, 269–70.

ing local matters finally compelled Notley to schedule a meeting of the assembly for the fall of 1678. Conscious of the lower house's strong sentiments regarding a full membership, the governor issued writs for by-elections to fill existing vacancies, without waiting first for the legislature to convene, and he summoned the full delegations of each county to attend the session. In Charles County, voters tried to elect Fendall to a vacant seat, but the council threatened the loss of a representative for the county if freeholders persisted in choosing the ineligible Fendall. The voters finally chose instead John Stone, possibly a stand-in for Fendall. Two other by-elections also suggest a mood of alienation. In Dorchester, freeholders elected Anthony Tall, an illiterate planter who owned only 100 acres and held no other office. In Calvert, Francis Billingsley won the endorsement of the voters; neither poor nor uneducated like Tall, Billingsley was an influential Quaker who had occupied no political office since serving as a constable under the regime of the parliamentary commissioners in the 1650s. The election of Clement Hill, a Catholic, in St. Mary's did not fit this pattern, however, since this adherent of the proprietary faction actually strengthened the governor's hand in the assembly. It is unclear how Notley, or even Lord Baltimore, regarded the election of Philemon Lloyd of Talbot to the now vacant speakership.[54]

The lower house immediately considered the numerous accumulated grievances of the colonists and picked up pointedly the complaints that had surfaced in 1676. The rare absence of Charles Calvert – this was the first assembly he had missed in two decades – emboldened many frustrated representatives to exploit this opportunity to the fullest. Notley, anxious not to offend needlessly any of the delegates, extended to the lower house substantially greater leeway in its deliberations and promotion of bills than Calvert had recently permitted. The governor's eventual approval of the resulting legislation probably forestalled a more aggressive expression of opposition. His generous cooperation soothed many angry assemblymen, especially after an alleged attempt to poison some of the legislators heightened the edginess of everyone present.[55]

The assembly's concerns ranged widely over numerous disputes regarding proprietary privileges and powers. Representatives lashed out in various ways against the absent proprietor and those who currently enjoyed his patronage. New laws tightened controls over sheriffs and other offi-

54. Ibid., 15:189–90, 192–93, 245. Fendall had served as guardian of the orphaned Stone. Wills 1, fols. 89–92, Hall of Records.
55. *Archives*, 7:1–105. Fendall later claimed "the business of poysoning the people at St. Maries . . . was a thing acted and Designed by the Papists" (ibid., 15:246). Carr and Jordan, *Maryland's Revolution of Government*, 22–26, also discuss this session in some detail.

cers and also limited more precisely their fees. A comprehensive statute on elections systematically restricted the proprietor's powers in that arena, placed the procedures of voting and the eligibility for membership under the jurisdiction of the assembly, and brought the local electoral practices more in line with parliamentary precedents. Another act stipulated more explicitly than ever before the proprietor's obligation to provide ample arms and ammunition and to distribute them more widely to the counties rather than storing them in a central magazine under the sole authority of the governor and council; this law also reiterated carefully the necessary role of delegates in approving any levies for war. To prevent expensive assemblies whose primary purpose was to handle the public accounts, the delegates empowered the governor and council to assess necessary levies for "the small charges of this Province," as long as the total did not exceed 50,000 pounds of tobacco per year. Most likely at the instigation of the Quaker members, the lower house also inserted a provision in this statute excusing from any fines for eighteen months those individuals currently without arms who failed to appear at musters. In other legislation, the assembly, or more pointedly the lower house, increased the civil jurisdiction of the county courts and struck further at the power of the Provincial Court by clever wording in one statute that attempted to diminish judicial discretion in the application of English laws in Maryland. The representatives could regard with pride the fact that they had achieved in this session the satisfactory resolution of so many of the concerns and grievances they had long harbored.

Charles Calvert returned to Maryland a few weeks after the close of this session. He declined for two and a half years to convene another meeting of the legislature and during this extended period also refrained from conveying publicly his negative response to most of the legislation passed in 1678. His silence misled many people. The failure of the assembly to gather again before 1681 certainly saved the colonists from paying additional taxes during desperate economic times, but Lord Baltimore's delays in meeting another session and in announcing his vetoes suggest more compellingly his desire to avoid as long as possible an unpleasant confrontation with what he knew would be disgruntled delegates. In the interim, he contained sporadic threats from hostile Indians and preserved domestic peace despite periodic manifestations of unrest and possible rebellion. The most serious internal threat occurred in the winter immediately after Calvert's return, and it is indicative of the proprietor's general effectiveness that as successive months passed by, the frequency of such challenges diminished and he presided more securely over the government.[56]

56. *Archives*, 15:211–378, covers activities of the years from Calvert's return to his decision on June 27, 1681, to summon the assembly again.

New Indian disturbances in the summer of 1681 finally prompted Calvert to summon the assembly a few months earlier than was necessary simply to protect the temporary laws from expiration. Fear of Indian attacks always provided a dangerous rallying point for aggravating internal unrest and fanning suspicions of the proprietary government. An ambitious dissident could usually gather some following simply by playing on these fears and circulating rumors of a conspiracy between the Catholic leadership and the Indians to murder Protestants. That summer, Calvert uncovered suggestive evidence that Josias Fendall was pursuing just such a course. This time, Fendall apparently had the assistance of a new accomplice, John Coode, a delegate from St. Mary's who like Fendall had initially enjoyed the patronage of the Calverts but had subsequently fallen out with the proprietary circle. Both men in their lengthy political careers had exploited religious tensions in the province and exhibited a frequent predisposition to oppose any authority, while also championing many legitimate grievances of their fellow colonists. In 1681, Fendall and Coode were behaving suspiciously and allegedly plotting to strike against the government of Maryland because of its purported conspiracy with the Indians. Calvert carefully collected depositions of the many public remarks and private conversations in which these two "rank Baconists" had expressed their opposition to the government and their suspicions of its malevolent intentions. The proprietor then issued a proclamation reminding colonists of his commitment to enforce the law against divulgers of false news, and he had the two men apprehended. Evidence of more widespread disaffection surfaced when George Godfrey, a justice and militia officer of Charles County, organized a band of men to free Fendall from jail. The attempt was foiled, and Godfrey was also imprisoned with a ruling from the council that his actions had been both rebellious and seditious.[57]

Additional actions by the proprietor soon created still more ill feelings. In proclaiming the forthcoming meeting of the assembly, Calvert finally announced his veto of the statute of 1678 regarding elections and explicitly disputed the assembly's right to legislate in this area. The proprietor also declined to fill the current vacancies in the lower house. Not long after the legislators drifted into St. Mary's City, they learned of still more disturbing news. Calvert revealed his vetoes of the statutes addressing defense issues and clerks' fees and, among other measures, a law calling for the recording of all statutes in a new volume. A seemingly innocuous law, the latter act, in keeping with recent efforts to review and codify all

---

57. Ibid., 388–92, 399, 400–5; 5:281 (quotation), 301, 302, 312–34 (trials of the three men); 20:xii–xiv; Jordan, "John Coode, Perennial Rebel," 10–13.

legislation, had provided for all statutes in effect at the end of the session of 1678 to be entered in a special volume. Although Calvert had authorized Notley in 1677 to extend tentative approval to new laws and to have them go into effect while awaiting the proprietor's ultimate judgment, Lord Baltimore apparently disliked the implication of recording these laws in the permanent book of statutes before his ruling. He publicly rejected these acts in 1681 but waited another three years before he finally clarified his opposition to some other laws passed in that session of 1678. Delegates bitterly resented Calvert's disallowance of laws they cherished so strongly, his duplicity in misleading them for almost three years, and his acting so independently and arbitrarily. The vetoes aroused an unprecedented reaction.

The resentful delegates first surveyed their membership and finding thirteen unavoidable vacancies argued that the lower house could not proceed until new elections filled the empty seats "according to Diverse and Manifold Presidents of the Lower house of Parliament in England." Furthermore, the representatives wanted the speaker, not the proprietor, to issue these writs. Calvert, arguing that enough members were present to act, wanted to avoid any by-elections. Extended debates ensued over the proprietor's powers and the importance or applicability of parliamentary precedents. Lord Baltimore argued that he had "the Sole Power to Dispose of his Conquests upon terms he Pleases." The representatives, "Extremely Grieved" by Calvert's remarks "To Liken us to a Conquered People," deplored his casual dismissal of the parliamentary example. The delegates finally gained the proprietor's agreement, for this assembly only, to issue writs for the election of a full contingent of delegates, but he insisted as a point of principle that he and not the speaker issue the writs.[58]

Two weeks elapsed before any replacements arrived in St. Mary's City. A bit cocksure, the lower house introduced its grievance that no act passed by both houses and assented to by the proprietor or his deputy should "be repealed but by the Consent of both houses." At issue was whether Notley's approval of the legislation from the Assembly of 1678 had in fact constituted proprietary sanction of those laws. Also, the delegates daringly questioned how much time the proprietor should have in order to express a disallowance. Did not passage of two years without a veto connote approval? In something of another concession, Lord Baltimore agreed during his future residence in Maryland to convey his ap-

---

58. *Archives*, 15:378–79; 5:405–6; 7:107–216, especially 114, 124 and 125 (quotations).

proval or veto immediately upon the close of a session and during his absence to provide a response within eighteen months.[59]

Calvert kept voicing his concerns about the Indians while the assembly-men debated privileges. A special defense bill finally came under discussion, but the lower house quickly amended several of its features. Calvert eventually settled for what he regarded as sufficient approval from the legislature for any forseeable contingency of war or peace with the Northern Indians. With this authority in hand, he wasted no time in adjourning the session on September 17; this action, rather than a prorogation, saved the temporary laws from automatic expiration. Meanwhile, Calvert vented his extreme displeasure in a proclamation released to the entire colony. "While the Enemy lay at our Doores," he noted, the representatives stubbornly neglected their true responsibility to the public. "It is evident that noe consideration of the Safety of their persons or property of their Estates and protection from plunder was soe Deare to them as an imaginary priviledge." Calvert lashed out especially at Quaker burgesses for being completely unresponsive to the Indian threats.[60]

Within six weeks, Calvert reconvened the same representatives he had so caustically chastized. He needed the legislature to appropriate additional funds to pay the soldiers and provide for the maintenance of prisoners captured in a recent expedition. This gathering is most noteworthy for its dispute over the current state of some permanent laws. By accident or calculated intent, the temporary Act for Reviving Laws in 1678 had included among its list of statutes the "Act for Ascertaining what Lawes are of force within this Province" from the previous assembly, which had been a listing of permanent legislation. If Calvert could manipulate the colony's laws, others could try to do so as well. Some parties now contended that by inclusion of this statute in the 1678 act, and by its omission from the revival legislation of 1681, all permanent legislation "were made Temporary Laws and since not revived." The upper house, investigating the matter, alleged "Divers Discourses held by Diverse Members of the Lower house about the Laws of this Province Endeavouring to wrest some Doubtful words in some Acts to this Sense that there are now no perpetuall Act but that all the Laws of this Province are Temporary."[61]

Some delegates may well have wished to see several permanent acts erased from the statute books, but everyone pleaded ignorance of any such discussions. Nonetheless, the lower house resisted efforts for a joint

59. Ibid., 7:152 (quotation), 153, 160–61, 182; 15:158.
60. Ibid., 7:172–73, 184, 188–95; 17:37–42, (quotations, 38, 39); William Richardson to George Fox, Apr. 2, 1681, Manuscripts, Portfolio 32, No. 118, Friends House, London; Jordan, " 'Gods Candle' within Government," 642–45.
61. *Archives*, 7:82–85, 226 (quotation) 227 (quotation).

meeting to consider the problem. The representatives, refusing to approve an act that would carefully list all permanent legislation and clarify any doubts, suggested postponing the matter until the next session with a promise that "this house will not take Advantage of any Mistakes or Errors." The upper house, however, demanded immediate resolution of the confusion and delayed the end of the session an extra day until a satisfactory act was passed.[62]

This legislature, first elected six years earlier, met once more in a fifth session on April 25, 1682. Again, a threat to the northern regions of the colony constituted the primary reason for the gathering, since Calvert wanted the assembly's advice on the proper response to this latest challenge. He urged upon the legislators a serious discussion of the problem and an avoidance of "Tedious and Long Debates in Matters of Small Concern." Although the two chambers did not fully concur on all matters, they dealt with each other cordially and completed the essential business with little overt disagreement.[63]

Calvert decided that summer to summon assemblies more frequently in the future in order to obtain joint responses to any threats to the province. Since he also hesitated to provoke complaints about the burdensome taxes necessitated by such gatherings, he dissolved the current assembly and in accordance with his ordinance of 1681 issued new writs for the election of only two delegates per county. No doubt Calvert carefully scheduled these elections to be held at a time when, in the absence of major threats or disputes, he could anticipate the least hostile response at the polls.[64]

The new assembly first met on October 26, 1682. The lower house now numbered twenty-two members; St. Mary's City, where the Calverts could easily influence elections, had retained both of its burgesses, and there were two representatives from each of the ten counties. Sixteen delegates had been returned from the recently dissolved legislature, but only eight members of this new body had served for more than one previous term. Missing were several men who had been especially active in recent sessions, including Christopher Rousby, John Coode, and Kenelm Cheseldyne, but reelected delegates Robert Carvile and John Rousby were present to continue their leadership.

Besides addressing the ever present Indian threat, the delegates tried again to secure control over elections and to reestablish delegations of four representatives per county. Lord Baltimore resisted any legislative challenge to his prerogatives in this area and another stalemate ensued.

62. Ibid., 228–29, 233, 234–35, 238.
63. Ibid., 257–330 (quotation, 260).
64. Ibid., 17:109–10.

Consequently, this three-week session passed no laws except the necessary act of revival of temporary acts, approval of the public levy, and two
private naturalization bills. The lower house, growing in confidence and
assertiveness, could not be cowed into submission to proprietary wishes.[65]

One year later, the assembly reconvened at the Ridge in Anne Arundel
County, a more convenient location for most members. The delegates
promptly renewed their call for an election law, and the proprietor, ignor-
ing this demand, similarly resumed his pressure for legislation to advance
trade and to establish ports in the colony. For days, the two houses
exchanged drafts of bills that the opposite chamber found unsatisfactory.
The burgesses were anxious to consider these two disputed bills and
defense legislation as a package. Perhaps to curry favor, they also proposed a gift to Calvert of 100,000 pounds of tobacco for having allowed
this session to meet in Anne Arundel County. If so, the tactic did not
work. The upper house, following the proprietor's wishes, blocked the
legislation being promoted by the representatives.

Calvert sternly lectured the lower house after almost a full month had
passed with still no legislation approved. The delegates made one last
attempt to gain their broader objectives by linking any approval of the
proprietor's bills with the full assembly's support of other acts. For a while,
it appeared that the upper house might cooperate in order to save the
corpus of temporary laws again threatened by no action at this session.
Calvert intervened, however, to adjourn rather than to prorogue the assembly and thereby protect the nonpermanent statutes. Before the members
dispersed, they had enacted only five laws, among them a modest proposal
for advancing trade that fell below the proprietor's expectations.[66]

Persisting uncertainty in many minds regarding the status of temporary
laws finally prompted Calvert to reconvene the legislature the following
spring. Furthermore, serious challenges to the charter in England required that Lord Baltimore return soon to London for what might well
become a lengthy absence from the province. Calvert wished to avoid the
necessity of any meeting of the assembly during his absence, especially in
light of the legislature's record in 1678.[67]

In preparation for this session, Calvert instructed clerks to transcribe
carefully all of the laws of Maryland for a thorough examination by the
legislature. This review and revision of statutes constituted the major
business of this third session. The lower house had its most knowledgeable members scrutinize the permanent laws, and only a slightly less

65. Ibid., 7:331–444.
66. Ibid., 445–619.
67. Ibid., 13:4–5.

impressive group investigated all of the temporary statutes. Still another committee worked to perfect the new bills before the current session.[68]

The assembly spent twenty-six days perusing the legislation. Members easily agreed on the value of most statutes and reaffirmed them. Similarly, a majority quickly concurred to repeal another set of laws now seen as unnecessary or duplicative. Four pieces of legislation, however, posed special problems. For some years, a portion of the lower house had wished to ensure that the laws of England always apply in the colony whenever the statutes of Maryland were silent on a particular subject. The Assembly of 1678 had attempted to prevent judicial discretion in applying English law, but uncertainty still prevailed. The delegates now proposed in 1684 to amend the Act Touching Judicature to gain this objective conclusively, but the proprietor demurred. He would allow an amendment explicitly invoking English law in the province only if a clause were added stating "if the Governor or Cheife Judge and the Justices of my Court shall find such lawes Consistent with the Condicon of this Province." The law was not amended. At the conclusion of this session Calvert announced his veto of all laws passed in 1678 except those he had publicly approved during the previous six years; this action eliminated the critical statute in which the lower house had earlier attempted indirectly to halt judicial discretion, and once again, the Provincial Court could claim unequivocally the power to determine which English laws might apply in the colony and in what manner they could be invoked.[69]

Differences also arose in this session over efforts of the lower house to amend the permanent act of 1649 regarding an oath of fidelity to the proprietor to include a "Salvo of allegiance to his Majesties." Again, some delegates resented such obligatory deference to the proprietor when no profession of loyalty to the Crown was either expected or demanded in Maryland. No agreement came on a satisfactory amendment, and the original language remained unchanged. Calvert was apprehensive about this wariness to swear allegiance to him. He informed the two houses that in the future he would expect all legislators to take a special oath of fidelity to the proprietor "before they be admitted to sitt" in the assembly, a measure often threatened in the past but never actually implemented.[70]

Calvert himself objected to the existing legislation regarding the "leavying of warr and defraying the publick charges," even without the stronger amendments under discussion by the delegates. He suspended

---

68. Ibid., 5–6, 11, 12–14, 16, 23.
69. Ibid., 1–126 (quotation, 39); Carr and Jordan, *Maryland's Revolution of Government*, 28–29.
70. *Archives*, 13:15 (quotation), 48, 49–50 (quotation).

the former act on this subject, which he apparently found in retrospect infringed too much on proprietary prerogatives. This unilateral rejection of a previously approved act left the colony without detailed legislation in this controversial area. Calvert proclaimed, however, his intention always to call an assembly when such necessities of defense arose, "soe desirous I am of giveing all manner of Satisfaccon in that particular to the freemen of my Province."[71]

Finally, this assembly was unable to agree on changes in the Act for Punishing of Certain Offenses, particularly the penalties for sedition against the proprietor. This was a sensitive issue in light of the executions of Daveys and Pate in 1676 and the recent punishments of Fendall and Godfrey in 1681. Differences persisted primarily over the leeway exercised by the court to impose more than one of the possible punishments enumerated in legislation regarding various crimes. When the pressures of time led Calvert to end this session, the two houses were still in dispute over this statute.[72]

Lord Baltimore sailed for England a month later. This time, he left the province in the care of the whole council as collective deputies to his minor son, Benedict Leonard Calvert. The proprietor extended special powers, however, to Henry Darnall and William Digges as joint commissaries, to Nicholas Sewall and John Darnall as joint secretaries, and to his cousin George Talbot as president of the council. All five men were related to Calvert and only Digges was a Protestant. The remaining members of the council included four other Protestants, who enjoyed less prominent roles and lacked much individual authority; as they died or left the colony during the next few years, only Catholics were to receive appointments to fill the vacant positions on the council. This consolidation of power in a narrow family circle was to exacerbate tensions, since none of these men could match either individually or collectively the performance of Thomas Notley during the proprietor's absence from 1676 to 1678.[73]

Three years earlier, a Virginia official had communicated to imperial bureaucrats his fears regarding Maryland's future. The colony was "now in Ferment," Thomas Lord Culpeper had noted in 1681. Part of the problem was "our Disease Poverty," but an additional threat hovered over the colony to the north: the very nature of its proprietary government. "Whether it be that the old Lord Baltimore's politick Maximes are not pursued and followed by the Sonne or that they will not doe in this

71. Ibid., 39–40.
72. Ibid., 39.
73. Ibid., 17:247–50, 252–53. Talbot was promoted to the head of the council over a Protestant, Thomas Taillor, who was actually the senior councillor in service in 1684.

Age" was uncertain to Culpeper, but he observed that Maryland was "worthy of your Lordships prudence to take care therein, as well for the sake of Virginia as his own."[74]

Charles Calvert was vigorously pursuing theories and practices increasingly unacceptable "in this Age" to most colonists. Such attitudes and procedures were endangering his authority within the colony and affecting his standing in England, where opponents of the Calverts' "Monarchical Government" were always scheming to overturn the charter of Maryland. Under the councillors officiating in Calvert's absence, these objectionable "Maximes" seemed all the more arbitrary and anachronistic to a population more and more insistent on a greater adherence to English practices and on a greater power residing with the elected representatives. Moreover, the Crown was starting to display a greater interest itself in what was transpiring in this Chesapeake colony.

Consequently, while Charles Calvert was anxiously defending his charter and colonial claims in Whitehall, his less capable deputy government confronted serious tests in Maryland. Immediately upon Lord Baltimore's departure, challenges arose from several of the perennial questioners of proprietary prerogatives. Robert Carvile did not even wait for Calvert to sail before launching strident verbal assaults on the proprietor's arrangements for the interim government. The deputies moved quickly against Carvile, but although he remained quietly under bond for good behavior through the summer of 1684, he continued to pose a potentially serious challenge to their authority. Another frequent threat, Josias Fendall, in exile since 1681, soon returned to Maryland. Frightened of what Fendall might do, the council issued a warrant for his immediate arrest, but this wily antagonist eluded capture and remained free to stir up possible trouble for the government. Christopher Rousby, a royal customs collector and former delegate who had recently carried his differences with the proprietor all the way to Whitehall, also returned about this time from England. With a royal commission still in hand, Rousby renewed his local opposition. It was he who aroused the deputy governors to commit their first irresponsible actions. During an argument and subsequent scuffle on board a royal naval vessel in November 1684, George Talbot murdered Rousby. This rash and probably drunken attack against a prominent local opponent and royal official inflamed sentiment throughout the colony.[75]

The other councillors hesitated to apprehend Talbot. Authorities in Virginia finally captured him, but Talbot managed to escape before any-

74. "The Present State of Virginia," Dec. 12, 1681, CO 1/47, No. 105i.
75. *Archives*, 17:181–84, 243–44, 271, 272, 298–300.

one could determine how to proceed jurisdictionally in this confused case. Rumors circulated that Talbot had returned to Maryland, where his friends were protecting him. The council compounded its problems by proroguing a meeting of the assembly scheduled for the spring of 1685. The eventual arrest and trial of Talbot helped slightly to still suspicions, but many resented that this proprietary relation, despite conviction by a jury in Virginia, received a pardon for his criminal deed.[76]

The government, remarkably, survived this episode, but opposition did not abate. Nehemiah Blakiston, Rousby's successor as customs collector, assumed a similar stance against the authorities and resumed the flow of complaints to England about the proprietary government, especially its failure to cooperate in enforcement of the navigation acts. Blakiston was also the son-in-law of the Calverts' old enemy Thomas Gerard and thereby the brother-in-law of the disaffected John Coode and Kenelm Cheseldyne, who also stood ready through these years to exact their revenge on the proprietary circle. A formidable opposition was slowly emerging in the Lower Western Shore counties.[77]

Events in the mother country were to shape decisively the course of the struggle for power in the colony over the next few years. News of the death of Charles II in 1685 persuaded the council to dissolve the current assembly. In subsequent months, differing allegiances with respect to Charles's successor would divide Marylanders just as conflicting loyalties pitted Englishmen against one another across the Atlantic. These particular tensions were not immediately apparent, however, in the new assembly. The deputies did not actually convene this body until October of 1686, but they could, surprisingly, draw some comfort from the outcome of these critical elections. The freeholders returned only five delegates from the previous assembly. Carvile and John Rousby were among those men not reelected, as were most of the other incumbents who had been outspoken in their disaffection. A significant exception to this trend was the victory of Cheseldyne, who soon replaced the deceased Philemon Lloyd as speaker of the lower house.[78]

No journal survives from either chamber for the first meeting of this assembly. Although the members sat for twenty-three days, they managed to approve only six statutes, including two private bills, the customary act for the public levy, and the necessary revival of temporary laws. Discussion apparently focused on an amendment to earlier legislation that had attempted to advance trade through the establishment of ports

76. Ibid., 300–11, 322–24, 326–48, 355–57, 359–60, 373, 410–12, 426, 475–83.
77. Ibid., 449–54, 455–57.
78. Ibid., 391, 398, 402, 457; 5:495; Papenfuse et al., eds., *Biographical Dictionary*, 1:30.

and towns. Protests had arisen concerning the location of these new sites. Some planters vigorously opposed the idea of carrying their tobacco to any place designated for shipping other than their own docks or perhaps the nearest landing to their plantations. The proposed amendments eventually passed, aided no doubt by the fact many of the delegates owned the land where the towns were now legislated to be built. Less easily resolved was the delegates' refusal to swear the special oath of fidelity that Calvert had stipulated in 1684 be taken by all future assemblymen. The representatives weakly argued that the request for the oath did not reach them until after they had begun the business of the session. They managed somehow to maintain this refusal, and the councillors reluctantly accepted the promise that members of the lower house would swear the oath at the opening of the next session.[79]

The colony drifted uneasily through another two years. Calvert, frustrated by circumstances that delayed his return, laced his correspondence with criticisms of the councillors and appeals for a greater unity within their ranks. In 1688 he even dispatched from England a new president of the council but seriously misjudged the impact his appointee was to have in Maryland. William Joseph, an arrogant Catholic from London, actually intensified the problems faced by the deputy government.[80]

The new executive arrived in October of 1688 with fresh instructions from the proprietor that included orders to summon an assembly as soon as possible. The freemen were certainly anxious for a legislature to meet. In addition to the general mounting of local concerns, many settlers were alarmed by news of the activities of James II, the new monarch, and by the implications of the recent birth of a Catholic prince who now became the immediate heir to the throne. Lord Baltimore had instructed his council that very autumn to proclaim the birth with a suitable celebration. Accordingly, great festivities were held on October 11 with Father Francis Pennington, a Jesuit priest, conducting a public service of thanksgiving. The government commanded additional celebrations to be held in the various counties, a round of festivities that numerous colonists felt little inclination to join. In a concurrent by-election, disturbed voters in St. Mary's County returned John Coode to the assembly.[81]

William Joseph made it surprisingly easy for Coode and others to forge an effective opposition in the lower house. The governor opened the assembly late that autumn with a lengthy address that managed to offend almost everyone. His speech began with an extended defense of the divine source of his power in Maryland, "Derived from God, to the King, and

79. *Archives*, 5:516; 8:15, 62; 13:129–44 (acts passed).
80. Ibid., 8:41–46.
81. Ibid., 40–41, 44–45, 57–60.

from the King to his Excellency the Lord Proprietary and from his said Lordship to Us." For Englishmen currently questioning the theory of divine right to rule, this treatise, arrogantly delivered, stirred new concerns, especially since Joseph in his brief tenure had already become closely identified with the glorification of James II and his Catholic son. Joseph then castigated the conditions he had discovered in the province, especially the rampant immorality and drunkenness. Without pause, he discoursed in a condescending tone on the purposes of the current session. The members were to pass an act requested by the king and Lord Baltimore prohibiting the export of bulk tobacco; Joseph lectured them not to question the wisdom of the measure or to follow the example of the Virginia legislature, which had recently declined to heed a similar request. As a "Second part of Duty," the assembly should approve an act of thanksgiving for the recent birth of the prince. In conclusion, Joseph expressed the "hope there are not any (in this present Generall Assembly) so Wicked as (by Machiavillian Principles) shall go about to divide the Interests of my Lord and his People" and that whoever should endeavor "to Divide the hearts of the People from my Lord, or my Lord from the People let him (by this Assembly) be Declared a Traitor to our God, King, Lord and People." Joseph dismissed the lower house with a parting admonition that "before you Begin to make Laws you do not begin to breake Laws" and with that requested each man to swear the oath of fidelity.[82]

Both the tone and the content of this opening speech incensed the delegates. They returned to their chamber combatively resolved to oppose the oath that they had never wanted to swear and that was not imposed by any law of the assembly. The representatives employed every argument they could muster to resist the oath, and the two chambers bickered for three days on this matter. Joseph further inflamed the members by asserting that "the refusing Allegiance implyes Rebellion" and reminding them that members of Parliament swore oaths of allegiance. The delegates quickly rejoined that they would gladly swear the same oath as Parliament required, an oath to the Crown; they professed their own allegiance to the proprietor and demanded any legitimate evidence of their actions to the contrary, insisting that "there is a great difference between the Oath of fidelity and allegiance." This standoff was finally resolved only by Joseph's proroguing the assembly over the weekend, during which time the men willingly took an oath of allegiance as private citizens rather than as members of the lower house, an important distinction in their minds.[83]

82. Ibid., 13:147–53.
83. Ibid., 154–65, especially 154–57, 159, 163.

This did not end the differences of this session, however. The lower house still bickered with the upper chamber for roughly three more weeks over various rights and privileges, among them the issuing of writs for additional by-elections, the appointment of clerks for joint committees, and numerous other actual and feigned hurts. The delegates rarely gained new ground, but they battled more vociferously than they had in some time. Reminiscent of the Assembly of 1669, they eventually came forth with eight complaints cataloguing popular grievances. These alleged that Calvert's officers were demanding sterling and refusing to accept tobacco in payment of rents and fines stipulated by law. The secretary's office was charging exorbitant fees not established by act of assembly. Calvert had unilaterally suspended a clause of the statute for advancement of trade without consulting the legislature, which alone had the power to alter laws. Illegal procedures had been followed in the arrest of some colonists without proper notification of charges, and people had been pressed into service or goods seized without appropriate authorization. Not even the council's scheduled meeting time for the Provincial Court passed without comment; it was, in the delegates' estimation, the "most perilous and incomodious time for the people to give their Attendance." For most of these complaints, the upper house attempted to provide some explanation and measure of satisfaction.

The representatives turned Joseph's own arguments on their head in opposing the requested act on the export of tobacco. Such a prohibition, they asserted, would be prejudicial to the interests of the king, the proprietor, and the people of England; accordingly, the house could not give its consent to such a bill. Several statutes did emerge from this session to encourage diversification of the economy, but Joseph failed to obtain the one law his instructions had explicitly ordered. In a letter a few weeks later to Lord Baltimore, the council provided a lengthy commentary on the "hot and high debates" the session had engendered and expressed the "distrust" that the upper house harbored of the elected members. The exasperated Joseph had concluded with some relief his first meeting with the assembly and had not scheduled the legislators to gather again until the following April. "What mind they will be of then wee know not," observed the proprietor's deputies.[84]

The "mind" of many of these delegates was certainly not any more favorable to Calvert's men by the next spring, and Joseph postponed the scheduled meeting. If the council had suspicioned rebellious sentiments in 1688, the government had to deal with an actual "risinge in Armes" the

84. Ibid., 165–227, for the surviving journal of the upper house and the legislation passed; the quoted passage appears on 172; ibid., 8:62–65, contains the council's letter.

following year. Coode and a company of rebels effectively exploited fears of an Indian attack, rumors of a Catholic conspiracy against the Protestants, an accumulation of grievances regarding various aspects of life in the colony, and the failure of the officials to proclaim the new monarchs William and Mary. Coode's forces marched on St. Mary's in July of 1689 and successfully overthrew the proprietary government.[85]

The delay in the assembly's meeting had removed the one possibility of the government's responding to current fears and rumors in an orderly, legitimate manner. In addition, Joseph and the council allowed three months to elapse with no official acknowledgment of the important news that had reached the Chesapeake in April concerning the recent revolution in England. Calvert's deputies made no public announcement of the change in government that had occurred in the mother country after the replacement of James II by William and Mary, nor did the council proclaim any allegiance to the new rulers, although authorities in Virginia quickly did so. These unexplained delays, while word-of-mouth reports spread throughout the colony, combined with the government's obvious disinclination to meet with the duly elected representatives, fueled the rumors already rife in the province of an Indian-Catholic-French plot. Some proprietary opponents were ready to exploit every possible weapon against the Calvert regime. When it became apparent that no assembly was to convene before October at the earliest, Coode, Cheseldyne, Blakiston, and a coalition that later identified themselves as the Protestant Associators gathered a small band of supporters and easily toppled the government in July without any bloodshed. By August 1, proprietary deputies had signed articles of surrender. One term of the settlement was indicative of what would follow – henceforth, no Catholic could occupy any office, civil or military, in the colony.

The victorious rebels quickly sent a congratulatory address to William and Mary, and in the monarchs' names issued a call for elections to a special convention, with each county to choose four representatives. Observers could not fail to detect the deliberate undoing of the proprietor's ordinance on elections. The countryside responded in some confusion. Many still adhered faithfully to the Calverts, and others, though less devoted to Lord Baltimore, nonetheless wondered about the authority of Coode to summon an assembly or gravely suspected his motives. Still,

85. The events leading immediately to the rebellion, the revolution itself, and the consequences of the overthrow of government are extensively discussed in Carr and Jordan, *Maryland's Revolution of Government*. See also David S. Lovejoy, *The Glorious Revolution in America* (New York, 1972), and J. M. Sosin, *English America and the Revolution of 1688* (Lincoln, Neb., 1982).

elections proceeded on schedule in all but one county, and the new delegates assembled in a one-house convention on August 22.

The membership consisted primarily of individuals fully supportive of
the revolution, but voters had returned some moderates not yet committed to the legitimacy of the new regime. A nucleus of seven men, primarily
from the Lower Western Shore and led by Coode, dominated the session
and amply rewarded themselves with new offices before the convention
concluded its business. At a second meeting the following spring, they
became influential members of the Grand Committee of Twenty established to oversee provincial affairs between meetings of the convention.
Beyond providing for the temporary governance of the colony, the convention's most important action was its appeal to the English Crown to
assume control of the colony.

The Protestant Associators governed Maryland for almost three years.
Local business proceeded on a reasonably normal basis, except in a few
counties where divisions hampered usual governmental activities. Coode
and his colleagues ventured cautiously in the conduct of provincial affairs, especially until word arrived of the Crown's decision to validate the
rebellion and to make Maryland a royal colony. Charles Calvert did not
relinquish his authority easily, and Coode and Cheseldyne finally journeyed to England to pursue in person the case against the proprietor and
to defend some of their own questionable activities. By the summer of
1690, English officials had decided to endorse the revolt and to assume
the reins of government as a "case of necessity." It still took almost two
years for the colonial bureaucracy to appoint a royal government, settle
some lingering questions, and send royal officers to the province.

Lord Baltimore lost all political control of Maryland with the overthrow
of his government and the Crown's subsequent intervention. The proprietor did succeed in preserving his jurisdiction over land affairs in the
colony. No longer, however, could he or his subordinates summon or
discharge assemblies, control election procedures, veto laws, or appoint
justices, sheriffs, and other officers. Without normal judicial proceedings,
Calvert no longer had effective oversight of his colony "by reason of great
neglects and miscarriages in the Government of Our Province and Territory of Maryland," in the words of the royal commission that appointed
Lionel Copley as the new governor. The Crown never completed official
judicial action against the charter. In the aftermath of the English revolution of 1688 and the heightened rivalry with Catholic France, Calvert had
no chance, as either a Catholic or an absolute sovereign proprietor, to
retain full powers in Maryland or to oppose successfully an illegal seizure
of his government.[86]

86. Carr and Jordan, *Maryland's Revolution of Government*, 146–79; *Archives*, 8:263
     (quotation).

Without a proprietor to invoke his charter in claiming princely prerogatives, proponents in Maryland of greater authority for the representative
branch of the assembly hoped finally to acquire those powers and privileges Charles Calvert had so effectively opposed. Parliamentary precedents, increasingly cited by the lower house in recent assemblies, would
surely command a greater validity, these colonists assumed, in a province
now directly under the Crown.

PART III

"Wee Your Majesties Most Humble and Loyall Subjects": 1689–1715

5

"By the Name of the Country Borne"

The Natives who are ignorant, and raw in busieness, and naturally proude, and obstinate, are not only the Representatives in Assembly, but the Justices of the County Courts: and by the name of the Country borne, distinguish themselves from the rest of her Majestys Subjects, and run into great heats and divisions, which may be of ill Consequence; for as they know little of the laws and good Manners they practice less.

> Governor John Seymour to Board of Trade, March 10, 1708/9

The people of Maryland would much rather have their cures supply'd by Persons of their own country whom they know, than by Strangers of whom they are not Known but are always Jealous that they come amongst them for no other End than to make purse and then Return home.

> "Memorial Representing the Necessity of Constituting a Suffragan Bishop in Maryland"

During the years of royal authority in Maryland from 1689 to 1715, dramatic changes occurred in the size and profile of the colony's population. Both Marylanders and outside observers noted the appearance of a sizable native-born population. Originally peopled primarily by young, single, white males, Maryland came to encompass a more natural proportion of women and a broader spectrum of age groups. In this quarter century the population was growing at an average rate of 2.5 percent per year and becoming more diversified, Africans or their descendants comprising almost one-third of the population and other Europeans, particularly those of Irish and Germanic stock, also now more numerous. A colony earlier consisting for the most part of "ordinary Householders," or of servants who could soon anticipate that status, now had a more heterogeneous economic profile, with growing disparities of wealth and poverty, declining opportunities for upward mobility, and a permanent status as slave, landless laborer, or tenant farmer characterizing perhaps a majority of the population.[1]

---

1. Menard, "Economy and Society," 153–212, 336–39, 366–85. See also Main, *Tobacco Colony*.

The population growth came despite a lower level of immigration than in previous years and a substantial outward migration, as poorer settlers, particularly recent freedmen, sought better fortunes in other frontier areas of the New World. Fewer immigrants of independent means now came to Maryland. Indentured servants also arrived in much diminished numbers and were more likely to be Irish, younger, and perhaps from a poorer background than their predecessors.[2]

A growing number of immigrants were not settling in Maryland voluntarily at all. Black slaves, now imported for the most part directly from Africa, outnumbered white servants in estate inventories by a ratio of 2.5:1 in the Lower Western Shore counties by the 1690s, and within a few years probate records from throughout the colony revealed a predominance of slave over servant labor. However enthusiastically or reluctantly the planters of the Chesapeake purchased African slaves, by 1710 these blacks numbered an estimated 7,945. This slave population, closely resembling the earlier demographic profile of white servants, consisted primarily of young adult males. It would be several more decades before the black community approached a balanced sex ratio and broader age spread.[3]

Despite the influx of Africans, the increase in total population from approximately 25,000 at the beginning of the period to almost 44,000 enumerated in a census of 1710 was primarily the result of natural growth. With the benefit of a more equitable sex ratio, the first generation of native-born Marylanders, reaching maturity without the restrictions of indenture, were indeed marrying at a much younger age. These creole couples had additional years for childbearing, and the size of families correspondingly increased. Kinship networks proliferated, and it was no longer so unusual for parents to survive to see their children enter adulthood. A significant number of native-born Marylanders first appeared in the older counties of the Lower Western Shore, but by the first decade of the eighteenth century most areas of the Eastern Shore had experienced a similar development. By 1710, if not a few years earlier, the majority of the colony's approximately 36,000 whites were native born.[4]

2. Carr and Menard, "Immigration and Opportunity," especially 233–42; David W. Jordan, "The Royal Period of Colonial Maryland, 1689–1715" (Ph.D. diss., Princeton University, 1966), 155–58. John Hart discussed the population increase in a letter to lords of trade, Aug. 25, 1720, CO5/717, No. 80.
3. Menard, "Maryland Slave Population, 1658 to 1730," and "From Servants to Slaves;" Allan Kulikoff, "The Beginning of the Afro-American Family in Maryland," 171–96, in Land et al.. eds., *Law, Society, and Politics in Early Maryland.*
4. Russell R. Menard, "Five Maryland Censuses, 1700–1712: A Note on the Quality of Quantities," *William and Mary Quarterly*, 3rd ser., 37 (1980), 615–26; Walsh, " 'Till Death Us Do Part,' " especially 150–52; Clemens, *The Atlantic Economy*, 41–79. The mean age at marriage fell from the middle and upper twenties to around twenty to twenty-two for native-born men and sixteen to seventeen for women.

These creoles were soon exercising a political influence upon local government. Immigrants, especially men of recent arrival, found entry into even minor offices increasingly difficult. A newcomer had to establish both his reputation and his fortune before he could expect to compete successfully, particularly with an individual who had inherited his land and entered the public arena at a relatively young age. For example, creoles in Charles County who gained access to local offices were consistently younger – by as much as fifteen years – than the average immigrant appointee; earlier commissions provided these natives an opportunity for longer periods of service, thereby reducing the turnover rate among incumbents and further limiting the prospects of appointment for any outside aspirant. Even immigrants with significant capital often had to wait patiently for a vacancy as patronage frequently favored a less affluent native over a more prosperous newcomer.[5]

This widespread bias received official expression in a statute of 1694 for "the Incouragement of Learning and Advancement of the Natives of this Province." The act established a minimum residency requirement of three years before any immigrant could hold a public office except under direct commission from the Crown.[6] Governor John Seymour, who never highly regarded the natives of Maryland, complained in 1708/9 that this law effectively discouraged the arrival of educated settlers. He reported to the Board of Trade that since the act's original passage only fourteen men

> have undergone that tedious Disability So that the Natives who are ignorant, and raw in busieness, and naturally proude, and obstinate, are not only the Representatives in Assembly, but the Justices of the County Courts: and by the name of the Country borne, distinguish themselves from the rest of her Majestys Subjects, and run into great heats and divisions, which may be of ill Consequence; for as they know little of the laws and good Manners they practice less.

Seymour lamented that the "Country borne" were so deficient that it was difficult even "to graft good manners on so barren a stock."[7] Ebenezer Cooke, later the colony's self-proclaimed poet laureate, similarly satirized the native politicians. *The Sot-Weed Factor*, published in 1708, portrayed

5. Walsh, "Charles County," 324–64, and Clemens, *The Atlantic Economy*, 120–67, illustrate well this pattern for Charles and Talbot counties. Governor John Seymour commented in 1707 on favoritism given to one individual "out of a foolish Conceipt of his being a Stout Fellow, and Country borne" (*Archives*, 25:263). Colonists similarly preferred a native-born clergy. See "A Memorial Representing the Necessity of Constituting a Suffragan Bishop in Maryland," Sion College Library, London.
6. *Archives*, 19:100–1. See David W. Jordan, "Sir Thomas Lawrence, Secretary of Maryland: A Royal Placeman's Fortunes in America," *Maryland Historical Magazine*, 66 (1981), 22–44.
7. *Archives*, 25:263, 267 and 269 (quotations).

the local justices of the peace as "Their Drunken Worships" and claimed that very few of them could read or write and

> As for Justice right or wrong,
> Not one amongst the numerous throng
> Knows what it means, or has the heart,
> To vindicate a Stranger's part.[8]

Both Cooke and Seymour, "Strangers" who never settled permanently in Maryland, played to the prejudices of their English readers and exaggerated the inabilities and crude deportment of the colonists. Although Maryland was no enlightened oasis, the colony was no longer so backward a wilderness. For example, the courts and their proceedings that Cooke so humorously lampooned compared favorably with most contemporary local courts of England.[9] In contrast to the more polished circles of genteel society in the mother country, Marylanders, with their rough, provincial mannerisms, undoubtedly cut a disappointing and often comical figure. Neither St. Mary's City nor later Annapolis pretended to be the equal of London, however, and the colony fared much better than rural England in any reasonable comparison with that region.

Maturing colonists, it is true, still had minimal opportunities for much formal education. Governor Francis Nicholson noted that before his arrival in 1694 there were "few schools and those but very mean ones either for Master or House."[10] Nicholson quickly promoted education, and soon the colony chartered King William's School in Annapolis. Church officials in England assisted in the collection of funds and recruitment of a schoolmaster. When Nicholson's successors, Seymour included, did much less to foster the school's progress, the institution floundered.[11] In 1715, Governor John Hart informed the assembly,

> It is with Compassion I observe so many young men of admirable natural Parts grow up without the least improvement of Art, to form their minds & make them more useful to their Country. It is more

8. *The Sot-Weed Factor* (London, 1708). Lemay, *Men of Letters*, 73–110, and Edward H. Cohen, *Ebenezer Cooke: The Sot-Weed Canon* (Athens, Ga., 1975) authoritatively address Cooke himself.
9. Joseph H. Smith and Philip A. Crowl, eds., *Court Records of Prince George's County, Maryland 1696–1699* (Washington, D.C., 1964), cxv. For other English descriptions, see David W. Jordan, ed., "Maryland Hoggs and Hyde Park Dutchesses: A Brief Account of Maryland in 1697," *Maryland Historical Magazine*, 73 (1978), 87–91, and Michael Kammen, ed., "Maryland in 1699: A Letter from the Reverend Hugh Jones," *Journal of Southern History*, 29 (1963), 362–72.
10. *Archives*, 23:81.
11. Ibid., 19:78, 290, 420–26; 23:77–78, 80, 81; 38:16, 27–31; Bernard C. Steiner, "Some Unpublished Manuscripts from Fulham Palace Relating to the Province of Maryland," *Maryland Historical Magazine*, 12 (1917), 121.

than Time to repair the great neglect that is shewn to Learning here.
It lies at your door to accomplish the good work of laying a foundation for Sufficient schools.[12]

Nonetheless, some natives made notable progress in their education.
Many clergy, more numerous by 1700, acquired extra income by teach-
ing, and affluent colonists more frequently hired tutors or occasionally
sent their sons to England or the Continent for further education. The
small community of professionally educated lawyers grew, and these men
plus others with special skills and knowledge personally schooled the
younger generation in fundamental subjects and prepared them for tasks
required by this society. Probate inventories indicate personal libraries of
greater occurrence, size, and quality, and the Society for the Propagation
of the Gospel contributed substantively to provide libraries in every parish throughout the colony, adopting the practice of establishing local
libraries first initiated by the Quakers in Maryland in the late seventeenth
century. The golden days of the Tuesday Club in Annapolis and other
impressive evidence of a cultured, intellectual life remained in the future,
but Marylanders could proudly point to many accomplishments, including gains in literacy, particularly among officeholders. For example, after
1696, no illiterate individual has been identified among the major officeholders of the four Lower Western Shore counties of Calvert, Charles,
Prince George's, and St. Mary's.[13]

Literate or unlettered, native or immigrant, most Marylanders continued to derive their livelihood from the production or exchange of tobacco. Despite a decline in profitability, this staple crop still dominated
the Chesapeake economy. Costs rose considerably during these years,
with higher prices for both land and labor, new duties on exported tobacco, and higher insurance fees because of the threats to transatlantic
shipping. Low prices for oronoco tobacco failed to increase demand, and
a period of serious stagnation prevailed for almost thirty years. Marginal
producers, the smaller landowners and some tenant farmers, as well as
landless freemen, suffered more severely than affluent planters, who controlled a larger percentage of the labor supply, had greater access to credit

12. *Archives*, 30:7. In 1717, the assembly legislated some financial assistance for schools
(ibid., 36:503–7).
13. Davis, *Intellectual Life in the Colonial South*, 1:282–83, 300–1, 328–29; 2:510–14;
Hall, ed., *St. Omer's and Bruge College, passim*; Day, "Lawyers in Colonial Maryland, 1660–1715;" Joseph T. Wheeler, "Thomas Bray and the Maryland Parochial
Libraries," *Maryland Historical Magazine*, 34 (1939), 111–37 and 246–65; Lorena
S. Walsh, "Development of Local Power Structures: Maryland's Lower Western Shore
in the Early Colonial Period" (unpublished manuscript, 1980).

and to unexhausted land, and could more easily weather any temporary crises.[14]

Disparities between wealth and poverty now began to grow. More adult males possessed no land, nor were most of them likely ever to become landowners. The majority of these men worked as laborers and lived permanently in the households of others. The more fortunate among these landless colonists eventually became tenant farmers. Comparative data on four counties in the first decade of the eighteenth century reveal that between 21 and 35 percent of the householders in each county were tenants, the majority with short-term leaseholds or tenancies at will, and evidence further suggests that tenancy was a permanent status for most of these individuals unless they left the colony.[15]

The typical landowner now possessed between 200 and 300 acres, on the lower side of this range for the Western Shore of the Chesapeake Bay and at the higher end for the Eastern Shore. Sixty to 70 percent of the landowners controlled fewer then 500 acres, and with more children surviving to adulthood, the prospects of diminishing holdings seemed certain, for few Marylanders practiced primogeniture. No longer could most Marylanders concur with the observer of 1676 that the colony was "a good poore man's Country." In contrast, roughly 10 percent of the landowners held more than 1,000 acres.[16]

A similar spread appears in the personal wealth of Marylanders as reflected by estate inventories and appraisals. Estates valued at £100 sterling or less, for example, total 75 percent of all estates inventoried in the 1690s, another 22 percent falling within the range of £100 to £500, but some deceased colonists were leaving personal belongings valued in the thousands of pounds sterling. The richest 10 percent of the population on the Lower Western Shore at the beginning of the eighteenth century owned approximately 54.6 percent of the wealth, and that pro-

14. Clemens, *The Atlantic Economy*, 29–40; Russell R. Menard, "Farm Prices of Maryland Tobacco, 1659–1710," *Maryland Historical Magazine*, 68 (1973), 80–85, and Menard, "The Chesapeake Tobacco Industry."
15. Menard, "Economy and Society," 424–29, and Menard, "Population, Economy, and Society;" also Main, *Tobacco Colony, passim.* The situation was compounded by the proprietor's ending the headright system and requiring after 1683 caution or purchase money, initially 100 pounds of tobacco for each 50 acres, then raised in 1684 to 120 pounds, and during the royal period to 480 pounds for every 100 acres. See Carr and Jordan, *Maryland's Revolution of Government*, 35–36; Kilty, *The Landholder's Assistant, passim.*
16. Carr and Jordan, *Maryland's Revolution of Government*, 181–82; Menard, "Economy and Society," 422–35; Clemens, *The Atlantic Economy*, 82; *Archives*, 5:145 (quotation).

portion was increasing. An even more dramatic break occurred with the wealthiest 2 percent or so.[17]

The major offices on the county and provincial levels of government were becoming a special preserve of this wealthy minority. Seldom did a sitting justice during the royal period own fewer than 1,000 acres at the time of appointment or possess an estate at death worth less than £500; even in a new frontier county, officeholding was increasingly the prerogative of the wealthiest 10 percent of the adult white males. For example, in Prince George's County, established in 1696, twenty-nine justices received appointment in the first thirteen years; fifteen of these men owned or were heirs to more than 1,000 acres, and four more possessed between 700 and 1,000. The few smaller landholders came from areas of the county without a great planter or were merchants with significant capital though little land. Of the twenty-one justices for whom inventories at death have survived, sixteen had wealth in excess of £500. Colonywide by the 1690s, major officeholding rarely went outside the wealthiest 300 or so men among an estimated 3,600 householders.[18] Religious considerations account for most exceptions to this concentration of political power. In some counties, many of the ablest and wealthiest men were Catholics or Quakers, who became ineligible to hold office after 1692. After their exclusion, some less affluent Protestants occasionally acquired positions they would not ordinarily have attained.[19]

Native status, wealth, and a more orthodox Protestant identification were increasingly joined by a fourth critical factor in determining which Marylanders were to gain access to political power and office on the local level of government. It became exceedingly advantageous to be related by blood or marriage to a previous justice, sheriff, or clerk. Among the young creoles, preference went frequently to those men whose fathers, brothers, and uncles had held or were currently occupying high office.

17. Aubrey C. Land, "Economic Base and Social Structure: The Northern Chesapeake in the Eighteenth Century," *Journal of Economic History*, 25 (1965), 639–54; Robert G. Schonfeld and Spencer Wilson, "The Value of Personal Estates in Maryland, 1700–1710," *Maryland Historical Magazine*, 58 (1963), 333–43; Main, *Tobacco Colony*, especially 48–96, 206–39; Menard, Harris, and Carr, "Opportunity and Inequality;" Lois Green Carr and Lorena S. Walsh, "Changing Life Styles in Colonial St. Mary's County," in Regional Economic History Research Center, *Working Papers*, Vol. 1, No. 3 (Greenville. Del., 1978), 72–118.
18. Carr, "County Government," and Walsh, "Charles County," examine in detail Prince George's and Charles, respectively. See also Carr and Jordan, *Maryland's Revolution of Government*, 181–86.
19. Carr and Jordan, *Maryland's Revolution of Government*, 212–15; Nicholson to lords of trade, Nov. 15, 1694, CO5/713/III, No. 114; Jordan, " 'Gods Candle' within Government," 647–48. In 1708 Catholics comprised more than one-third of the white population of St. Mary's (*Archives*, 25:258).

Political participation as an officeholder was narrowing to a considerably smaller segment of the population.[20]

The membership of the Maryland legislature between 1689 and 1715 reflects these changes. A total of 276 men gained election or appointment to sit in the two houses or to serve on the council for this period. The freeholders returned 270 of these individuals as their representatives, 27 of whom had also served before the revolution. Thirty-seven men occupied seats in the council, all but six of whom also sat as elected delegates; four of these exceptions were royal placemen. For the first time, the elected branch of the government had become the preeminent training ground for the powerful upper house and council.

Analysis of the assembly's membership underscores the emergence of a true governing elite set apart from the general citizenry by wealth and status and clearly distinguishable from previous legislators by lengthening tenure of office, by evolving bonds of kinship, and by the new ability to transfer political power to sons, brothers, and other relatives. By the end of the royal period, a relatively small number of related families unquestionably dominated the assembly and stood at the apex of the political life of their respective counties.

The mounting evidence of wealth, clearly surpassing that of the typical householder, continued a trend in progress by the late 1660s but was characteristic of the entire assembly at the turn of the century (Table 5). Excluding the four royal placemen who apparently never owned land in the colony, no councillor at the time of appointment possessed fewer then 750 acres and only four men owned fewer than 1,000 acres. Two of the lesser landowners acquired their commissions immediately after the revolution of 1689 as a reward for their support, and a third individual was the son of one of these men. Furthermore, at no time between 1692 and 1715 did less than 50 percent of the men currently sitting on the council or in the upper house own less than 2,000 acres, and the proportion increased to two-thirds by 1698, nine-tenths by 1708, and a full 100 percent in 1715. By that year, one-half of the councillors possessed more than 5,000 acres each.

The elected chamber, though somewhat less affluent, still stood clearly apart from more than 90 percent of the white population. At least 211, or 78 percent of the 270 men chosen by the freeholders, controlled more than 500 acres at their initial election. In the first royal assembly, approximately half of the membership owned 1,000 acres or more, and thereafter the proportion persisted at between two-thirds and three-fifths of the

---

20. The ties of kinship are an important theme in the case studies of individual counties conducted by Carr, Walsh, and Clemens cited in footnotes above.

Table 5. Landownership at election of assembly members, 1689–1715

Assembly	Total members	Unknown	None	1–500 acres	501–1,000 acres	1,001–2,000 acres	2,001–5,000 acres	More than 5,000 acres
1689–92	38 (5)	0	0	5	9 (1)	10 (4)	12	2
1692–93								
UH	12	0	1	0	2	3	5	1
LH	42 (7)	3 (2)	1	7	10 (2)	11 (3)	7	3
1694–97								
UH	12	0	2	0	1	3	4	2
LH	42 (19)	3 (1)	0	3 (1)	10 (2)	12 (6)	10 (8)	4 (1)
1697/98–1700								
UH	9 (5)	0	1	0	0	2 (1)	3 (3)	3 (1)
LH	46 (12)	5 (3)	0	2 (1)	7 (1)	15 (2)	15 (4)	2 (1)
1701–4								
UH	8 (7)	0	0 (1)	0	0 (1)	1 (1)	4 (2)	3 (2)
LH	46 (5)	6 (2)	0	2	5 (2)	17	11 (1)	5 (0)
1704–7								
UH	13	0	1	0	1	1	5	5
LH	46 (6)	5 (2)	0	6	9	15 (2)	11 (2)	0
1708								
UH	10	0	1	0	0	0	6	3
LH	50	5	1	4	6	25	7	2
1708–11								
UH	9 (7)	0	1	0	0 (1)	0	5 (3)	3 (3)
LH	50 (8)	4 (1)	1	5	9	1 (6)	10 (1)	0
1712–14								
UH	14	0	1	0	1	0	6	6
LH	50 (8)	3 (1)	1	4	11 (2)	18 (3)	12 (1)	1 (1)
1715								
UH	11	0	0	0	0	0	5	6
LH	50	8	0	0	10	14	16	2

Note: Numbers in parentheses represent men appointed or elected after the start of an assembly. UH denotes upper house; LH, lower house.

delegates. A sizable number of these men were the barons of 2,000 or more acres.

Several additional men undoubtedly belong in the category of large landowners. A reasonably precise determination of acreage cannot be established for thirty-four burgesses, but most of them owned at least two plantations. This number includes individuals like St. Leger Codd, Sr. and Jr., Thomas Smith, and George Gale, clearly among the wealthiest men in their areas. Probate materials confirm that at death – and almost certainly at the time of election as well – at least twelve of these thirty-four men held more than 1,000 acres, some of them considerably more.[21]

Just three delegates were apparently landless when they entered the legislature. Young Thomas Brooke, Jr., the fourth generation of his family to hold a provincial office, was heir-at-law to thousands of acres when elected in 1712. Edward Wynn, a lawyer and recently appointed attorney general chosen to represent St. Mary's City in 1692, had arrived with Governor Lionel Copley only a few weeks earlier with little opportunity as yet to purchase any property. Finally, there is no evidence of a land patent or warrant for Wornell Hunt "Esq.," a lawyer educated at Lincoln's Inn, when the voters of Annapolis first elected him in 1708; by 1711 he possessed at least 480 acres.

A mere twenty-one delegates probably owned fewer than 500 acres. A majority won their first, and often only, election in the years just after the revolution of 1689 and usually represented counties with a large, ineligible Catholic population. A few individuals in this category, however, were clearly upwardly mobile; John Bradford, for example, owned 452 acres when first elected in 1708 but through profitable marriages and his own resources commanded 14,000 acres by the mid-1720s.

The estates of the delegates at death confirm the new domination of Maryland's assembly by men of exceeding wealth (Table 6). At least ninety-three of the representatives, or approximately 35 percent, owned more than 2,000 acres at the end of their lives, many presiding over domains several times larger. An additional seventy-two burgesses, or another 26.7 percent, possessed between 1,000 and 2,000 acres at death. These numbers would be appreciably higher if they included those individuals for whom an accurate total is unavailable but who definitely had landholdings exceeding 1,000 acres during their legislative service; a minimum of ten of these forty-one men almost certainly had more than 1,000 acres at death. Only nineteen delegates serving during the royal period definitely held no more than 500 acres at death. Eight of these individuals

21. Solomon Clayton, Joseph Harrison, Thomas Bordley, Alexander Warfield, Charles Wright, Edward Scott, Philemon Hemsley, and Richard Johns, in addition to the Codds, Gale, and Smith, owned more than 1,000 acres at death.

Table 6. Wealth at death of assembly members, 1689–1715

	Landed estate (acres)						
	Amount unknown	None	1–500	501–1,000	1,001–2,000	2,001–5,000	More than 5,000
Members of upper house (35)	4[a]	0	0	4	4	12	11
Members of lower house (270)	41	3[b]	16	45	72	67	26

	Personal estate (pounds sterling)[c]						
	Amount unknown	None	Less than 300	301–500	501–1,000	1,001–2,000	More than 2,000
Members of upper house (35)	5	0	2	2	4	11	11
Members of lower house (270)	27	2[d]	47	37	64	56	37

[a] Three men — Lawrence, Quarry, and Randolph — were royal placemen who never settled permanently in Maryland and probably owned no land; the fourth, Thomas Brooke, was greatly in debt and his land heavily mortgaged.

[b] Two men had given a substantial quantity of land to descendants before their deaths; a third individual died penniless.

[c] Based on appraisal of total estate value.

[d] One individual died penniless, and the other had given away all his property before death.

served for only one term, and an additional seven won reelection only once.

The powerful gentlemen who served in the upper house commanded at their deaths vast estates seldom amounting to less than 1,000 acres. At least eleven individuals possessed more than 5,000 acres, and fully two-thirds of the membership bequeathed landed property in excess of 2,000 acres. Again, the nonresident royal placemen provide the major exceptions.

Total estate values survive for thirty of the thirty-five councillors who actually received a summons to sit in the legislature. Eleven of these men possessed personalty assessed at their deaths as worth more than £2,000 and another eleven had such wealth in excess of £1,000. Those individuals with smaller personal estates are primarily the councillors who rose to office as a result of their participation in the revolution of 1689. The five men for whom precise estate valuations are unknown include prominent figures like Philemon Lloyd and Richard Tilghman, who obviously ranked among the wealthiest residents of Maryland.

Valuations exist for 243 of the elected delegates. At least 194 left estates specifically valued at more than £300, placing them among the most affluent 10 percent of the inventoried population, and 157 of these estates were worth £500 or more, rendering their former owners among the upper 4 percent. Finally, 93 surpassed the £1,000 valuation. Not surprisingly, 17 of the 37 individuals with estates appraised at more than £2,000 were among the few representatives who eventually received an appointment to the council, and numerous others in this range were also at one time nominees to that distinguished body.

The twenty-seven individuals without a known estate valuation include persons indisputably among the most prosperous colonists. Nine definitely possessed more than 1,000 acres of land, and another seven clearly owned more than 500 acres. The remaining twelve delegates include a disproportionate number, five, elected from St. Mary's County. Similarly, the category of delegates with estates valued at less than £300 also contains an unusually high number from St. Mary's, where ineligible Catholics were among the wealthiest residents. More than half of these relatively poorer men won their first election before 1700, and those who entered the assembly thereafter usually had ties by blood or marriage to an earlier delegate.

These high standards of wealth placed individuals of modest social origin or affluence at a great disadvantage in gaining preferment at the polls, much less in gaining appointment from the Crown to serve in the upper house. Rarely after 1689 did a former servant attain a provincial office, and the few men who overcame the substantial odds required many more years and considerably greater personal connections to climb the political ladder than had their predecessors. Thirteen freedmen still achieved this notable success in the decade following the revolution, but more of these men possessed skills that rendered them atypical servants. Between 1700 and 1715, only three former servants won initial elections. As one of the few sons of former servants to acquire high office in the eighteenth century, Charles Wright became something of an exception when chosen by the voters in 1712.[22] Even with such restricted opportunities for advancement, former servants or their descendants in Maryland still enjoyed a greater likelihood of political participation and officeholding than did their counterparts in Virginia.[23]

As a concomitant of greater wealth, the members of the assembly now also possessed a better education than their predecessors. Despite Governor Seymour's protest that there was no "person of liberall Education" in the legislature, at least fifteen men serving during the royal period had studied at a university in England or Scotland or at the Inns of Court in London.[24] Another ten to twelve individuals probably had formal schooling of some kind abroad, and still others had studied with tutors in Maryland. Literacy has been conclusively established for at least 263 of the 270 delegates and for all of the councillors. The definite instances of proved illiteracy come primarily at the start of the period, among prominent supporters of the revolution. Only one delegate initially elected after 1698 was even possibly illiterate.[25]

The most striking aspects of the collective profile of assemblymen, like that of local officeholders, are the growing number of native-born delegates, the increasing bonds of kinship uniting the members, and the longer tenures they served in the legislature. Creoles clearly captured control of the assembly and council by the early 1700s. The decade of the 1690s marked the transition period; immigrants still dominated the membership of provincial institutions, constituting a majority of the 112 men

22. Former servants sitting in the assembly between 1660 and 1689 had spent an average of sixteen years in the colony before their first election; after 1689, that average period of residence extended to twenty-three years, only four men accomplishing the feat in less than fourteen years. James Crawford, William Blanckenstein, Ninian Beale, and Philip Lynes are examples of such atypical freedmen. See also Lorena S. Walsh, "Servitude and Opportunity in Charles County Maryland, 1658–1705."

23. In Virginia, no servant arriving after 1640 served in the assembly between 1660 and 1706, nor was any burgess during these years descended from a freedman (Quitt, "Virginia House of Burgesses," 159–79, 274).

24. *Archives*, 25:267. These well-educated men include William Bladen, David Browne, Kenelm Cheseldyne, St. Leger Codd, John Coode, Thomas Greenfield, Andrew Hamilton, Wornell Hunt, Henry Jowles, George Muschamp, Robert Smith, Thomas Tench, Sir Thomas Lawrence, Robert Quarry, and Edward Randolph.

25. Edward Larremore of Cecil, elected in 1708, was apparently illiterate and made his mark. He died during his first term.

who first served between 1689 and the end of the century (Appendix C), but their percentage was noticeably declining, just as had been the pattern a decade earlier in Virginia.[26] In the Maryland Assembly of 1704–7, for the first time a majority of the elected members were natives or had immigrated to the colony as very young children. In the Assembly of 1712–14 and again of 1715, at the close of the royal period, immigrants coming to Maryland as either adults or minors and every person of unknown origin comprised no more than 29 percent of the total elected membership of either body. Many of these immigrants, moreover, were by now residents of long standing, like Matthias Vanderheyden, who had lived in Maryland at least thirty-three years. The council and upper house, where natives became a majority by 1710, experienced the same change. When the Calverts regained the province in 1715, the council of eleven men included seven natives of Maryland and two natives of Virginia who had moved to Maryland as young children.

The family names so familiar to students of the eighteenth century Chesapeake seldom appeared either in the legislature or even among county officers before the 1680s and 1690s; the founders of the well-known family dynasties, in both Virginia and Maryland, immigrated primarily late in the seventeenth century and first established their own places in the social and political world of the two colonists during the last two or three decades of the 1600s.[27] The first real wave of second-generation officeholders in Maryland entered the assembly between 1689 and 1700, when nine sons of former provincial officeholders achieved similarly high position (Table 7). Their ranks were enlarged by an additional seventeen men in the first decade of the new century and twenty more in the following six years. By 1715, nine men had even become the third generation of their families to hold provincial office, and the unusual Brookes had a fourth-generation representative for one term.

The membership of the last royal assembly in 1715 illustrates convincingly the new supremacy of a prominent cluster of families whose political leadership was to be so familiar for the remainder of the colonial period. The surnames of Addison, Bordley, Dashiell, Dent, Ennalls, Hall,

26. In Virginia, the percentage of native-born delegates increased from about 20% of the members of the Long Assembly (1662–76), to 36% of the 285 men first sitting between 1676 and 1706. Some 60% of the burgesses serving during these thirty years had arrived in the colony in 1660 or later or were descendants of such men. The last legislature elected in Virginia in the 1690s had only nine immigrants among the forty-two burgesses for whom a place of birth has been determined. See Quitt, "Virginia House of Burgesses," 9–12; Rainbolt, "Relationship Between Leadership and Constituents," 430.

27. Quitt, "Virginia House of Burgesses," 20–26, and Bailyn, "Politics and Social Structure." The emergence of distinctive political elites, particularly in the years after 1689, is also a central theme of Greene, *The Quest for Power*, especially 19–50.

Table 7. *Appointive and elective service by direct descendants of provincial officeholders*

Generation of family to hold provincial office	Before 1660	1660–69	1670–79	1680–88	1689–99	1700–9	1710–15
Second	2 (2)	4 (2)	6	5 (1)	9	17	20
Third	0	0	0	1[a]	2	3	3
Fourth	0	0	0	0	0	0	1

Note: This table records the first election or appointment only. Numbers in parentheses indicate individuals whose fathers held provincial office in another colony (Virginia in all cases).

[a] Richard Gardiner, son of burgess Luke Gardiner, is listed here as third generation and his father as second generation (in "before 1660" group). The first Richard Gardiner sat as an unelected member in several early assemblies when attendance was open to all freemen.

Harris, Harrison, Holland, Lloyd, Mackall, Purnell, Robins, Stone, Tasker, Taylor, Tilghman, Ward, and Woolford, all represented at Annapolis that spring, were already well known to the residents of the respective counties and were to remain prominent for decades to come. In the upper house, five of the eleven councillors were second-generation assemblymen, and among them Edward and Philemon Lloyd constituted the third generation of their influential family to serve in the assembly. Three of these eleven councillors later died without male heirs, but the sons of seven other men served in subsequent legislatures and descendants of the eleventh member also became provincial officeholders. Seventeen of the fifty delegates sitting in the lower chamber in 1715 were themselves at least second-generation assembly members, and two of that number represented the third generation of their families to serve.

In addition to several prominent families not then sitting in the assembly – like the Frisbys, Hammonds, Pearces, and Smiths – the families represented by these legislators in 1715 solidly established themselves in their respective counties during the royal period. These families further concentrated their influence through extensive intermarriage; some unions, assisted by the passage of time, ended political rivalries that had divided members of the first generation during the proprietary years and the early royal period.[28]

Elaborate kinship networks, extending through sons- and brothers-in-law, connected members of the assembly and council on the provincial level and justices on the county bench below. For example, the Assembly of 1701–4 included Elisha Hall and his two brothers-in-law, Walter Smith and John Smith, representing Calvert; a third brother-in-law, Robert Bradley, sat for Prince George's; and Elisha's own brother, Benjamin Hall, served from Charles County. Such familial connections became increasingly common.

The council by 1715 resembled the closely related family enclave of Lord Baltimore's advisory body of the 1670s and 1680s, but this time it was a more broadly based Protestant elite whose power was to continue through subsequent generations. Unlike Calvert's councillors, these men also had close family ties with numerous members of the lower house.

---

28. For example, Thomas Addison, son of Councillor John Addison, who owed his success in provincial politics to an active role in the revolution of 1689, married Elinor Smith, whose uncle Richard Smith was even imprisoned for opposing the rebels. King George's Parish Register, 1701–1801, fol. 243; Wills 13, fols. 244–48, both on deposit at Hall of Records, Annapolis, Md.; Christopher Johnston, "Smith Family of Calvert County," *Maryland Historical Magazine*, 3 (1908), 68–70. Other examples include the marriage of Thomas Truman Greenfield to the daughter of Kenelm Cheseldyne and a union bringing together the Thomas Brooke and Ninian Beale families.

Two different families, the Lloyds of Talbot County and the Addisons of Prince George's, possessed the widest political base of power in the colony and constituted the apex of Maryland's emerging elite.[29] Similar family networks, though less extensive and powerful, prevailed in other areas of the colony. Prior service in local offices and familial ties bound these men with county government more extensively than ever before, and governors started to complain bitterly of the troublesome "Native" or "Country" party. Governor Francis Nicholson astutely perceived this new configuration of political leadership as early as 1699. He observed that year that the interests of the mother country and the colony were rapidly diverging, and a major cause was the increasingly local orientation of the assembly with its growing native-born membership. Henceforth, Nicholson cautioned, it would be absolutely necessary that any governor "be esteemed by the people, or at least the major part of them, to be a lover to them and their Country." He further remarked that councillors as well as elected assemblymen "by Nature and Self Interest" would promote legislation considered to be "for the good of their Country," even when these acts might be "very prejudicial to his Majesty's Interest and Service."[30]

As that "native" interest became more pronounced in the next decade, Nicholson's successors learned just how formidable this emerging power structure could be. Governor John Seymour battled this "Country borne" elite vigorously and unsuccessfully for almost five years. He had virtually no control over whom the freeholders elected and scarcely more power with the county justices, whom he directly appointed himself. The ties between the county bench and the county delegations were now too close. In exasperation, Seymour confessed in 1708/9 that the justices "almost believe themselves independent of the Queens Governour, and were I to change them for others, there is so little Choice, the remedie might be worse than the disease." A governor's leeway in appointing justices was indeed increasingly circumscribed; it was becoming a matter of which sons, brothers, or nephews he would commission, just as the voters were similarly making their choices among members of the same families.[31]

As members of a new generation came of age, they gradually assumed management of parts of their families' wide-ranging planting and mer-

29. See the Legislative History Project's files on these families, and Jordan, "Emergence of a Native Elite," 270.
30. Nicholson to lords of trade, July 1, 1699, CO5/1310, No. 2.
31. For Seymour's complaints, see *Archives*, 25:262–67, 267–70 (quotation, 269); and for similar observations from Alexander Spotswood, governor of Virginia, see R. A. Brock, ed., *The Official Letters of Alexander Spotswood, Lieutenant Governor of the Colony of Virginia, 1710–1722*, Virginia Historical Society, Collections, N.S., Vols. 1 and 2 (Richmond, Va., 1882–85), *passim*.

cantile affairs, just as they made their debuts in public service as justices, vestrymen, and militia officers and in other important positions. They worked their way through a variety of such offices to establish their abilities, and in the process those who were less capable were winnowed out. If an older son were not suitable or worthy, his younger brother emerged to take his place, and sometimes brothers would serve concurrently. Service in the assembly followed for those individuals who commanded the highest regard of the electorate; wealth alone was not usually sufficient, for most counties by the early eighteenth century had several affluent families among whom the voters could choose. The ablest men, or those with the most influential connections, eventually served as well on the council or highest court in the province. Rarely after 1700 were these leading families of Maryland not represented on the county bench, in the assembly, or in other ranking provincial offices, and families like the Lloyds and Addisons could expect to have many representatives.[32]

The emergence of this elite and its more assured access to office directly influenced the profile of assemblymen in several respects. The average age of delegates, as of the opening of each new assembly, declined over the course of the royal period from 47.6 in 1692 to approximately 40 years of age for each of the last four assemblies starting in 1708. On at least twenty-seven occasions between 1689 and 1715, freeholders returned men who were not yet 30 years old. The voters of Cecil County even elected Thomas Frisby in 1702 when he was just 20. The Committee of Elections and Privileges voided the election, ruling that this son of a sitting councillor was underage; the voters simply waited a few months until the young Frisby turned 21 and then reelected him. A larger number of delegates than before appeared at the capital to take seats in the lower house while still in their 30s; this occurred on at least 109 occasions. Each of the last four assemblies of the royal period averaged twenty-one members who are known to have been under 40 years of age.[33]

The majority of terms throughout these years were still served by men in their 40s, but the number was diminishing. Moreover, such delegates were now more frequently experienced legislators serving recurring terms, rather than the older newcomers who had prevailed in earlier periods. For example, Ninian Beale and James Smallwood established precedents with their service in the lower house into their seventy-fifth

---

32. Charles Sydnor, *Gentlemen Freeholders: Political Practices in Washington's Virginia* (Chapel Hill, N.C., 1952), engagingly describes a similar society in neighboring Virginia.

33. *Archives*, 24:298, 356, on Frisby. Five different assemblies had at least four delegates under thirty years of age. For comparisons with the age structure of the House of Commons, see Henning, ed., *The Commons, 1660–1690*, 1:44–47.

years, respectively. Smallwood sat continuously as a delegate for Charles County from 1692 through 1714, the longest uninterrupted service to that time. Beale, first elected in 1689, was still serving a decade later, when the lower house, acknowledging the "many Signall Services and Laborious Endeavors . . . which he still continues Willingly Even beyond what his age seems Capable of," voted £75 to buy three slaves for the veteran public servant and delegate.[34] Such seniority was most unusual, but it was no longer uncommon for a delegate to serve into his 50s or 60s. At least seven men in the Assembly of 1704–7, and again in 1708–11, were 50 years of age or older, and the precise age remains unverifiable for several other individuals who almost certainly belong in the same age category.

The continuing service of more delegates into their 50s and beyond, as well as the increasingly frequent election of representatives at a much younger age, contributed to the steady accumulation in the assembly of men with greater experience and longer tenures. Lower life expectancies still prevented the extensive service familiar to students of the Congress in the present century, with its many veterans of thirty or more years. Still, the contrast to the first five decades of the Maryland assembly is significant (Appendix A). Among the 478 delegates chosen between 1637 and 1715, only 23 won election six or more times; 18 of them first sat after 1689, and 13 for the first time after 1700. The more numerous representatives serving three to five terms likewise sat disproportionately after 1689. Although the turnover of delegates, especially those men serving only one or two terms, continued to be high, these legislators of brief duration do occur less frequently after 1689.

Recurring service, with its potential impact on the assembly's organization and business, is illustrated more clearly in a further analysis of legislative service (Table 8). Between 1660 and 1715, first-term elected members constituted 50 percent or more of the delegates of eight of the nineteen different assemblies, but significantly in only one of the eight convened after 1693. Conversely, members returning from the immediately prior assembly exceeded one-third of the original burgesses in only three of the nine legislatures meeting between 1660 and 1689, but after that year, reelected incumbents fell below that proportion only once, never comprised less than 30 percent of the delegates, and totaled 40 percent or more of the original membership in five of the ten assemblies sitting during the royal period.

Many representatives sat for additional terms but not in consecutive assemblies. The combination of reelected incumbents and other delegates

34. *Archives*, 22:335 (quotation), 337.

Table 8. *Turnover and continuity among elected assembly members, 1661–1715*

Assembly	Total number of delegates	Members serving in first term	Members reelected from last assembly	All members with prior service
1661	16	10	4	6
1662	17	5	7	12[a]
1663–64	20	11	4 .	9
1666	21	8	6	13[b]
1669	27	13	8	14
1671–74/75				
Original	31	19	8	12
By-elections	14[c]	10	0	4
1676–82				
Original	42	25	14	17
By-elections	15[d]	14	0	1
1682–84				
Original	22	6	16	16
By-elections	1	1	0	0
1686–88				
Original	21[e]	11	5	10
By-elections	5	2	0	3
1689–92				
Original	38	23	13	15
By-elections	5	5	0	0
1692–94				
Original	42	26	14	16
By-elections	7	6	0	1
1694–97				
Original	42	18[f]	16	24
By-elections	17	10	0	7
1697/98–1700				
Original	46	17	26	29
By-elections	10	7	0	3
1701–4				
Original	46	14	25	32
By-elections	5	5	0	0
1704–7				
Original	46	23	13	23
By-elections	6	4	0	2
1708A	50	22[g]	20	28
1708B–1711				
Original	50	8	41	42
By-elections	8	6	0	2
1712–14				
Original	50	23	19	27
By-elections	8	6	0	2
1715	50	18	24	32

with prior service grew impressively in number. Their total never represented less than one-half of the lower house's membership after 1693. Table 9 demonstrates further the increase in collective experience, especially for assemblies meeting after 1700, and shows the cumulative longevity of all delegates grouped approximately by decade. After the 1660s, when members had somewhat greater experience owing to the frequent convening of one-session legislatures, only 6.6 to 8.1 percent of delegates to the assemblies of the next three decades had served in four or more bodies and 12.7 to 24.4 percent in three or more legislatures. However, 14.3 percent of the burgesses in the three assemblies of 1701–8 had served in four or more legislatures, and 32.4 percent in three or more, and the comparable figures for 1708–15 were 22.4 and 34.5 percent, respectively. These higher percentages do not fully reveal the greater accumulation of experience, for assemblies now met in lengthier and more frequent sessions than was usually the case in the proprietary period; during the years of royal rule, the typical legislature had a life of three years and convened for four or five separate sessions.

The upper house, without a fixed term of service or the need for reelection, similarly experienced longer tenures (Appendix B). Less frequently than under proprietary rule did governors and the Crown make mistakes in selecting councillors; new members usually came under care-

Table 8 (*cont.*)

Note: With the exception of four men at the 1708A assembly, which was dissolved before an election could be rescheduled, this table does not include individuals whose elections were declared void, unless the person was subsequently reelected.

*a*Includes Nathaniel Utie, who previously served as an appointed member in the upper house.

*b*Includes James Neale, who previously served as an appointed member in the unicameral assembly.

*c*Does not include John Vanhack, an original member of this assembly and reelected after the creation of Cecil County altered his county of residence.

*d*Does not include Thomas Smith, mentioned in the journal as attending the fifth session but possibly a clerical error.

*e*The identity of one elected delegate from Anne Arundel to this assembly remains unknown.

*f*Includes Henry Coursey, who previously served as an appointed member in the upper house, and Thomas Smith, who may have served in 1682.

*g*Includes Thomas Brooke, who previously served as an appointed member in the upper house.

Table 9. *Cumulative experience of elected assembly members by approximate decades*

Terms of service	1661–69	1671–82	1682–89	1689–1700	1701–8	1708–15
1	31 (47.6)	60 (68.9)	19 (42.2)	73 (54.1)	42 (40.0)	49 (42.2)
2	19 (29.0)	16 (18.4)	16 (35.6)	29 (21.5)	29 (27.6)	27 (23.2)
3	6 (9.2)	4 (4.6)	7 (15.6)	24 (17.8)	19 (18.1)	14 (12.1)
4	7 (10.7)	4 (4.6)	0	5 (3.7)	8 (7.6)	13 (11.2)
5	1 (1.5)	1 (1.2)	2 (4.4)	4 (2.9)	5 (4.8)	9 (7.8)
6	0	2 (2.3)	0	0	2 (1.9)	3 (2.6)
7	0	0	1 (2.2)	0	0	0
8	1 (1.5)	0	0	0	0	1 (0.8)

Note: Individuals are not included who were elected but either were never allowed to take their seats or died before the assembly convened. Dates represent the beginning and end of groups of assemblies, arranged approximately by decade. Numbers in parentheses are percentages.

ful scrutiny for longer periods before appointment, and consequently there were fewer dismissals. The average tenure of the thirty-two councillors serving between 1660 and 1689 barely exceeded seven years, only six men sitting for longer than a decade. For the seventeen men appointed between the revolution and 1700, the average tenure increased only slightly to nine years, but thereafter substantially longer periods of service became the rule. The twenty individuals receiving their first commissions between 1700 and 1715 sat for an average of thirteen years, and the council of eleven men serving in 1715, at the conclusion of the royal period, were to enjoy an average tenure of nineteen and a half years.

The freeholders, like the governors, had a clearer idea of whom they were selecting, and the performances of most assemblymen rarely surprised the public. The phenomenon of men receiving either election or appointment quite soon after arrival in the colony had virtually disappeared. Seldom did an individual enter the assembly who had not lived in Maryland for ten or more years; only thirteen men won seats before seven years of residence. With but two exceptions, these were men of very high status, and eight of them had dwelled in the province for at least four years. The overwhelming majority of delegates were individuals with at least twenty years in Maryland. By the early 1700s, generally four-fifths of the delegates of any given assembly were in this category and three-fifths had lived for more than thirty years in the colony.

Such extended residence and the greater opportunity it fostered for knowing more about these men and their abilities enabled freeholders to cast a more discriminating vote, and certainly they were not blindly electing anyone who had wealth, ability, or previous service. Two different assembly elections in 1708 illustrate the choices that freeholders were exercising. Governor Seymour had attempted throughout the Assembly of 1704–7 to obtain a thorough reform of the colony's judicial system. Frustrated by the resistance of the delegates, who in turn reflected popular wishes as well as their own concerns, Seymour proceeded unilaterally to effect his objectives. In the summer of 1708, freeholders elected to a new assembly men firmly resolved to resist the governor; Seymour's supporters by and large lost at the polls. This lower house fought the governor so strenuously that he angrily dissolved them after only a week and called for another election. Forty-one of the fifty dismissed delegates were promptly reelected, and the nine new members represented no gains for Seymour's position. Voters again declined to support those individuals who had closely cooperated with him. It is interesting that the behavior of the Maryland electorate in this instance resembled the response of voters in Virginia to comparable attempts about the same time by Governor Alexander Spotswood to reform the tobacco inspection system and to gain votes by his patronage. The Virginia freeholders wreaked a similar vengeance on their governor.[35]

The evolving relationship between constituents and representatives proceeded during these years in directions first apparent in the 1670s and 1680s. Although many facets remain frustratingly cloudy, more detailed legislation governing elections, extensive reports by a more active Committee on Elections and Privileges, and very full accounts of a series of elections in Kent County, combined with occasional and incidental remarks scattered through various records, provide a richer canvas of electoral activity.

In 1692, the first royal assembly, achieving the much desired goal of delegates for years, finally brought the electoral procedure completely under the legislature's control. The statute substantially retained the property qualifications in effect for the past two decades but restored representation to four delegates per county. Citing the value of the parliamentary example, which their predecessors had futilely included in the vetoed act of 1678, these lawmakers incorporated basically the same procedures for elections employed under the proprietor but eliminated the special writ of summons he had required before one could attend the assembly. Sheriffs remained ineligible for election and ordinarykeepers also became disqualified.[36] By custom, but not yet by law, the speaker of the lower house routinely issued warrants for new elections to fill any vacancies, in accord with the English practice; the proprietor's earlier control of such writs had been a continual source of friction.[37] With the act for the advancement of natives in 1694, the assembly also established a three-year residency requirement for eligibility to stand for election. In 1708, a revised law defined in greater detail the procedures for conducting elections, especially their timing, and added to those already ineligible for office "any other Person disabled by any Law of England from sitting in parliament." This clause aimed further at excluding Catholics, as did a stricter enforcement of the oath requirements. Unrecognized by Marylanders at the time, the new provision also extended to the colony an English law rendering naturalized citizens ineligible for election. This implication of the law was not perceived, however, until the celebrated battles of the 1770s over the seating of Jonathan Hagar.[38]

35. Ibid., 27:179–374, contains the journals of these two assemblies. Jordan, "Royal Period," 249–60, discusses these elections in more detail; Morgan, *American Slavery, American Freedom*, 359–61, describes Virginia's election.
36. *Archives*, 13:541–44. The legislature defeated efforts in 1696 and 1715 to reduce once again the number of delegates to two or three in order to cut expenses (ibid., 19:305; 30:60, 142, 160). Virginia had only two burgesses per county.
37. *Archives*, 19:4; Mereness, *Maryland as a Proprietary Province*, 205.
38. *Archives*, 27:352–55; Jordan, "Elections and Voting," 249–50, explores this law, its intention, and its implications.

The assembly also asserted successfully in 1708 the sole authority to establish or abolish representation in the legislature. Earlier in the royal period, it had reclaimed the right to create new counties, which the Lords Baltimore had tended to accomplish through proprietary ordinances after the 1650s. Then, Governor Seymour, following Charles Calvert's precedent in extending representation to St. Mary's City, issued a charter in 1708 to Annapolis, and one of its provisions allowed for the election of two burgesses to the assembly. The delegates refused to seat the two individuals, who appeared at the next legislature; the lower house astutely claimed English precedent to support their position, for since 1671 the House of Commons had successfully challenged similar efforts by the Crown to create seats in its chamber. Eventually, the assembly itself bestowed representation on Annapolis but did so through legislation, not an executive charter, and only after revising the electoral qualifications that Seymour had decreed.[39]

In 1715, the assembly introduced a residency requirement, one of the few instances in which the legislature's action contrasted with English practices, which it had otherwise sought so carefully to emulate. Candidates now had to reside within the county that they wished to represent. Such a legal stipulation first appeared implicitly with respect to representation for Annapolis in 1708, but until 1715 an individual could clearly qualify to vote in more than one county, and presumably, with the exception of Annapolis, one could represent a district other than that in which one primarily resided. Before passage of the new restriction, at least twenty-eight delegates had represented more than one constituency during their careers. However, the vast majority and perhaps all had moved their residences, found themselves in different counties through the alteration of boundaries, or sat from either St. Mary's City or Annapolis, as well as from the counties in which these towns were located.[40] Precedent seems to have opposed a man's sitting for a county in which he did not have a primary residence, but why the assembly legislated the residency requirement in 1715 remains uncertain, except that it underscores the evolving relationship between representatives and the electorate, especially the expectation of most freeholders that the delegates be, quite literally, one of them.[41]

39. Jordan, "Elections and Voting," 250–51. Representation for St. Mary's City ceased in 1708, when the town had no residents to receive a writ for a new election.
40. *Archives*, 30:270–74. A proprietary ordinance on elections in 1681 had spoken of burgesses "now liveing and resideing within their said county," but if this was intended to be a residency requirement, it was not included in the assembly's act of 1692 or subsequent election laws before 1715, except for the Annapolis charter (ibid., 15:379; 27:358–59; Chancery Records, PC, fol. 600, Hall of Records).
41. Jordan, "Elections and Voting," 251–52.

With the return of proprietary rule, the Assembly of 1716 reconfirmed explicitly the gains of the royal period in a statute that summarized the new election procedures and practices effected in recent years. With a few exceptions, these provisions remained basically unchanged for the remainder of the colonial era. In a supplementary election act in 1718, the assembly did legislatively sanction a practice that had prevailed unofficially since the 1690s whereby the speaker issued warrants for any elections to fill vacancies and also dispensed with the usual stipulation of time for such by-elections. In a significant departure from previous practice, the statute also effectively excluded Catholics from the franchise unless they took the qualifying oaths.[42]

Opposition to Catholic participation in the political process had persisted even after the removal of Catholics from all offices in 1689. Throughout the 1690s, complaints surfaced that Catholics were wielding great influence with their votes. One disgruntled colonist in 1698 asserted that papists "Choose all such Persons as are disaffected to the King and Government" and that Catholics' votes were often decisive at the polls. Governor Francis Nicholson, who battled to ensure the establishment of the Church of England and other measures occasionally unpopular with large segments of the electorate, also observed that "other enemyes also to our church and state are most of the rude and dissolute people of the Province who are managed by the Papists."[43]

In 1708/9, Governor Seymour similarly asserted that "declared Enemys of our Church and State," among whom he particularly included Catholics and Quakers, were "the busiest at the Severall Elections in the Countys where they reside." Seymour accelerated the campaign against Catholics. He particularly disliked the noticeable increase in their number with the influx of servants from Ireland, and he gathered census data on the precise number and location of Catholics throughout the province.[44]

The lower house, in introducing its bill in 1718, again noted the continued growth and active politicking of Catholics. The delegates argued that the denial of the suffrage to Catholics would make the colony's practices more consonant with those of the mother country, a position heartily endorsed by Governor John Hart. The eventual law stipulated that the

---

42. *Archives*, 30:617–22 (act of 1716); 33:287–89 (act of 1718).
43. Ibid., 23:414 (quotation), 451; 25:582–83 (quotation). Nicholson also categorized papists as "our profess'd Enemyes."
44. *Archives*, 25:268 (quotation), but see also 26:289–92; 27:371, and Seymour's census of Catholics, Seymour to lords of trade, Sept. 17, 1708, and enclosure, CO5/716/III.

sheriff could tender the oath as often as he wished to any individual suspected of disguising his papist beliefs.[45]

Catholics were not to play a direct role in Maryland politics again until the American Revolution. The law of 1718 expressly stated that Quakers were still eligible to vote and were not affected by this oath requirement, but of course devout Friends, like Catholics, could not hold office. Occasionally, a former adherent or the son of a Quaker or Catholic would convert, swear the requisite oaths, and hold office, but for the most part politics in Maryland became the domain of those colonists who had won the political and religious struggles of the 1690s on behalf of the Church of England and had then legislated less tolerant policies toward nonestablished religions.[46]

The final significant change came four years later and built upon the earlier exclusion of sheriffs from the assembly. Proprietary patronage had remained an important means of persuading burgesses to support unpopular bills. In addressing a disputed election directed to the Committee of Elections and Privileges in 1722, the lower house ruled that "for the future any person Chosen to Serve as a member Delegate or Burgess that shall after such his Election accept of any office or Pension from or under the Government shall (According to the practice of the British Parliament) be incapable to sit or serve as a Member in this House by Virtue of such Election." The House of Commons had fought vigorously in recent decades to attain an effective act against placemen, but these efforts had actually been much less successful than their Maryland imitators realized. In the struggle to limit executive influence over assemblymen, the lower house in this instance exceeded the accomplishments of the House of Commons in controlling its own membership.[47]

Elections became more ritualized during the royal period, just as they became more standardized in procedure.[48] Election day was a special occasion for county residents, who rarely gathered together and looked forward to this break in their normal routines. Court days generally

45. *Archives*, 33:144, 211, 219, 222, 223–24, 278–79. Proponents of the legislation cited the Act of Parliament of 7th-8th William, Chap. 27, Sect. 19. The statute was rushed through the assembly to affect an upcoming by-election.
46. For example, Thomas Edmundson, raised as a Quaker, and Charles Carroll Barrister, from a Catholic family, served in the assembly after 1715.
47. *Archives*, 34:447; Betty Kemp, *Kings and Commons, 1660–1832* (London, 1965), 22–23, 52–64. An act excluding pensioners for a brief period had finally passed in 1716 in England, but its effect was less than intended by the lawmakers. The assembly in Virginia and other southern colonies also lagged behind the lower house of Maryland in effectively excluding placemen (Greene, *The Quest for Power*, 187–88).
48. Carr, "County Government," 380–91, also discusses these procedures with helpful references to parallels in England and Virginia.

attracted a large number of colonists for a variety of legal and commercial transactions in addition to judicial proceedings, and much visiting, hospitality, and good times attended such occasions. An even more festive air seemed to prevail at those courts that included elections.[49]

More extensive accounts describing election days survive for Virginia, especially in the eighteenth century, but comments in the Maryland records corroborate these descriptions of elections in the Old Dominion.[50] Certainly, alcohol was abundantly a part of the election process in both colonies, as well as in England. One observer in St. Mary's City in 1698 later testified that a certain person might not have noticed a particular event "by reason he was much Concerned that time in drink being the day the City Burgessess were Chosen." Another colonist had complained in 1689 about a candidate's getting men "in drinke." Nonetheless, the Maryland legislature never resorted during these years, as did its counterpart in Virginia, to passing a law restricting treats in order to combat the drinking problem.[51]

By the 1690s, if not before, differences were sufficiently pronounced that with or without the additional stimulus of alcohol tempers might flare out of control. For example, in Talbot County in 1692, a discontented party came into the election court "with a great Multitude in a Riotous & Tumultuous manner" and made "Menacing Speeches to the Justices and Sheriff." In 1699, "fighting and Riotous accons" attended an election in St. Mary's County. Similarly, in Prince George's during the taking of a poll in 1714/15, William Taneyhill used his horsewhip against the Reverend Jacob Henderson and told him to "begone from this side or words to that effect."[52]

With such exceptions, Marylanders left little private commentary on their elections. Most county clerks even failed to record the transactions

49. Rhys Isaac, *The Transformation of Virginia, 1740–1790* (Chapel Hill, N.C. 1982), 88–114, interprets the importance of "occasions," such as election day in the Chesapeake world.

50. Sydnor, *Gentleman Freeholders*, especially Chaps. 3 and 4; Pierre Marambaud, *William Byrd of Westover, 1674–1744* (Charlottesville, Va., 1975), 207. The most extensive discussion of eighteenth century elections in Maryland appears in David Curtis Skaggs, *Roots of Maryland Democracy 1753–1776* (Westport, Conn., 1973).

51. *Archives*, 23:412; 8:120. On election days in England, see Hirst, *Representative of the People?* 109–56. The Virginia experiment is discussed in Robert E. Brown and B. Katherine Brown, *Virginia, 1705–1786: Democracy or Aristocracy?* (East Lansing, Mich., 1964), 153, and Morgan, *American Slavery, American Freedom*, 358. Maryland finally, and in vain, attempted such a prohibition in 1768 (Skaggs, *Roots of Maryland Democracy*, 24).

52. Talbot County Records, NN No. 6, fol. 32b (rear); *Archives*, 22:445; Prince George's Court Records, Liber I (G), fol. 718. The problem in Talbot arose from the frustrations of freeholders who wanted to reelect Quaker John Edmundson, recently disqualified for his inability to swear required oaths. His supporters failed on this occasion but did elect him again in 1694, when he was once more disqualified.

of the election courts, so knowledge is based largely on incidental mention, usually reported in conjunction with disputed elections reviewed by the lower house's Committee of Elections and Privileges. Its deliberations suggest much about what was either commonplace or unusual about election day activities and procedures. Fortunately, the clerks in one county, Kent, did record more extensive accounts of seven elections held over two decades beginning in 1698. Those accounts answer many questions while also presenting new puzzles.[53]

The Kent elections, and presumably those held elsewhere, followed the same stylized procedure. The court convened on election day at about 9 a.m., when the writ and proclamation were read to "a very large appearance" of the gathered electorate or, as a clerk in Cecil later observed on several occasions, to "A Great Concourse of the Freeholders."[54] After the sheriff read the writ, the Court "giveth the Electors som Caution and Advice and then ordered them to proceed to their Election." Generally the election was completed by the end of the day, the sheriff deciding when to close the poll. Occasionally, however, it became necessary to adjourn the election court to a second day or over a weekend. Bad weather, procedural complications, or disagreements among the voters might account for the adjournment. In Kent in November of 1708, for example, the clerk noted that "there being Severall heats and Disturbances amongst the people, the Sheriff with the advice of the Court thinks fitt to adjourn till Monday Tenn o'clock and that they may be the better to consult there Intrests for the advantage of there County."[55]

It is nowhere stated what advice the justices gave to the freeholders. Probably they instructed voters routinely on the importance of choosing wisely, but no doubt from time to time less scrupulous justices sought to set the mood or to influence voters through implicit if not explicit comments made on or off the bench. The decision to adjourn the election court in Kent in 1708 may have constituted such a case. Did justices use the weekend to electioneer among the voters, to inform them of Seymour's recent actions against local courts, and thereby insinuate the proper "Intrests for the advantage of there County?" When the court

53. See Kent Court Proceedings I, fol. 877 (1697/98); ibid., ID No. 2, fol. 57 (1701); ibid., GL I, fol. 378 (1704); ibid., 1707–1709, fols. 150, 157 (1708); ibid., JS No. W, fols. 28–29 (1714), 51–52 (1714/15), 122–24 (1715/16). These elections to 1708 have also been discussed in Carr, "County Government," 383–88.

54. Cecil Judgments, SK No. 1, fols. 46, 240, 382, speaking of election courts in 1719, 1720, and 1721.

55. It was perhaps the adjournment in November 1708 that later caused the lower house to question the sheriff of Kent for irregular proceedings in the election (*Archives*, 27:293). Cecil also had a two-day election, Apr. 3–4, 1719. Cecil Judgments, SK No. 1, fol. 6.

reconvened on Monday morning, the "heats and Disturbances" had apparently been resolved, or at least the clerk provides no evidence of continuing conflict.[56]

Freeholders voted generally by voice or a show of hands. Only when the outcome was in doubt, or electors on one side or the other so requested, was there a formal poll, in which case each voter publicly indicated his preference. The candidates did not need to be present, but on at least one occasion in Kent, they were brought into the court before the poll was taken. If in attendance, the winning candidate entered after the vote to be presented, to watch the signing of indentures, and to receive any grievances his constituents might want carried to the assembly.[57]

The possibility of there having been slates of candidates, like the continuing question of electoral subdivisions within counties, remains unsettled, but the Kent County records leave no doubt that opposition was common and that some form of pairing or districting was quite likely. Between 1694 and 1716, contests occurred for at least seventeen and perhaps several more of the thirty-two available seats in Kent for which election records survive. Voting on a given election day proceeded with four separate elections, one seat determined after another, although on one occasion in 1714/15, in a closely contested match that had to be adjourned overnight, the clerk recorded that "Mr. William Frisby sheriff proceeds to examine the Poles that was given on both sides – being near a like that by a Generall Voice both the Said Parties are to go as Delegates." Then the freeholders selected a third and fourth representative in separate voting. However, in numerous other elections, candidates who were close contenders for the first or second seats failed to vie for any of the remaining positions. Postulating the existence of geographical districts does not readily solve the mystery, nor does it seem that the failure to win a first seat made losers unwilling to accept a lower place.[58]

Over the twenty-two years, eight men won election "Nemine Contradicente" on one or more occasions, Thomas Smith doing so three times and William Frisby, Daniel Pearce, and St. Leger Codd, Jr., each accomplishing the feat at least twice. They were indisputably among the most

56. The question of the justices' advice is all the more pertinent since candidates by this period usually came from among the justices themselves. In at least one election in Somerset County, "the Justices arose from the Bench" before voting actually began. Otherwise, nothing further is known of their activity (Somerset Judicial Record, 1693–94, fol. 110). A few decades later, leading residents, including justices, were speaking on behalf of certain candidates (Skaggs, *Roots of Maryland Democracy*, 22).

57. For example, in 1708 in Kent, in the case of two of the four seats, candidates appeared before the crowd before the poll was taken. On the interaction of representatives and constituents, see *Archives*, 23:372–73; 7:369, 424; 19:577; and Hall, ed., *Narratives*, 350.

58. Kent Court Proceedings, JS No. W, fols. 51–52.

eminent men in the county. Wealth and education were not an automatic guarantee of election, however, as veteran burgesses Smith and Pearce personally discovered. Smith had won a contested election in 1694, but then had been unopposed in 1697/98, 1701, and 1704, and in these assemblies played a leading role, serving finally as speaker from 1704 to 1707. In this last term, Smith sided frequently with Seymour rather than with popular sentiment on several issues, and Smith accepted a controversial commission from Seymour for an office the lower house had adamantly refused to support. This allegiance with the governor likely led to Smith's inactivity in the elections of 1708 and 1712. When he stood again in a by-election in 1714, it was undoubtedly an embarrassment for this experienced and distinguished legislator, militia colonel, and Provincial Court justice to lose to young William Blay, a candidate standing for the first time. Pearce, the son of a burgess, won unanimous election the first two times he stood in 1708, and perhaps again in 1712, but he lost in 1714/15 and again in 1715/16 for unexplained reasons; the clerk simply noted that voters "wholly declined" to support Pearce's candidacy in the latter election.[59]

A few men in the colony apparently had sufficient stature to discourage opposition except in the most heated of times. Whenever William Frisby chose to run, he was elected without opposition – although he often chose not to be a candidate. Other would-be burgesses had a more arduous path to victory. That opposition was more the rule than the exception is suggested further by the lower house's questioning of the returns from Baltimore County in 1697/98. The Committee of Elections and Privileges was suspicious of the report that four men had been elected without any opposition. The assembly seated the four individuals only after interrogation of six men from the county provided sufficient sworn testimony of a proper election procedure and of unopposed candidates.[60]

Although opposition might center upon personalities, and an individual's reputation and general manner were critical, elections were also affected by politicking over issues such as proprietary prerogatives, establishment of the Church of England, appropriate jurisdiction for the courts, tobacco regulation, taxation, and control of appointed officers. Candidates apparently indicated their positions on occasion and spoke directly to voters' concerns, for Governor Nicholson in 1698 cautioned the delegates in strong language against "promising what great things they would doe (in Redressing Grievances if they were chose)."[61]

59. Papenfuse et al., eds., *Biographical Dictionary*, and Kent election court records cited in note 60. Smith was ultimately appointed to the council in 1716.
60. *Archives*, 22:78–79. In 1666, Charles County had unanimously elected three of its four burgesses (ibid., 2:8).
61. Ibid., 22:71 (quotation), 108.

Complaints of irregular procedures, especially on the part of sheriffs and clerks, mounted in the closing years of the century. The Committee of Elections and Privileges between 1692 and 1715 investigated charges of illegal procedures in at least forty-two elections and voided the returns in thirteen instances. Among the grievances were failure to notify all eligible voters, refusal to allow a poll when requested, and scheduling of courts at inaccessible places, as in 1699 in St. Mary's County, when the sheriff held a by-election "at a place of noe resort but a neck of land all together out of the way."[62]

Because the committee did not function regularly before 1692, its surviving records may skew the picture of disputed elections toward the later period. However, except for a dispute over the attempted election of Fendall in 1678, little mention of challenged elections and even of alleged misconduct in an election, survives before 1689. Patterns of membership, as well as Charles Calvert's granting of representation to St. Mary's City to guarantee seats for his supporters, argue persuasively that increased competition was starting to occur by the late 1670s, and after 1689, both direct and indirect evidence becomes quite pronounced for contested and disputed elections.[63]

In one election, voters in a particular county might turn out in large numbers and carry differences all the way to the assembly in protest against the outcome of the voting; then in the next election, apathy might reign supreme. No consistency prevailed in voter activity. Governor Nicholson proposed in 1694 a fine on any freeholder who failed to appear at an election court without a lawful excuse, and he wanted to require freeholders to remain until the election was over.[64] Nothing came of this bill, but concern arose again two years later when a by-election in Talbot attracted fewer than forty people and only twenty-two or twenty-three actually signed election indentures. With much shorter notice and other

62. These cases do not include invalidation of elections in which candidates were not qualified or were not seated by virtue of age, religious beliefs, etc. See *Archives*, 13:353, 355, 358; 19:23, 314; 22:78–79, 413, 414, 416, 445 (quotation); 24:166–67; 27:205, 209, 210, 290, 293, 333, 417, 455, 457, 520; 29:136–37, 144–45; 30:113. In Virginia, between 1684 and 1706, the lower house had to settle eighteen election disputes (Quitt, "Virginia House of Burgesses," 238).

63. In 1659/60, three delegates from St. Mary's were ruled unduly elected for unspecified reasons; two of the three were immediately reelected (*Archives*, 1:383). In Somerset in 1669, voters had elected two burgesses, but the sheriff returned indentures for just one; the sheriff was fined (ibid., 2:187–88). Finally, there was some confusion, unstated, about returns from Kent in 1642 (ibid., 1:129–30). No doubt, sheriffs and justices before 1689, as well as after, failed on occasion to show due concern for full participation. In October, 1683, for example, Baltimore county officials apparently made no attempt to inform all voters of a by-election that was held one day after the court of proclamation (Baltimore Court Proceedings, D, fol. 85).

64. *Archives*, 19:51.

special circumstances attending by-elections, participation might understandably fall below that expected when all four seats were to be determined, but even so the Talbot turnout in a county of 1,397 taxables was lamentably low. Coming simultaneously with a Calvert election of unseemly haste and low turnout as well, Nicholson again questioned ways to elicit more participation. The possibility of accepting sealed absentee ballots arose, but the lower house eventually concluded that the election law already provided sufficiently for procedures and no change should be legislated.[65]

The matter did not die. In 1708, the upper house, noting that freeholders were often "very indifferent & remiss," pushed again for legislation to encourage greater participation. The lower house once more resisted and noted that such laws were not customary in England. The revised election law of that year did include measures to improve voter awareness of the time of elections and to schedule them at more convenient places. Finally in 1715, again at the instigation of the upper house, an amendment to the act on elections established a penalty of 100 pounds of tobacco for any qualified voter who failed to appear at an election, one-half of the fine going toward county expenses and one-half to the informer. There is little indication of the act's success or failure. Meanwhile, large turnouts for other elections revealed that voters were willing to participate when motivated by particular issues, crises or candidates; when the outcome seemed to be of little importance to them, they did not bother to vote.[66]

The greater activity of the Committee of Elections and Privileges illustrates the general development of a more effective internal organization within the lower house. An elaborate structure of committees had evolved and that in turn led to a more sophisticated phrasing of laws, a more successful devising of strategy, and the slow but sure establishment of influential precedents contributing to achievement of the delegates' objectives. Not accidentally, many of these accomplishments had depended on the initiative and expertise of a powerful nucleus of members. The timing of these critical advances correlates with the appearance in Maryland politics of more men well trained in the law and other individuals whose education and experience qualified them to introduce different practices into the assembly's conduct of business. Such men tended to win

65. Nicholson to lords of trade, Mar. 27, 1697, Co5/714; *Archives*, 19:312–13, 314, 361–62.
66. Ibid., 27:249–50, 251 (quotation), 317; 30:173, 273. A by-election in Baltimore County in 1721 drew only 107 voters; the population of the county in 1720 has been estimated as 4,100. See Baltimore Court Proceedings, IS No. C, fol. 615; Karinen, "Maryland Population: 1631–1730," 405. Virginia in 1662 had established a fine of 200 pounds of tobacco for failure to vote and included this provision in the codified election law of 1705 (Quitt, "Virginia House of Burgesses," 202).

the support of freeholders more rapidly and more consistently than did the average burgess and were quicker to receive deference from other delegates. Seven professional lawyers had served before 1689, and among them Kenelm Cheseldyne, Robert Carvile, Thomas Burford, and the two Rousbys had been especially influential. Cheseldyne continued to have an impact after the revolution, when he served in four more assemblies as an elected delegate; he presided as speaker of the lower house for much of the critical decade between 1685 and 1697.[67]

Three other professional lawyers with extensive training, Robert Smith, Philip Clarke, and William Dent, joined Cheseldyne in the early legislatures of the royal period, won frequent reelection, and became central figures in the assembly's conduct of business. Smith replaced Cheseldyne as speaker for four sessions between 1694 and 1696. At other times, he served as a prominent member of the Committee of Aggrievances and the Committee of Laws. Clarke became chairman of the Committee of Laws by 1697 in his second term and reputedly drafted much legislation single-handedly. A former clerk of the lower house, Dent served as chairman first of the Committee of Laws and second of the Committee of Aggrievances during his first term in the assembly. In three later terms, he usually presided as chairman of the Committee of Laws, before rising to the speaker's chair and leadership of the entire lower house for the last two sessions preceding his death. Shortly after the turn of the century, other professional members of the bar, among them the astute Thomas Bordley, took seats in the legislature and began prominent careers there.[68]

Expertise and leadership were by no means limited to the professional lawyers. Other representatives practiced actively as attorneys in the courts and in additional ways demonstrated a knowledge of the law and of procedure.[69] Even the average delegate was better informed than had been the case just a few decades earlier. The governor and council were no longer as likely to monopolize information nor to provide what little continuity existed. Indeed, royal governors, themselves now the officials least familiar with the province, frequently called upon members of both

67. Day, "Lawyers in Colonial Maryland," and entries for these men in Papenfuse et al., eds., *Biographical Dictionary.*
68. Papenfuse et al., eds., *Biographical Dictionary.* Aubrey C. Land, *The Dulaneys of Maryland* (Baltimore, 1955), provides an extended study of Daniel Dulaney the Elder, another such individual, who first served in the assembly soon after 1715.
69. Thomas Smithson, for example, the son of an English justice and member of Parliament, served six successive terms in the lower house, playing an active role on both the Committee of Aggrievances and Committee of Laws, as well as becoming speaker. Through many of these years, he was also chief justice of the Provincial Court. The assembly awarded him a special gratuity in 1702 to discourage his retirement (Smithson file, Legislative History Project).

houses to provide perspective and detail on earlier laws and practices. Some delegates were always as knowledgeable as, and occasionally more so than, the consulted councillors.[70]

Legislative committees enabled talented men to extend their influence in provincial politics. Quite irregular and ad hoc in their functioning before the 1680s, these internal working groups assumed a greater role in the business of the lower house during the royal period. Beginning in 1692, each assembly regularly appointed four committees at the start of each session — Accounts, Aggrievances, Elections and Privileges, and Laws. Any given committee might have between five and eleven members, but the usual size was six or seven. Membership generally remained similar from one session to another, although some delegates served only briefly for one session. In the first two royal assemblies, the lower house's committees on Laws and Accounts met jointly with members from the upper house, but that practice ceased by 1697/98.[71]

Rarely did more than half of the elected membership of any assembly receive a committee assignment, although some valued individuals might serve on as many as three different committees over the course of an assembly's life and often gained appointment to two committees during the same session. Dominating the list of forty-four delegates who held such multiple assignments are those men who eventually became speaker or gained appointment to the upper house.

Toward the end of the royal period, double assignments became less common. Similarly, after 1700, greater stability and continuity characterized committee membership. For example, Joseph Hill of Anne Arundel served continuously on the Committee of Accounts from his first term in 1704 until 1724 and for most of that period presided as its chairman. James Phillips of Baltimore joined Hill for five of those eight legislatures. Concurrently, John Mackall of Calvert, also first elected in 1704, began service that year on the Committee of Elections and Privileges, where he continued through 1724; in the next assembly, he became the speaker, a post he retained for five assemblies. Finally, Robert Tyler of Prince George's first sat on the Committee of Aggrievances in the Assembly of 1704–7; he won reelection to six of the next seven assemblies, during each of which he served on this important committee, usually as its chairman. He was joined on the committee in four of these legislatures by his colleague Daniel Mariartee of Anne Arundel.

70. Day, "Lawyers in Colonial Maryland," 147–50, distinguishes carefully between lawyers, who were professionally educated, and attorneys, who had received less rigorous training. On governors' consulting burgesses, see *Archives*, 20:135, 148.
71. Papenfuse et al., eds., *Biographical Dictionary*, 1:31–41, provides membership lists of major committees, 1689–1715.

The Committee of Laws clearly stands out as the most influential body, closely followed by the Committee of Aggrievances. Often, individuals served on both committees or graduated from Aggrievances to Laws. Twelve of the men who became councillors during the royal period had previously served on the Committee of Laws, six of them presiding as its chairman. Eleven councillors had prior duty on the Committee of Aggrievances. Membership on the other committees led much less frequently to higher appointments, and these delegates usually displayed less evidence of extensive education. Still, the appointees were respected planters or merchants, but rarely with any experience as lawyers or attorneys. The Committee of Elections and Privileges seems especially to have provided the means for screening and testing new burgesses. Its membership turned over more rapidly than did that of any other committee.

Delegates from a few counties proved more likely to acquire committee assignments and leadership roles. Representatives from Anne Arundel, Kent, Talbot, and Calvert account for half of all committee assignments during the royal period. Early in these years, St. Mary's delegates were unusually active, but after 1700 they rarely won appointment. Analysis by separate committee reveals interesting patterns. Apparently four-fifths of all assignments for delegates from Talbot County were to Laws or Aggrievances, where a representative from that county was almost invariably included. Kent's delegates served disproportionately on Elections and Privileges and on Accounts, but a committee assignment for a delegate from Charles was most likely to be Laws. Of those counties most frequently represented on committees, only Anne Arundel maintained a balance of delegations over the four standing bodies.

In internal organization, the assembly more closely resembled the esteemed model of Parliament. The ancient struggle to emulate that body, and especially the House of Commons, found a welcomed source of strength in the royal governors. Unlike the proprietary officers, these chief executives considered it natural and desirable to pattern the Maryland legislature more directly on the English model. For example, in 1697, Governor Nicholson automatically extended to Maryland the English practice of dissolving any assembly that had sat for three years, "since this Generall assembly was in the like nature of the Parliament of England as to this province." He constantly prodded the lower house to alter its procedures so that they conformed to those of Parliament. In 1697/98, the delegates, in declining to pass a new law the governor requested, insisted that "as they shall gain Experience will endeavor to come nearer and nearer to the practice of parliament in England as the constitution of this province will admitt." Nicholson promptly rejoined that the lower house could not legitimately insist on any matter of local custom that was not agreeable to the laws of England.[72]

The situation had completely reversed since delegates had battled the proprietor to abandon local custom and embrace English practices. Almost ten years after this exchange with Nicholson, Governor Seymour opened a session of the assembly by reminding the delegates that "Wee are obliged to follow, and observe the sanctions of our great Pattern the Parliament of England."[73] Such admonitions and unsolicited actions by the governors fostered significant advances for the assembly; even if a change was not always welcomed, the closer analogy to Parliament proved salutary in other ways.

The governor might not always extend support, however, as delegates learned in their persistent attempts to acquire undisputed power to appoint the clerk of the lower house. Since at least 1674/75, the proprietor had claimed the prerogative of nominating the clerk. Imposing an oath of secrecy had been the only control the house could effectively assert over the clerk. In 1692, however, the delegates ignored the nomination submitted by Lionel Copley and simply elected and installed a man of their own choice. The issue came under discussion again during Nicholson's tenure, when the lower house apparently chose from among nominations submitted by the governor. The delegates still fought with him over the clerk's allegiance and the privacy of house records.[74]

In Nathaniel Blakiston, the lower house found a more obliging governor. Professing unfamiliarity with local placemen, Blakiston curried favor in 1700 with his willingness "to leave it to your house to nominate such Clarke and present him to him for his Approbacon no one having as yett addressed his Excellency for that Office." The house promptly appointed one of its own members, William Taylard, who subsequently resigned his seat. Taylard served through 1707, and the following year the lower house rejected Seymour's nominee and chose Richard Dallam as the replacement. Seymour and the upper chamber reluctantly accepted this situation. In 1714, a new governor, John Hart, also accepted the lower house's choice of Thomas Macnemara to succeed the deceased Dallam,

72. *Archives*, 19:589 (quotation); 22:39, 40, 96 (quotation). This exchange came on the heels of the lower house's questioning Nicholson's presence in the assembly and seeing some of his remarks and other actions as "soe unparliamentary." The governor and upper house in response called the elected chamber on a series of points whereby it was not acting "According to the Customs of Parliament." See ibid., 11, 34 (quotation), 47, 55 (quotation), 67. Nicholson also repeatedly asked the delegates to follow the example of the Commons and report their exact votes on bills (ibid., 39, 182).
73. Ibid., 27:3.
74. Ibid., 13:252, 350; 19:25–26 (quotation), 143, 172; 22:156–58, 186, 209, 240; Owings, *His Lordship's Patronage*, 138.

after asking only if the council had any objections to the man, who had
been the *bête noir* of Hart's predecessor. With Macnemara's appointment, the lower house effectively established a precedent that would
prevail thereafter without serious challenge.[75]

With respect to positions of patronage outside the assembly itself, the
legislature continued to seek greater control over eligibility for appointment, tenures in office, and fees. The celebrated contest over the powers
of Secretary Thomas Lawrence, a struggle that stretched over the entire
royal period, most dramatically reveals the assembly's increasing success
in rendering placemen less independent. The delegates had learned well
the potent power of refusing to pass necessary legislation governing
public offices and fees for more than a brief period, usually a maximum
of three years. Either temporary statutes or an indefinite deferring of
proposals repugnant to the representatives worked very effectively in
securing greater authority for the assembly. Members employed both
tactics in resisting the efforts of Lawrence to claim powers and revenues
the majority of the delegates did not wish him to possess. Not even the
unwavering support of the Crown on Lawrence's behalf dissuaded the
delegates. Resisting adamantly calls for permanent legislation embody-
ing the secretary's claims, the lower house proclaimed in 1697/98 that
"in this Infant Country we hold it best not to enact perpetuall Laws."
They might have added, of course, especially laws not favorable to the
perceived interest of the representative branch of government. The delegates had less hesitation when the law in question secured a gain for
themselves. Governor Seymour later commented ruefully on the effectiveness of the tactic in rendering "those who are dependent on the
Government" more beholden to the assembly. Lawrence never gained
the satisfaction that he, his agents, and two successive monarchs repeatedly demanded from the legislature.[76]

Meanwhile, by 1709 the representatives were also reclaiming a greater
role for county courts in the selection of sheriffs, and of course directly or
indirectly the members of the lower house usually exercised influence on
the county court. By informal arrangement not officially enacted into
law, the justices would nominate two or three men from whom the
governor would select a sheriff. This had been the practice established in
law in the mid-seventeenth century before Charles Calvert effected a
change that left him freer to choose whomever he wished. From 1709 to
1715, years for the most part without a resident governor in the colony,

75. *Archives*, 24:6 (quotation), 7, 36–37; 27:185–86 (quotation), 200–1; 29:350, 391–
      92, 394.
76. Jordan, "Sir Thomas Lawrence," examines in detail this continuing battle. See also
      Archives, 22:134 (quotation); 25:268 (quotation); 26:523.

the courts apparently played this nominating role, but the situation is not as clear after the restoration of proprietary government.[77]

Perhaps most striking, however, was the growing strength of the elected lower house vis-à-vis the appointed upper chamber, a strength visible in many areas. Whenever members of the two houses met in joint committee after 1692, one of the delegates almost invariably served as chairman; this had rarely occurred before 1689.[78] To curtail the skirting of the full assembly, the lower house avoided the practice of convening interim committees appointed by the legislature or the council to conduct important business arising between meetings of the assembly. The delegates went officially on record at the turn of the century as opposing these committees summoned "in the Vacancy of Assembly" and held successfully to that resolve when Governor Seymour tried to revive the practice. Delegates had previously learned that the governor and councillors too easily prevailed in such committees.[79]

During the later years of Charles Calvert's rule, the lower house had repeatedly insisted on the presence of some delegates whenever the council or a portion of that body met to apportion taxes. In the royal period, the representatives went farther in establishing their primary role "to lay the Publick Levy." This critical business became the subject of regular legislation guaranteeing a predominant voice for the delegates, and briefly the lower house even asserted sole authority in this activity. The Assembly of 1692 passed a statute that assigned to a specific delegate from each county the responsibility to apportion the levy; this committee was to include no councillor, and no member of the upper house sat on the Committee of Accounts during that session either. A committee of such delegates was to meet annually even when the assembly was not convened. Francis Nicholson challenged this exclusion of councillors from any apportioning of the levy when the lower house attempted to pass a similar law again in 1697/98. The delegates defended their procedure, citing the precedent of 1692 and arguing that councillors "not being Elected or being representatives of the Country have noe right to dispose of the Publique Assessm[ts]." The governor and upper house declined to approve the proposed law. Whenever subsequent assemblies legislated on this subject, two or three councillors were again included in the special committee. The Committee of Accounts meeting during a session remained solely a lower house body, however, although occasionally a joint committee inspected the records. In addition, the delegates elected a public treasurer for each shore, usually members of the lower

77. Ibid., 25:74, 125; 22:442, 504–09; 27:388–89, 391; 29:254, 380, 381–83.
78. See, for example, ibid., 13:16; 22:322; 24:403.
79. Ibid., 24:192 (quotation), 381.

house, to oversee the collection and disbursement of all funds voted by the assembly. These posts became quite important.[80]

In face-to-face conferences while the assembly was in session, the lower house now more frequently held its own and by the later years of the royal period actually won numerous battles. In 1692 following such a meeting, the delegates expressed their gratitude to Speaker Cheseldyne for his excellent handling of the conference.[81] This new success owed much to the fact that in the aftermath of the revolution, the upper house lacked the aura of superiority it had earlier possessed. The total turnover of the council after 1689 stripped that body at once of its continuity, experience, and special distinction. Although as a group the new royal councillors remained the beneficiaries of an inherited tradition of power and deference, as individuals they lacked the eminence of the extended proprietary family. They had too much in common with their neighbors, fellow rebels, and the men who currently sat in the lower house. For a brief period in the 1690s, many members of the elected chamber could accurately boast of possessing experience in government that was greater than or equal to that of most councillors, and many could also claim superior ability or wealth.

By the early 1700s, when the council again constituted a clique that clearly stood out in wealth, ability, and experience, the elected lower house had successfully established its special role as a body representing the people, as the branch of the assembly truly independent of the governor, and as the equal if not yet the superior of the upper house. The delegates increasingly chided the councillors for standing in the way of the "Good of the Country," and for being a "stumbling Block" in the path of desired legislation. In essence, the delegates were more persistently demanding the upper house's acquiescence in whatever direction the representatives might lead, even against instructions from England.[82] Now more frequently, a majority of the councillors did concur with the prevailing sentiments of the delegates.

The tension between local interests and royal directives, so central to disputes between the two houses and the governors during this period, gradually encouraged some men to regard service in the lower house as more appealing and commendable than a seat on the council, where one must swear a special oath to uphold the royal interest. Such an attitude

80. Ibid., 13:465 (quotation); 22:65 (quotation), 146, 165; 24:85, 322–33; 38:109–10, 186–87; Owings, *His Lordship's Patronage*, 60–61, 157–59. The House of Burgesses in Virginia had successfully claimed the right to lay the public levy without interference from the governor or council in the 1660s. See Billings, " 'Virginia's Deploured Condition,' " 94.
81. *Archives*, 13:382.
82. Ibid., 27:319; 29:188–89.

appears toward the end of the royal period, when men hesitated to accept appointment as councillors. Governor Seymour reported in 1707 that some men whom he wished to nominate "refuse to act having streight lac'd Consciences." Men who did accept commissions demanded more remuneration and benefits to offset the additional pressures and burdens of serving. Plural officeholding among councillors reached levels once again comparable to those in Lord Baltimore's council.[83]

Even additional patronage did not always ensure fidelity. Robert Quarry, often the ranking royal placeman in the Chesapeake during these years, noted in 1709 that "the generallity of the Councills being Gentlemen of the Country are wholly in the Interest of the Assembly and as ready to lessen the Prerogative in all things as they [the assembly] are." Quarry stressed the importance of selecting councillors carefully, but he also observed it was essential that a governor always be in residence and that councils not have the power to pass acts after the death of a governor and before a new chief executive arrived. He astutely perceived the source of much of the new strength of the assembly and the so-called Country or Native Party.[84]

Although royal governors, with their encouragement of the parliamentary model, often fostered the development of the assembly, the rising strength of the legislature, especially after 1700, indeed depended fundamentally on the frequent absence or ineffectiveness of governors. Significantly, Maryland was without a resident governor for seven of the twelve years between 1702 and 1714, the critical period when the new elite of native-born Marylanders was firmly establishing its influence. Particularly between 1709 and 1714, the years after Seymour's death and before the arrival of John Hart, the lower house effectively pressured the upper house on several important issues. Generally attentive to royal wishes and conscientious about performing expected duties, the council under the leadership of Edward Lloyd lacked the authority or impact of a royal governor, nor did these men always disagree so fundamentally with the positions of the delegates. During these five years, earlier gains of a more modest nature and the internal changes of the assembly membership came together with the absence of a governor and unusual provincial and transatlantic circumstances to provide the lower house with advances it might not otherwise have enjoyed.[85]

83. Ibid., 25:265; Jordan, "Maryland's Privy Council," 79–83. A later proprietary governor observed "such men as ought to be Chosen, are not Easily got, and few men Care for an Empty Honor attended with trouble without some recompense" (*Calvert Papers, Number Two*, Maryland Historical Society, Fund Publication No. 35 [Baltimore, 1899], 80).
84. Quarry to [David Pulteney, Lord of Trade], Dec. 2, 1709, CO323/7, 1.
85. See below, pp. 221–22, 225–29.

When the colony returned to proprietary control in 1715, the elected branch of the assembly occupied a much different place in the provincial political structure than it had in 1689. No one would have argued that the delegates yet comprised the superior house of the legislature, but no observant individual could have failed to note that the chosen representatives were now the equal of the upper house in political power. Representative government under the fourth Lord Baltimore and his heirs was to be quite advanced in comparison with the voice of the freemen or their deputies under Cecilius and Charles Calvert.

6

"We More Immediately Represent the People"

Your familiarity and pretended Equallity with the Right honble the House of Comons in England is enough to provoke and surprize us at once . . . .we are far from pretending to that Rt hon^{ble} house of Lords or Rt hon^{ble} house of comons in England. We do not desire you should be abridged of the least priviledge belonging to you, but when your demands are better Tempered with Justice or Modesty they will better become you to aske or his Majestys Governor to grant.

> Members of the upper house to delegates of the lower house,
> October 1698

We cannot help your differing in Judgement from us but since you must own we more immediately represent the People than your Honble Board you must allow us to know more of their Oppressions and we offer the properest Remedies we can to relieve them.

> Delegates of the lower house to members of the upper house,
> November 1712

During the second week of May 1692, St. Mary's City thronged with its largest gathering in years. The legislature's sitting always occasioned special opportunities for business transactions and for pleasure, but this spring an unusual air of anticipation and curiosity prevailed. Sir Lionel Copley, the new governor, was convening the first royal assembly. Most people were anxious to observe the chief executive and to commemorate the inauguration of royal rule.

Copley had moved quickly upon arrival that spring to establish his authority. Within days of reaching St. Mary's, he met with the council, hastily convened and dissolved the last session of the Convention of Protestant Associators, made initial appointments to the colony's courts and other offices, and hosted various Indian chiefs who visited the capital in full ceremonial dress to conclude new articles of peace. Copley also promptly issued writs for the election of a new assembly.

Three years had passed since Maryland's government had functioned very extensively above the county level. The Associators' convention had limited its business at semiannual meetings to appointing and dismissing local officeholders and to passing a few ordinances that addressed only the most pressing concerns. The Grand Committee of Twenty, appointed by the convention in 1690 to oversee provincial affairs in the absence of a governor or council, had similarly restricted the exercise of its authority. Although county government had proceeded remarkably smoothly in most areas of the colony, a backlog of both routine and extraordinary items awaited the attention of Copley and a new council and legislature.[1]

By the time members of the assembly converged on the small village, the governor was already aggressively addressing the most pressing matters and establishing his control. His rough, soldierly manner, tempered with some Old World graces and trappings, readily charmed many Marylanders. Still others quickly accepted him simply because he officially represented the king and queen and promised a legitimate executive authority. For those colonists awed neither by Copley's presence nor his commission, the governor had ample patronage with which to woo or to punish reluctant individuals.

Copley had immediately demonstrated an unwillingness to court the most stalwart members of the proprietary faction. His early appointments distinctly favored those men whom the revolution had brought to power and others who had enthusiastically supported the Protestant Associators. The governor removed from office a few prominent men whose support of the revolution had been lukewarm, but whom the Associators had felt compelled to continue in office. Otherwise, only the dismissal of Quaker John Edmundson from the Provincial Court was a surprise; this action hinted at the stricter policy of sworn oaths Copley was soon to require of all officeholders.[2]

Nine former Protestant Associators dominated the upper house of the first royal assembly. Two proprietary nominees, Thomas Brooke and James Frisby, had been added to the council at the last minute in England.

1. *Archives*, 8:305–23, encompasses the council's journal for the first month of Copley's tenure. See also Bacon, *Laws of Maryland*, under "Charles Lord Baltimore," Chap. 11, for the last meeting of the Protestant Associators' convention, and Carr and Jordan, *Maryland's Revolution of Government*, for the most extensive treatment of the years between 1689 and 1692.
2. *Archives*, 8:306–7; Provincial Court Judgments, DSC, fols. 10–11. On Copley's reshuffling of local judicial appointments, see Cecil County Judgments, 1683–92, fol. 121, and Baltimore County Court Proceedings, F No. 1, fol. 170. Edward Randolph described this period in numerous letters printed in Robert Noxon Toppan and Alfred T. S. Goodrick, eds., *Edward Randolph: Including His Letters and Official Papers . . . 1676–1703*, 7 vols. (Boston, 1898–1909), 7:353–55, 377 (cited hereafter as *Randolph Letters*). Annie Leakin Sioussat, "Lionel Copley, First Royal Governor of Maryland," *Maryland Historical Magazine*, 17 (1922), 163–77, is informative but contains numerous errors. Jordan, "Royal Period," 67–130, provides the fullest discussion of Copley's tenure.

A royal placeman, the new secretary Thomas Lawrence, completed the appointed membership, but he had not yet arrived in Maryland. The elected delegates as a group had been somewhat less committed to the recent revolution, but the victorious party of 1689 still clearly held sway in the lower house as well. Approximately half of the forty-two representatives had actively supported the revolution, including Kenelm Cheseldyne, who soon became the speaker. Ranged against these men was a smaller corps of individuals, six or seven delegates led by William Whittington and St. Leger Codd, who had openly resisted the Associators at substantial personal risk. The remaining burgesses had apparently been neutral during the past three years.

Among the full membership, twenty-six men were serving their first term in the legislature, and twelve of these representatives had never held any major county position. The previous officeholding of another six delegates was limited to membership in the recent convention. All together, less than one-fourth of the lower house could claim any significant prior governmental experience. Similarly, only one-fourth of the upper house had served in any assembly before 1689, and for the time being that chamber had no more expertise than the elected house. A few quite knowledgeable individuals were to provide critical leadership during the month-long meeting.[3]

Members of the assembly, much less the general public, had an unexpectedly brief and scarcely awe-inspiring exposure to Copley during this first session. After an undistinguished opening speech to both houses, the governor fell "under some indisposition," probably the "seasoning," which left him bedridden for the next nine days and limited him to very irregular attendance thereafter. Copley exercised his authority primarily through Nehemiah Blakiston, whom he appointed to preside over the upper house, noticeably passing over Henry Jowles, the senior councillor and the more experienced legislator.[4]

The representatives themselves provided the drama and excitement in the governor's absence. Scarcely had the delegates taken their seats than the lower house dismissed five members on technical grounds of ineligibility, four as Quakers and John Huett as an ordained minister. Three of the five, as most people were keenly aware, had opposed the recent revolution. Certainly partisan motivation spurred subsequent action against several delegates from Cecil County for their "denying the Authority of

3. Papenfuse et al., eds., *Biographical Dictionary*, 1:32; Carr and Jordan, *Maryland's Revolution of Government*, 163–76.
4. *Archives*, 13:251–52, 253 (quotation). Jowles's cooperation in 1689 had been critical to the success of the revolution.

the Late Convention." The surveyor general of customs, Edward Randolph, then present in Maryland, sarcastically commented that the assembly sent home better men than he found sitting in the council chamber. He termed the proceedings a purge designed as "the Good Methode to obtain . . . their laws." Indeed, by the time replacements had been elected for seven expelled men, the most important business of the session had been decided.[5]

That business rendered this first royal assembly a turning point in the political history of the colony. In organization and procedure, this body accomplished gains for the legislature, and especially for the lower house, that the proprietor had resolutely opposed for decades. Elected representatives more confidently asserted equality with the appointed upper house than ever before. Finally, this legislature enacted an impressive array of statutes, several of which fundamentally affected the assembly's development and significantly altered life in the colony.[6]

The final harvest of the assembly's debates was eighty-six laws, the majority familiar acts now only slightly amended.[7] Several, however, bore the clear imprint of recent events and the turnover of power. Formal recognition of the new English rulers achieved a major goal of the revolution of 1689, with victorious colonists jubilantly identifying themselves as "Wee your Majesties most humble and Loyall Subjects." Laws addressing the loss of property and the inactivity of some courts and governmental offices since 1689 testified to the conclusion of those unsettling years.

Through other statutes, the assembly redressed many of the grievances articulated by the rebels. Elections finally came under the exclusive control of the assembly, which also enacted an official return to four delegates per county. The legislature responded at last to the repeated pleas of some vocal colonists for the support of the Church of England. The Act for the Service of Almighty God and the Establishment of the Protestant Religion Within this Province extended official status to the Church of England, instituted a compulsory annual tax of forty pounds of tobacco per poll for support of that church, and provided for the division of the province into parishes and the election of vestries.

Excessive fees had constituted another persistent complaint. Opposing Copley's request that the power of establishing and limiting fees be vested in the council, the lower house unanimously insisted "that noe Officers ffees ought to be imposed upon them but by the Consent of the Represen-

5. *Archives*, 13:254, 257, 352, 354, 361, 364–68 (quotation, 365); *Randolph Letters*, 7:375–76.
6. *Archives*, 13:251–424; 8:312; Jordan, "Royal Period," 88–97.
7. *Archives*, 13:425–561.

tatives in an Assembly."[8] Copley and the upper house acquiesced when the delegates forwarded copies of the parliamentary legislation upon which the lower house based its claims.

Since the lengthy tenure of some sheriffs had been a frequent subject of protest, the assembly also enacted a maximum term of two years for that office and limited its perquisites. Clerks and justices became bound by new restrictions as well, although the assembly hesitated to go as far as earlier grievances might have warranted in attacking plural officeholding; too many members of both houses were already enjoying the benefits of multiple posts stripped from the proprietor's favorites. A statute on the militia and security of the colony restated the central role of the assembly in approving any levies for defense, and the new act concerning proceedings at law explicitly noted that where provincial laws were "silent," justice was to be administered according to the laws of England.

Several revenue measures drew particular attention. The assembly granted to Copley the traditional revenues that had gone to the proprietor, despite the recent explicit denial of some of these fees to him by English colonial officials. A mutually supportive arrangement was evolving between Copley and members of the assembly. He further managed to convince them to transfer to him the income from the fees for ordinary licenses, previously the perquisite of the secretary and again explicitly denied Copley by officials in England. The assembly also disregarded a compromise reached in England on other of Lord Baltimore's rights and transferred most of them to the Crown. Similarly, the assembly declined to return to Calvert's agents the land records seized in 1689; they would remain on deposit in the secretary's office. The assembly fully vented its long-standing but previously checked opposition to Lord Baltimore and his circle. These various financial arrangements were to embroil the government of Maryland, the Crown, and the proprietary faction in intense controversy for decades to come.[9]

Copley's flagrant violation of instructions from the Crown, evident in numerous laws he approved at this assembly, and his lax enforcement of Parliament's Navigation Acts and some local legislation soon spawned a vigorous opposition to the governor's leadership. Blatant favoritism to a few individuals, especially to Blakiston, generated further animosity and suspicion of his actions. However, the first outward expressions of discontent came not from the assembly, which seemed willing to accommodate any enemy of proprietary rule, but from two other imperial placemen, Randolph and Lawrence.

8. Ibid., 382.
9. Ibid., 311–14, 321, 411–12; 8:309–13. Carr and Jordan, *Maryland's Revolution of Government*, 173–75, discuss the earlier decisions in England regarding these revenues.

Edward Randolph, never overly politic when he confronted resistance or suspected dishonesty in colonial governments, launched the assault. His local campaign to prosecute illegal traders, some of whom he found sitting comfortably on the council, had met staunch opposition from Copley and Blakiston. Randolph was already ill-disposed toward the two men for their rude reception upon his arrival in Maryland. The customs collector became increasingly agitated by developments during the meeting of the assembly and subsequently by the executive's deliberate attempts to foil Randolph's investigations and prosecutions. Letters to English officials soon detailed the governor's misdeeds and savagely attacked other leading officeholders as well. Randolph disparaged the "contemptable crew" in charge of the provincial government. "The Council is composed of shreds like a Taylor's cushion," he wrote, calling the new authorities "Sylly animals" who "strut it like New Beadles of St. Martin's Parish." Randolph obviously voiced his objections within the colony as well, for he soon attracted support from some Marylanders predisposed by policy differences or jealousies to dislike those currently in power.[10]

With little difficulty, however, Copley rallied ample support from other colonists antagonized by this obnoxious intruder who viewed the colony so disdainfully and who threatened to halt profitable trading practices in the Chesapeake. Copley gained illegal access to Randolph's correspondence and publicly distributed some of the seized letters with their caustic observations on the colony and its local leaders. These disclosures galvanized considerable opposition to Randolph.[11] By the end of the summer, the customs collector had a valuable ally in Lawrence, who discovered upon arrival that Copley had acquired for his own enjoyment revenues and powers that rightfully belonged by royal directive to the secretary's office. Lawrence provided a stronger magnet than the unpopular Randolph for attracting colonists disenchanted with the governor. The secretary was a royal official commissioned directly to the province, the ranking member of the council, and not a prosecutor of trade violations.

As the colony's two top officials renewed their personal warfare, the council became divided in its loyalties. Henry Jowles, snubbed repeatedly by Copley, enlisted in Lawrence's camp, as did James Frisby, who had always viewed Copley and the leading Associators warily. The governor, counting firmly on Blakiston and several other councillors to discourage any further opposition, swiftly dismissed Jowles and Frisby from the council and actually imprisoned Lawrence. To elude a similar fate, Ran-

10. *Randolph Letters*, 7:353–85; Michael G. Hall, *Edward Randolph and the American Colonies* (Chapel Hill, N.C., 1960), 138–44.
11. For Copley's perspective, see his letters to Blathwayt, June 20 and 25 and July 30, 1692, Blathwayt Papers, Colonial Williamsburg, and Copley to lords of trade, July 29, 1692, *Archives*, 8:335–37.

dolph hid ignominiously in nearby swamps for several days before he too finally fell into the hands of his pursuers.[12]

Copley's forceful measures greatly restricted his opponents' potential to amass a wide following. So long as the governor remained unchallenged from England, his position in the colony seemed secure. Copley's days proved to be numbered, however. Bedridden most of the spring and summer of 1693, he finally died on September 9. For the second time in four years, Maryland was without a properly commissioned chief executive.[13] Neither faction could muster sufficient strength to establish immediate control, and when members of the assembly began arriving in St. Mary's City a week later for a previously scheduled meeting, the struggle for power moved into a larger arena.[14]

The lower house, after a quick investigation of conflicting claims, indicated its support for Lawrence, who had been released from custody. The influence of Cheseldyne and other delegates suspicious of Copley's entourage proved decisive, and a majority of the council appeared ready to break with Blakiston and to concur with this judgment by the representatives. However, the unexpected arrival of Edmund Andros, the governor of Virginia, interrupted the session. In an action later overturned in England, Andros claimed the vacant office of chief executive for himself. Some Marylanders questioned his faulty reading of royal commissions, but Andros overrode these objections and perhaps drew the support of uneasy legislators who welcomed an alternative to both Lawrence and Blakiston. Dissolving the assembly, Andros bypassed both men as well as the still dismissed Jowles to install Nicholas Greenberry as acting president of the council; Andros also pointedly denied Lawrence reinstatement as secretary.[15]

Over the next six months, the council met periodically to attend to pressing matters, but once again the colony drifted with a provincial government that avoided tackling controversial issues. Most attention focused on efforts to untangle the financial accounts of the colony that had become confusingly mixed with Copley's personal estate; Edward

---

12. Jordan, "Royal Period," 104–14, and "Sir Thomas Lawrence, Secretary of Maryland," 27–28; Hall, *Edward Randolph*, 145–47; *Archives*, 8:410, 424–25, 437–43, 482–83, 493–96, 499–502, 504–5, 529, 544–45, 549–55.
13. *Archives*, 8:414; 20:127. Francis Nicholson, the lieutenant governor, was currently in England.
14. Richard Lee to the Virginia council, Sept. 18, 1693, in H. R. McIlwaine, ed., *Executive Journals of the Council of Colonial Virginia* (Richmond, Va., 1925), 1:298; *Randolph Letters*, 7:451–53; *Archives*, 19:5, 15, 60.
15. Ibid., 8–10, 60–61, 62–63, 66; 20:6–8, 22, 27–30; *Randolph Letters*, 7:454–55; Andros to lords of trade, Oct. 23, 1693, in W. Noel Sainsbury et al., eds., *Calendar of State Papers, Colonial Series, America and West Indies*, 44 vols. to date (London, 1860–), *1693–1696*, No. 637 (cited hereafter as *CSP, 1693–1696*).

Randolph's earlier suspicions of mismanagement and embezzlement had been accurate. Meanwhile, word reached America of the Crown's vindication of Lawrence. The royal directive compelled Andros to return to Maryland, where he reluctantly reappointed the secretary to all his former powers. Lawrence, in collaboration with Randolph, also now free, began amassing the documentation necessary to prove their serious charges against the former regime. The two men eagerly awaited the arrival of Nicholson, whom the Crown had officially commissioned as the colony's governor.[16] With a mixture of relief and continuing uneasiness, on July 26, 1694, Marylanders once more greeted a new chief executive. Nicholson was "received with a hearty welcome of the most of the Inhabitants, those of Governor Copley's party as well as they can," Edward Randolph reported.[17]

A thirty-nine-year-old bachelor, Nicholson was the veteran of prior colonial assignments in New York and Virginia as well as sixteen years of service in the English army.[18] His career owed much to influential connections within English governing circles, contacts he assiduously cultivated. Dedicated to the causes of "Religion, Service of the King & Interest of the Countrey," as he early articulated his convictions and priorities to the assembly, Nicholson provided Maryland with probably the ablest administration in the province's first sixty years of existence. Fundamentally efficient, honest, and conscientious, the governor demanded the same commitment and capable performance of duty from all subordinate officials, an attitude and behavior many failed to display consistently. Nicholson had little patience with those civil or religious officeholders who abused the public's trust or the Crown's faith by a lack of integrity or ability. Normally fair and reasonable, the governor could become narrowly vindictive toward persistent opponents or irresponsible officials.[19]

Nicholson immediately tackled an array of thorny issues in a fury of governmental activity. Believing that ultimate solutions lay in an improved educational and moral climate, Nicholson sponsored the estab-

16. Jordan, "Royal Period," 121–30.
17. Randolph to Blathwayt, Aug. 22, 1694, *Randolph Letters*, 7:466.
18. Bruce T. McCully, "From the North Riding to Morocco: The Early Years of Governor Francis Nicholson, 1655–1686," *William and Mary Quarterly*, 3rd ser., 19 (1962), 534–56; McCully, "Governor Francis Nicholson, Patron Par Excellence of Religion and Learning in Colonial America," ibid., 39 (1982), 310–33; Stephen Saunders Webb, "The Strange Career of Francis Nicholson," ibid., 23 (1966), 513–48; Richard L. Morton, *Colonial Virginia*, 2 vols. (Chapel Hill, N.C., 1960), 1:334–88.
19. For an excellent appraisal of Nicholson by a contemporary, see James Blair to [Earl of Nottingham?], Mar. 29, 1693, *CSP, 1693–1696*, No. 227. Jordan, "Royal Period," 132–200, details Nicholson's tenure in Maryland. For his comment to the assembly, see *Archives*, 19:29.

lishment of an educational system, the building of churches, and recruitment of clergy. He also proposed specific reforms of various institutions.
Although dedicated to improving the local situation, he nonetheless approached all problems with a paramount commitment to English interests and an intercolonial, rather than a narrowly provincial, vision. In
areas of the economy, defense, or religion, for example, he believed the
interests of the mother country could not be compromised. Usually, Nicholson successfully avoided situations in which a direct conflict might exist
between the self-perceived interests of the colonists and any objectives of
the Crown, or he was careful to address such issues only at the most
propitious times. For example, after an early assembly declined to vote as
much aid for beleaguered New York as the governor had requested, the
disappointed Nicholson reported to his counterpart in that colony that he
was presently unwilling to hazard the peace of the province and his own
good will with the legislators on this matter. Later, he was to bear down
harder on them for contributions toward the defense of northern colonies
after he had accomplished more fundamental objectives.[20]

Nicholson believed a restored confidence in government was essential if
officials were to take forceful action in alleviating economic woes and
other problems. Therefore, first he prodded Marylanders to strengthen
their political institutions, particularly to place courts and other public
bodies on uniform and announced schedules, and to demand a more responsible level of public service from officeholders. Nicholson substantially enhanced both the quality and quantity of information available to
the governor, the assembly, other officials, and the public regarding local
and provincial business in a campaign to ensure fuller and more accurate
record keeping. In turn, he employed these records to improve the quality
of decision making, to encourage responsible officials, and to upbraid or
even dismiss the incompetent or uncooperative. In early letters to his superiors in England, Nicholson lamented the poor quality of records of past
administrations, the people here, he wrote, "not expecting (as I suppose)
ever to be called to account." Any such expectation received a jolt during
Nicholson's tenure. He demanded a regular submission of records, which
he studied carefully, and he periodically toured the counties and visited
local officials for on-the-scene inspections. Little escaped his vigilant eye.[21]

20. Nicholson to Gov. Benjamin Fletcher, Nov. 29, 1695, *CSP, 1688–1696*, addendum
(typed), Public Record Office (London, 1935).
21. Nicholson to Blathwayt, Nov. 16, 1694, Blathwayt Papers. See also, *Archives*, 20:83,
105–13, 127, 133, 189–90, 201–12, 235, 254, 419–20, 510; 19:386; 23:372–74.
Nicholson made periodic tours of the counties for additional personal inspections.
Nicholson to [?], June 14, 1695, CO5/713/III, and *Archives*, 20:162; 23:336. Carr,
"County Government," Text, 545–53, perceptively discusses Nicholson's attempts to
improve local administration.

The governor's most immediate impact, perhaps, was made by his careful recruitment and encouragement of more capable public servants. Complaining of "the great scarcity of good Clarks; (so that I am allmost forced to make according to the proverb Bricks without straw)," Nicholson fostered the careers of young men like William Bladen, an immigrant who became the long-term clerk first of the lower house and later of the council, and William Dent, a native who began with clerkships and later received appointments as solicitor general, attorney general, and naval officer. Both men were also to serve in the assembly. They stand out among the able individuals whom Nicholson identified and rewarded with patronage. In turn, they themselves trained other men in improved methods of record keeping.[22]

Moreover, Nicholson brought back into the political arena capable colonists whose opposition to the revolution of 1689 had subsequently restricted their political service, particularly in appointive positions. His patronage policy sought to improve the calibre of justices, sheriffs, and other officers, but it also addressed a larger problem as well. "I found the country very much . . . in Divisions which caused great Heats and animosities," Nicholson early observed, "but I have used all possible means to reconcile them and hope in God that it is very nigh, if not altogether done." He enjoyed some degree of immediate success, but the challenge confronted him throughout his tenure, particularly as new divisions arose to supplant older fractures.[23]

At the highest level, Nicholson quickly restored to the council Jowles and Frisby, who had remained in political limbo since their dismissal by Copley. Jowles particularly rose in importance as Nicholson filled posts previously monopolized by Blakiston, now deceased, or others of Copley's clique. Commissions for local and provincial offices soon combined the names of old proprietary supporters with those of active revolutionaries of recent years. As Nicholson became more familiar with his appointees and assessed their performances, he did not hesitate to alter the commissions frequently with dismissals and new appointments. He abolished the worst examples of plural officeholding, in particular eliminating the substantial duplication of the membership of the council and the Provincial Court; the new justices brought representation from all counties to the colony's highest court. Significantly, the Provincial Court under Nicholson overlapped more extensively with membership of the lower house, rather than exhibiting its traditional congruence with the

22. *Archives*, 23:489 (quotation). See entries on Bladen and Dent in Papenfuse et al., eds., *Biographical Dictionary*.
23. Nicholson to lords of trade, Nov. 15, 1694, CO5/713/III.

upper chamber. This fact lent additional prestige and power to the delegate-justices and to the legislative chamber in which they served.[24]

The assembly played a prominent role in Nicholson's program. He issued writs for the election of a new legislature just four days after his arrival in Maryland. Both in Maryland and in earlier and later tenures in neighboring Virginia, Nicholson relied extensively on the institution of representative government, and he occasionally appealed over the members of the council, usually a governor's most trusted allies, for support in the elected lower house. Nicholson's reforms frequently alienated entrenched power while enjoying a greater response and popularity among the colonists at large.

The election returns for Nicholson's first assembly reflected the new political climate he had signaled in his initial commissions for the county courts. Only eighteen of the forty-two delegates in Copley's legislature retained their seats, the greatest turnover occurring in Kent, Calvert, Talbot, and Cecil counties, areas of strong resistance or hesitancy toward the Protestant Associators in 1689. At least half of the twenty-four new members had openly opposed the revolution of 1689, and six were former burgesses who had played no official political role since the proprietor's overthrow. Their election and the new alignments that emerged in this assembly marked the conclusion of the worst years of intense factionalism. Henceforth, political leadership within the assembly and in local government no longer resided exclusively with either side of the revolutionary divisions of the late 1680s and early 1690s.[25]

Recognizing the validity of complaints regarding the inaccessibility of St. Mary's City for most colonists and astutely perceiving that area's identification with past divisions, Nicholson allied with delegates seeking to relocate the seat of government. He had recently sponsored a similar move in Virginia, and his support led to the passage of a law in November of 1694 to designate a new capital for Maryland. The assembly moved to temporary facilities in Annapolis in early 1695, and construction began soon thereafter on a permanent statehouse.[26]

The early sessions of Nicholson's first legislature wrestled with serious

24. Nicholson was unable, of course, to appoint Quakers and Catholics, although he noted that they were among the "ablest men for Estates and Parts in this Country" (ibid.). For his appointments, see *Archives*, 8:129; 20:106–11, 115, 128, 132, 137, 155–56; 19:40–41; *Randolph Letters*, 7:466–67; Provincial Court Judgments, TL No. 1, fol. 120. For a fuller discussion of this patronage, see Jordan, "Royal Period," 145–46.

25. *Archives*, 20:126–28; Papenfuse et al., eds., *Biographical Dictionary*, 1:33–34; Webb, "The Strange Career of Francis Nicholson," 529–32, 535–41.

26. *Archives*, 7:318, 445; 13:356, 369; 19:71–78; 20:68, 76, 192. Elihu S. Riley, *The Ancient City* (Annapolis, Md., 1887), 1–68, describes the early history of "ann arrundeltown."

problems. The colony's finances were in shambles, the province "very much in debt" and the crisis worsening daily. The impact of the stagnating tobacco economy was pervasive. Moreover, a severe winter in 1693–94 had decimated the colony's livestock, and a shortage of corn and wheat throughout the middle years of the decade left numerous families "destitute of bread for some months." The irregularity of the English fleet's appearances in Chesapeake waters compounded matters, for necessary provisions were frequently unavailable or prohibitively expensive and a vast quantity of tobacco was spoiling. Many colonists sought an alternative income and raw materials for clothing by turning to the planting of fibers and to woolen and linen manufacturing, especially on the Eastern Shore. Others, burdened by mounting debts, migrated to Pennsylvania and the Carolinas drawn by "rumors or lies of prosperity there."[27]

Nicholson set before each gathering of the assembly a sheaf of proposals addressing these economic matters and other important issues. The governor offered both specific and general solutions for the legislators' debate and action. He wanted to discourage economic diversification that might reduce tobacco production – the Crown was firm on this matter – but Nicholson also realized that a satisfactory economic recovery was essential to accomplish other aims and to prevent further suffering. He desired greater assistance from Maryland in the intercolonial struggle against the French and Indians, but this too depended directly on progress both in the economy and in defense measures closer to home. Nicholson proceeded simultaneously on multiple fronts, using his legislative initiative and his administrative discretion. Assembly members became dazed by the sheer volume of proposals and concerns. The assembly elected in 1694 met with an unparalleled frequency, gathering for six sessions in its first two years alone. Nicholson would actually have preferred that it meet more often, but he realized that the tax burden would constitute an impossible hardship under present circumstances.[28]

The delegates and councillors initially responded cooperatively and enacted statutes that greatly increased governmental revenues to meet current expenses and to discharge the large public debt. Despite a wariness regarding new taxes, the two houses legislated several import and export duties, including an additional three pence per hogshead tax on exported tobacco, new levies on the exportation of animal skins, beef,

27. Nicholson to lords of trade and to [?], June 14, 1695, and Lawrence Memorandum to lords of trade, June 25, 1695, CO5/713/III; *Archives*, 19:237; 20:191–92, 327–29; 23:84; Margaret S. Morriss, *Colonial Trade of Maryland, 1689–1715* (Baltimore, 1914).

28. *Archives*, 19:23–596, covers eight sessions. For a typical agenda from 1696, see ibid., 288–92.

and pork, and new fees on the importation of indentured servants, Negroes, and liquors. By stringent taxing measures and a strict supervision of expenditures, the colony slowly gained control of its financial situation, with the help as well of an improvement in the general state of the economy. Within three years, Nicholson proudly announced that all of Maryland's debts were finally paid, and for the first time in more than a decade a slight surplus began to accumulate in the treasury.[29]

The greatest challenge to Nicholson's political skills came in the spring of 1696, when he received word of the Crown's veto of the act of 1692 establishing the Church of England and disallowance of two more recent statutes, passed under his own administration, refining the establishment legislation and founding a school in the province. More serious was the Crown's objection to a clause in the establishment act stating that "the Church of England within this Province shall have and Enjoy all her Rights Liberties and Franchises wholly inviolable as is now or shall be hereafter Established by Law, and also that the Great Charter of England be kept and observed in all points." Royal advisers worried about the consequences of a full application of English rights to the colonists and feared that this clause both conflicted with the constitution of the province and threatened the Crown's prerogatives there.[30]

Nicholson lamented to Henry Compton, the bishop of London, that he did not dare be candid with the assembly or communicate directly word of the repeals for fear the legislature would decline to pass new acts. If such laws could be secured, he confided, "I must attribute it to a more immediate influence from Heaven than any politicks I can use with them."[31] Summoning, however, the full power of his "politicks," Nicholson called for the assembly to reconvene on July 1, just forty-five days after the last session had adjourned. He deliberately withheld the disappointing news of the vetoes from the two houses. After surveying a range of problems, the governor casually referred a dozen proposals to the attention of the Committee of Laws, including a recommendation that it "draw up the Acts of Religion anew and abbreviate the same" and also that the colony pay tribute to the king by altering the school statute to

29. Ibid., 19:193, 276–79, 459–60; 22:16, 97–98; 38:9–11, 16–19, 49–51 (quotation), 51–52, 63–69, 97–100, 109–10, 125–26. The conclusion of the War of the League of Augsburg reopened transatlantic trade routes and brought sufficient English shipping and goods to the colony (ibid., 20:474–76, 485, 503; 23:488–503).
30. *CSP, 1693–1696*, Nos. 2190, 2230. For the text of the three vetoed acts and their predecessors, see *Archives*, 13:425–30 (quotation, 425–26); 38:1–2, 27–31, 37–41. Kenneth L. Carroll, "Quaker Opposition to the Establishment of a State Church in Maryland," *Maryland Historical Magazine*, 65 (1970), 149–70, describes efforts to overturn these laws.
31. Bernard C. Steiner, ed., "Some Unpublished Manuscripts from Fulham Palace Relating to the Province of Maryland," *Maryland Historical Magazine*, 12 (1917), 117–18.

make William the supreme patron with power to appoint some trustees and to have the school bear his name. By July 4, the obliging lower house had discussed and submitted the requested legislation, but to Nicholson's dismay, the church bill still contained the disputed clause.[32]

The governor requested a slight rephrasing and volunteered to pay the cost of the new act himself if the change were made. Becoming suspicious, the burgesses voted instead to refer the bill to the next session. Nicholson, meanwhile, confided to the upper house that the king would not approve the act as currently phrased, for fear it would lead Marylanders "to carry all their causes to Westminster Hall." The governor lectured the lower house for being "so stiff" and prorogued the assembly overnight, a popular device of governors when deadlocks occurred.[33]

Neither side had weakened in its resolve when Nicholson met the legislature the next day. He tried as persuasively as possible to enunciate why the temporal and spiritual issues should not be combined in the same statute and even agreed to endorse a separate bill setting forth "their liberties." "As God Almighty moved the hearts of the Children of Israel," Nicholson pleaded, so he hoped their hearts would be open to pass a law that might attain royal assent. The delegates instead reasserted their traditional association of the "Priviledges and Liberties of the Church and State together," by citing King Henry's charter, Lord Baltimore's charter, and their own 1692 act of religion. By this, they explained, they meant to ensure that "where the Laws of this province are silent Justice shall be administered according to the Laws of England." Reluctantly, Nicholson settled for the only bill he could obtain and assented to the legislation as originally written by the lower house.[34]

The governor apologetically rationalized his capitulation in another letter to Compton. It was impossible to get the act, he wrote, "without some Clause about Liberty and property which your Grace very well knows Englishmen are fond of." Nicholson stated again that he dared not inform the assembly of the king's vetoes. The statute of 1696, still containing the disputed clause, was doomed to disallowance, but at least any act on the law books for the time being, Nicholson explained, would enable him to proceed with advancing the church's program.[35]

The assembly members soon learned, as they were bound to do, of the royal vetoes and reacted in an "ill humor" to Nicholson's lack of candor.

32. *Archives*, 19:379ff., especially 381–82, 387, 389, 404 (quotation), 406, and 420–26 (final school statute).
33. Ibid., 390, 393.
34. Ibid., 393, 394 (quotation), 395–96 (quotation), 398, and 426–30 (the final act).
35. Nicholson to bishop of London, July 14, 1696, Fulham Palace Papers, Mar. 1696–1769, Lambert Palace Library, London. See also Lawrence to Earl of Bridgewater, Mar. 25, 1697, CO5/714/l, and *Archives*, 23:79–80.

The unpleasant nature of this interaction in the summer of 1696 seriously impaired previously amicable relations. This issue coalesced other isolated discontents that had been festering among a minority of the delegates and colonists. Nicholson's systematic investigation of every phase of provincial and county administration had embarrassed numerous officials, whom the governor had not hesitated to replace and often to prosecute for their violations of the laws. Guilty justices, sheriffs, and vestrymen, as well as some innocent people, became alarmed about an exceptionally aggressive provincial government that might sharply curtail local autonomy.[36] Furthermore, the extremely frequent assembly meetings had alienated many taxpayers, who resented any additional charges in such troubled times and little understood or sometimes opposed the accomplishments of these lengthy sessions. The assembly, increasingly weary and less enthusiastic about his proposals, began to stall on several items that the governor considered critical, particularly a major remodeling of the militia and a costly revision of all legislation.

Knowledge of Nicholson's explicit withholding of critical information provided effective ammunition for his opponents, who seized this opportunity to distort the governor's intentions and program. During the following months, dissidents distributed considerable propaganda that attempted to discredit Nicholson's administration. With the depression not yet over, popular spirits remained low and some people quite willing to find a scapegoat. "So please God there don't come better times," Nicholson wrote William Blathwayt, the imperial bureaucrat, "I may shutt up Shopp."[37]

John Coode, among other Marylanders, was especially determined to end Nicholson's tenure. The perennial rebel, as a reward for aiding Lawrence in 1693, had received appointment from Nicholson as sheriff of St. Mary's and second in command, under the secretary, of the county's militia. Persisting indiscretions and an inability ever to work very long within any government soon wrought Coode's downfall, however. A drunken appearance at a church service provoked an indignant caning by the governor, but more serious were the discoveries that Coode had embezzled public money during the period he headed the government of the Protestant Associators and that he owed the Crown more than £439 from his tenure as collector of customs for the Potomac district. Finally, Coode's "excessive drinking, Blasphemous lewd talking cursing and

36. For Nicholson's mounting attacks against lax and corrupt officeholders in the spring of 1696, see *Archives*, 20:448, 453, 579–81; Provincial Court Judgments, IL, fols. 92–93.
37. Nicholson to Blathwayt, July 14, 1696, Blathwayt Papers.

swearing" constituted the very behavior Nicholson could not tolerate in public officials.[38]

The governor's disenchantment with Coode was no secret when the latter, currently under prosecution, stood successfully for a by-election in the summer of 1696. As the assembly gathered for its seventh session in September, the governor gave the highest priority to avenging what he regarded as a direct challenge from Coode and the voters of St. Mary's County. In a recent harangue against religion and the established church, Coode had admitted to having been ordained as an Anglican priest in England before his coming to Maryland twenty-four years earlier. Nicholson shrewdly employed this surprising information to contend that Coode was therefore ineligible to sit in the assembly, according to the English precedent the lower house had itself invoked to disqualify the Reverend John Huett from membership in 1692. The lower chamber, having already routinely seated Coode, sensitive to the least affront from the governor, and four of its members no doubt recalling their role in defending Coode's right to sit in 1681 when an earlier executive tried to obtain his dismissal, curtly responded, "We humbly conceive ourselves proper Judges of our own members." Several days later, after testimony from lawyers and a review of the precedents, the Committee of Elections and Privileges recommended that Coode be expelled, but the full house, influenced by his friends and supporters, overruled the motion. The irascible Coode then gloatingly admitted that he had indeed once been ordained. Many chastened delegates, who had discounted that charge or reasoned that Coode was no longer in orders if he had ever been so, resented Coode's lack of candor and modesty; they now rescinded their former vote and grudgingly conceded the governor had been right. Meanwhile, stripped of offices and facing double suits in the province's courts for embezzlement and blasphemy, Coode fled to Virginia, from where he continued to pester Nicholson.[39]

Local leadership of opposition to the governor descended upon Philip Clarke, another delegate from St. Mary's, an old friend of Coode, and a decided firebrand in the assembly. Clarke had arrived in Maryland in 1676 but gained his first political position from the Protestant Associators in 1689. Active in the colony's courts, Clarke became one of numerous lawyers in the first royal assembly, where he sat on the Committee of

38. Jordan, "John Coode, Perennial Rebel," 1–28; *Archives*, 20:453, 514–15 (quotation).
39. Ibid., 19:435–40, 476 (quotation), 477–82; 20:489–94, 511, 561–62. Coode had reputedly sought election and entered the lower house "on purpose by his atheism and debaucht designs to have corrupted them [delegates] to the overthrow of all publick spirited understandings" (Lawrence to Archbishop Thomas Tenison, Feb. 20, 1696/97, Fulham Palace Papers, Vol. 2, fols. 85–86).

Elections and Privileges and the Committee of Laws. Reelected in 1694, Clarke failed to retain his committee assignments under a new speaker, although Nicholson frequently consulted him for legal advice and appointed him a Provincial Court justice in July 1696. Two months later, Clarke emerged as leader of restless delegates and became a pronounced defender of the privileges of the lower house; in the special summer session his role eclipsed that of any other member. Robert Smith, speaker for the first four sessions and apparently not an admirer of Clarke, was ill and absent from that session. Smith's replacement was Cheseldyne, who had earlier favored Clarke and now reappointed him to his former committee posts. Clarke reputedly drafted the new religion bill personally.[40]

Following the September meeting, Clarke bided his time while coconspirators in St. Mary's circulated charges against the governor. Opposition to Nicholson centered in that county which had recently lost the capital and owing to the ineligibility of Catholics remained under the political domination of Coode's faction, many of whom Nicholson had attempted to discredit. Their attacks on the governor sufficiently disturbed Nicholson that he determined by mid-December to confront the ringleaders personally and to press court action. Appearing before the Provincial Court, he charged Clarke with "several crimes and misdemeanors," dismissed him as a justice, and suspended his legal practice. Nicholson further offered a reward for the apprehension of Coode and promised a pass and money to any troublemaker who would go to England and officially register a grievance. Meanwhile, Nicholson carefully collected depositions from people throughout the government attesting that he had never required anything illegal of them as the rumors were charging.[41]

An unusually severe winter placed a temporary freeze on the incipient rebellion, but Indian disturbances, always a potential excuse for uprisings, prompted Nicholson to summon the assembly again in May of 1697. In addition to proposing defense measures, the governor pressed again for his unfinished reforms. Although the lower house opposed his various legislative recommendations, it responded tamely in comparison with the two previous sessions. Invoking English precedent, Nicholson then dissolved this body at the end of the session, since three years had passed since its election.[42]

Clarke admitted at his trial that summer authorship of a "scandalous defamatory Writing" that had cast aspersions on the governor. With a public apology from Clarke and the colony reasonably quiet, Nicholson

---

40. Papenfuse et al., eds., *Biographical Dictionary*, 1:224; *Archives*, 23:501.
41. Ibid., 19:464–67, 471; 20:561–65, 574–83; Provincial Court Judgments, TL No. 2, fol. 174.
42. *Archives*, 19:507–96.

indulgently released his opponent on the promise of good behavior.[43] The governor soon regretted this generosity, for he subsequently learned that during recent months Coode and Clarke had also been operating indirectly through Gerard Slye, Coode's stepson, and Robert Mason, a colleague from the rebellion of 1689 whom the lower house had appointed as treasurer of the Western Shore in 1695. Slye had dispatched a list of complaints to English authorities. The charges were generally vague, often absurd, and hardly convincing to anyone who knew Nicholson, but their circulation still alarmed the governor to the extent that he initiated judicial proceedings against Slye for spreading false information.[44]

Provincial business necessitated the election of a new assembly during the winter. When sheriffs returned the indentures, Nicholson perceived how widespread dissatisfaction with his administration had become. Many of his staunchest supporters were missing when the new assembly convened on March 10, 1697/98. William Dent, Robert Smith, Edward Dorsey, Edward Boothby, John Hynson, William Frisby, Thomas Tasker, and Edward Blay were no longer delegates. Clarke gloatingly remarked following the elections that "the Jacobite Burgesses, who are the Governor's friends, are now out." The absence of these men certainly constituted a serious blow to Nicholson. Turnover since the last assembly had reached 44 percent, the governor's enemies clearly predominating among those representatives returned from the previous legislature. Moreover, many of the seventeen delegates now taking seats for the first time were anxious to embarrass Nicholson and oppose his programs. After learning of the full composition of the new house, Clarke accurately boasted, "I will warrant I will manage them well enough."[45]

Leadership in the new assembly indeed rested securely in the hands of the Clarke-Coode faction and of "Lord Baltimore's agents and dependants," as the council loosely styled a second group of delegates. The latter individuals belonged to families that possessed strong ties to the old proprietary interests, and many of these men remained especially close to discontented Catholics and Quakers so disadvantaged by various policies of the royal government.[46] Thomas Smithson, no intimate of the governor, now occupied the speaker's seat. He shared leadership in the lower house, however, with Clarke, for whenever the chamber went into a committee of the whole for deliberations – a frequent occurrence in this

43. A copy of the proceedings was entered in the Charles County Court Records, V No. 1, fol. 371.
44. The governor observed the shrewdness of "one of Cood's principles that Fling a great deal of Dirt, and some will stick" (*Archives*, 23:374–80, 502).
45. Ibid., 371; Provincial Court Judgments, IL, fol. 83 (quotation); Papenfuse et al., eds., *Biographical Dictionary*, 1:34–35.
46. Council to Board of Trade, May 28, 1698, CO5/714/II.

session – the delegates invariably elected Clarke and not Smithson as chairman. Clarke also presided as chairman of the influential Committee of Laws. Other particularly active burgesses included James Crawford, William Taylard, and Elisha Hall. Crawford, earlier barred from his legal practice by Nicholson, was a vocal member of the Committee of Aggrievances, an assignment shared by Taylard, who also sat on the Committee of Laws. Notorious for previous associations with Copley, Taylard resented that Nicholson and Lawrence had dismissed him from several profitable clerkships. Hall, a delegate from Calvert, linked the two groups opposing Nicholson. A close friend of Crawford and the individual who had posted security for Gerard Slye upon the latter's arrest the previous December for spreading the charges against Nicholson, Hall headed the old proprietary faction. The current coalition represented an interesting alliance of men who had bitterly opposed one another less than a decade earlier during the revolution of 1689.[47]

Not surprisingly, this lower house was the most recalcitrant body Nicholson ever faced in Maryland. The only pleasant moment, perhaps a strained one at that, came at a "Gen[ll] Entertainment" that Nicholson hosted on the evening of the first day's session.[48] The delegates had come armed with a volley of grievances, most of which they aimed personally at Nicholson, including his arrest of vestrymen and justices "for very slight occasions," his dismissal of attorneys from their practices "without being Legally convicted of any crime," his attendance at the Provincial Court, which "strikes an awfull fear upon Attorneys, Jurors and Suitors," and his persistent requests for new taxes.[49]

The governor, disregarding the temper of the burgesses, foolishly tried to promote his favorite reforms, particularly a new militia law, and to obtain vindication against the charges distributed by Slye. Nicholson was also anxious to squelch rumors that the government of Maryland was being restored to Lord Baltimore. Business degenerated into petty bickering; the assembly dispersed after one month without passing any of the laws for which it was summoned and without acting on the allegations of Slye. Nicholson, in turn, had refused to approve a levy bill, because the lower house would not officially include some councillors on the committee, and declined to support a reviving bill, because of disputes over which laws it should cite.[50]

47. Jordan, "Royal Period," 186–88. The second group also included Benjamin Hall, Edward Lloyd, William Hemsley, Richard Tilghman, Simon Wilmer, and John Whittington.
48. *Archives*, 22:7.
49. Ibid., 7–151, especially 86–87 (first two quotations), 109 (third quotation). For Nicholson's responses, ibid., 56–57.
50. Ibid., 59, 62–63, 65, 70–71.

Immediately upon conclusion of the session, Nicholson moved personally against his principal adversaries. The assembly had refused to discharge Mason as treasurer, as the governor had requested, but Nicholson, noting Mason "to be a Busy Man of Coods party," rescinded Mason's commission as sheriff of St. Mary's, an appointment that was in the governor's power to terminate. The council interrogated clerks of the lower house about the recent session and then summoned Clarke to answer accusations that he had introduced false information during the recent debates.[51] Slye had, in the interim, circulated a second set of nineteen charges, primarily ludicrous slanders of Nicholson's private character. Whatever their impact on Marylanders, these smears little impressed Whitehall officials, who proceeded confidently with arrangements to appoint Nicholson as governor of the larger colony of Virginia.[52]

Before receiving the gratifying news of this promotion, Nicholson gained a different kind of satisfaction in exacting revenge on his opponents locally. He arrested Slye, Mason, Clarke, and other associates. In pretrial interrogations, Slye proved anxious to shift all blame to Coode, and later that summer in the trials of both Slye and Clarke, a full account of the conspiracy emerged. To Nicholson's discredit, the trials were high-handed and procedurally irregular. Despite an inaccurate and sloppy prosecution, one jury found Clarke guilty; another ruled Slye innocent. The justices, on weak grounds, threw out the latter verdict and called another jury, not accidentally composed of the same men who had earlier convicted Clarke. This panel obligingly returned the desired guilty verdict of Slye, who immediately threw himself on the council's mercy and made a full confession. Clarke and Mason soon followed, and all three men fully incriminated Coode. Nicholson responded most harshly toward Clarke, the legislator among the group and probably the individual beyond Coode most responsible for directing the attacks and strategy against the chief executive. Nicholson imprisoned Clarke, while merely fining the other two men.[53]

With some emotional distance from the heat of the trials, Nicholson later appraised more perceptively the sources of discontent. In a letter to the Board of Trade, he wrote:

51. Ibid., 33, 39, 44, 50; 23:406 (quotation), 410–18.
52. Slye to James Vernon, May 26 and June 23, 1698, CO5/719/VI; "A True Account of a Conference at Lambeth, Dec. 27, 1697," in William Stevens Perry, ed., *Historical Collections Relating to the American Colonial Church*, 4 vols. (Hartford, Conn., 1870–78), 1:36–65.
53. *Archives*, 23:435–37, 441–43, 447–55, 471–73, 504–10, 519–20, 524–25, 528–29, 531; 25:4, 5, 13, 20, 39, 161, 166, 212–18; Provincial Court Judgments, IL, fols. 52–65, 142–43; WT No. 3, fol. 5.

Some were willing that his Majesty should deliver them from Popery and slavery, and protect them in time of War: because they were not then able to preserve them selves. But, now it hath pleased God, by his Majesty's unimitable Valour & Conduct, and indefatigable pains, that these troubles and fears are ceased; they are not Satisfied with his Majestys Government; because it curbs them in their former athiestical, loose, and vitious way of living; and debars them of that Darling, illegal trade . . . .I fancy that these dissatisfied People here, design to have a tryal of skill, whether they can by their own, and their accomplices, ways, and means, get my Lord [Baltimore] his Government again. And I think they would either be Governors them selves, or have such an one as they might rule.[54]

The assertiveness of the lower house, an assertiveness Nicholson him-self had helped to foster, had overreached proper constitutional bounds, he believed. Addressing the delegates in April of 1698, the governor observed "by the Actions and Behaviour of the House they think them-selves to have an Arbitrary and unbounded power."[55] The councillors joined Nicholson in further admonishing the burgesses at the next session the following October:

Your familiarity and pretended Equallity with the Right honble the House of Comons in England is enough to provoke and surprize us at once. We take the Government of this Province in its farest and Largest Extent to be a power derived from and depending on his Maj[ty] the King of England . . . and although we have the hon[r] to be of his Majesties Councill of this province, yett we are far from pretend-ing to that Rt hon[ble] house of Lords or Rt hon[ble] house of comons in England, and how you came to pretend to it we know nott. We do not desire you should be abridged of the least priviledge belonging to you, but when your demands are better Tempered with Justice or modesty they will better become you to aske or his Majestys Gover-nor to grant.[56]

The lower house was treading a difficult line. The struggle to define the place of representative government in the local polity as well as in the imperial structure always ran the risk of offending governors and coun-cillors in Maryland and alienating advisers of the Crown across the Atlan-tic. And inevitably, any power accruing to the elected branch heightened the expectations of the colonists to have their concerns forcefully pre-

54. Nicholson to Board of Trade, Aug. 20, 1698, *Archives*, 23:488–502 (quotations, 491–92); also Nicholson to [Vernon?], Aug. 18 and Nov. 12, 1698, Nicholson Let-ters, Colonial Williamsburg.
55. *Archives*, 22:70
56. Ibid., 248–49.

sented and their interests vigorously defended against whomever stood in the way. Conflicts could not be avoided even among the best intentioned of men, and not all officeholders were equally conscientious. Numerous delegates wanted power more to pursue their own interests than to promote altruistically the public good. In this intense struggle, the lower house understandably invoked whatever models and precedents it could to achieve equality or supremacy within the assembly, and that model most powerfully before them at all times was the Parliament. The stern rebuke from the upper house had been prompted by the delegates resolutely claiming that "the house of Delegates in this province have all wayes claymed as their Birthright the Same priviledges as the House [of] Commons clayme in England." How could tempers not flare when the delegates were lectured in one session to adhere more closely to that model and then in the following assembly were chastized for promoting such an adherence? In actuality, both sides looked selectively to the parliamentary model to take what best suited their respective purposes.[57]

Nicholson, on reflection later, did not so much blame the lower house as a body for his problems, nor did he attribute the unpleasant disturbances to the general populace. Rather, he condemned a few headstrong discontents, whom he described as curses upon society, for overstepping legitimate bounds and manipulating others for base, personal ends. Nicholson especially branded Coode as "a diminutive Ferguson, in point of Government; and a Hobbist, or worse, in point of religion." This persistent rebel and his closest associates were not, in the governor's estimation, sincere proponents of any alternative political or religious theories. Nicholson ascribed Coode's motivation to the fact that he was heavily in debt, as was his stepson Slye. Mason was "a great pretender of honesty; but hath cheated and oppressed most of those that lay in his power to serve so," and Clarke, "a mighty pretender to Law," was in fact "one of the great Incendiarys in the house of Delegates" and also out primarily for his own personal gain.[58]

Nicholson's observations were at least partially correct. There were distinctly unappealing and highly questionable aspects of the public and private lives of these men. Furthermore, they never attracted the same degree of personal following outside St. Mary's County that the Protestant Associators had earlier mustered, partially because conditions were not so oppressive and unjust as they had been in 1689 but just as importantly because most colonists were no longer so naive about Coode and his coterie. The cooperation that Clarke impressively enlisted in the lower

57. Ibid., 166.
58. See Nicholson's long letter of Aug. 20, 1698, ibid., 23:488–502, especially 501 (quotations) speaking of these "mutinous and rebellious Fellows."

house was a different form of opposition to the governor than the traditional rebellion Coode had usually championed. Clarke's temporary alliance with other discontented colonists operated primarily within a legal framework, an important advance in provincial politics as a consequence of the earlier revolution, the introduction of royal authority, and the significant developments of the assembly itself. An opposition was now able to resist unpopular executive actions and pursue various alternatives through the legislature and not be forced to respond completely outside the official organs of government.

Furthermore, most colonists never felt the same personal antipathy toward Nicholson that they had earlier registered against the proprietor and his deputy governors. Despite charges of arbitrary government and dictatorial measures, accusations that most informed colonists quickly qualified or dismissed, the governor retained at least the tolerant support of Marylanders because of his solid accomplishments. "I neither pretend to be infallible nor wise at all times," Nicholson once remarked. "I very well know that 'tis in man to err, & none lives without faults: but . . . mine are of the Understanding, and not of the will; especially those concerning this his most sacred Majestys Government." Nicholson had become heavy-handed at times and indeed poked his nose into every phase of provincial life, but never for his own financial gain. The evidences of his self-denial and of his generosity toward the colony were too numerous to ignore or discount. The public, by and large, realized that, as did the majority of his detractors within the assembly. They opposed particular measures and wanted changes in policy more than a total change in government.[59]

Nicholson's last meeting with the assembly in late October was not particularly productive. He had irrevocably passed the point of effective cooperation with these delegates, and everyone knew that Nicholson was soon to leave the colony. The assembly had no intentions of enacting the ambitious reforms the governor still envisioned as being in the best interests of the colony, and he would never retreat from the progressive stance he had established in his first year. This last session eventually settled into a critique of his cherished bills for further support of the clergy, church, and school, no favorable action being taken on any of these issues.[60]

The delegates, having asserted their independence, were magnanimous

59. Ibid., 502. Nicholson had contributed generously to church and school projects, lent the province money at no interest, held council meetings in his own quarters to avoid the expense of rent elsewhere, and had never openly sought or received monetary "bequests" from the assembly. Such observations could never be made about either his predecessor or his successor.
60. *Archives*, 22:156–278, especially 179–87.

in their parting words. They congratulated Nicholson on his new appointment and acknowledged as "one of Our greatest temporall Blessings that it hath pleased Allmighty God to send soe Gracious a Prince to Reigne and Rule over us." "If debate concerning our priviledge have been beyond what is really our Right of which we are not yet sencible," they said, "We desire they may rather be imputed to our Misunderstandings then Stubbornness." Their declaration overstated their true feelings about both Nicholson and the jurisdictional squabbles within the assembly, but it was nonetheless a testimony of at least grudging respect for Nicholson and indicative of the remarkable change that had occurred in the colony's political life. All but a few of Nicholson's most unbending critics signed a parting tribute that traced the positive accomplishments of the governor's tenure and appropriately credited him for leadership in achieving these improvements.[61]

Nicholson, happily anticipating the resumption of projects he had initiated several years earlier in Virginia as lieutenant governor, transferred the reins of government in Maryland to Nathaniel Blakiston, his successor, on January 2, 1698/99. Nicholson carefully briefed the new chief executive and promised full cooperation and an active correspondence.[62] In a final report filed July 1, 1699, to the lords of trade, Nicholson reflected further on his experiences and astutely commented on the problems that were increasingly to plague his successors in Maryland, as elsewhere in New World colonies. The emergence of a native interest accompanied by a greater concern in the mother country for involvement in many critical areas of provincial life ensured disagreement and intense battles between governors and assemblies. Nicholson wisely advised the Board of Trade to screen candidates for royal governorships carefully. In the future, it would be absolutely necessary that any governor "be esteemed by the people, or at least the major part of them, to be a lover of them and their Country, and not that he be Sent or comes to make or retrieve a fortune."[63]

Nathaniel Blakiston was subsequently regarded by most Marylanders as "a lover of their Country." Although Blakiston clearly came to America to "seek a fortune" and prospered during his brief sojourn in the colony, he never aroused the level of opposition or hostility that Nicholson had eventually engendered. Part of Blakiston's popular success derived from his shorter stay; Nicholson too had been popular in his first

---

61. Ibid., 197 (quotation); 25:38–39. Among those not signing were Thomas Smithson, Edward Lloyd, James Crawford, Walter Smith, Elisha and Benjamin Hall, Philip Clarke, and William Hemsley.
62. *Archives*, 25:43–47.
63. Nicholson to lords of trade, July 1, 1699, CO5/1310, 2.

two or three years. But a more persuasive explanation arises from the differing styles of the two men and Blakiston's less than wholehearted commitment to the provisions of his instructions and commission. The contrasts between the two men are instructive in understanding the further evolution of the assembly.

Blakiston arrived with some preestablished ties to the colony of Maryland. His family came from the same area of England as many of the province's earliest immigrants, and an ancestor had married one of the Calverts. Blakiston was himself the nephew of Nehemiah Blakiston, the former customs collector, rebel, and confidant of Copley. Although Blakiston had also served in two other colonies before his appointment to Maryland, any similarity to Nicholson ended there. Blakiston lacked his predecessor's reforming zeal and adhered more closely to a calculated policy of cooperation with and deference to local leaders; Blakiston rarely prodded them into actions they did not welcome or initiate themselves. Nicholson described Blakiston accurately: "I find he is not over much publick spirited, especially when it is any charge to him, for he openly declares that he doth not like the Country; that he comes to make up his fortune, therefore would endeavor to do it as soon as possible."[64]

Wary Marylanders, assessing their third royal governor in seven years, quickly concluded that they had little to fear and much to gain from Blakiston. With a more prosperous economy and Nicholson's successful financial measures having retired the provincial debt, the colony was not suffering as severely as it had earlier in the 1690s. Blakiston's tenure of three years encompassed a peaceful period without major problems or gubernatorial reforms. The new executive consistently avoided any conflict, and the assembly, exhausted from the frequent and often heated sessions under Nicholson, welcomed a respite. Blakiston deliberately refrained from summoning any meeting except on a "speciall Occasion." In practice, this meant that the council met only for a day or two approximately every three months, and the legislature convened briefly once each year. The governor proudly boasted of the great expenses these restricted sessions saved the colony. At the same time, he remained highly solicitous of the opinions of both councillors and delegates upon matters of policy and patronage, and he heeded his promise to "Always go along with the Gentlemen of the Council & be glad upon all Occasions to take their advice for his Majestys Service."[65] With such infrequent formal meetings

---

64. See entry for Blakiston in Papenfuse et al., eds., *Biographical Dictionary*; also Nicholson to Archbishop Thomas Tenison, July 23, 1700, in Perry, ed., *Historical Collections*, 1:122.
65. *Archives*, 25:52–53 (quotation); Blakiston to Board of Trade, Apr. 8, 1699, and Mar. 12, 1699/1700, CO5/719/VII and CO5/715/I.

of either the council or the assembly, Blakiston relied most heavily upon individuals from Anne Arundel and neighboring counties, and his major appointments reflected a heightened dependence on certain families living nearer the capital. A careful concern for geographical distribution of power and a broader development of talent, practiced by Nicholson, gave way to a more concentrated leadership by a few individuals and further fostered the emergence of the new provincial elite in Maryland, its most prominent members residing in counties close to Annapolis on both sides of Chesapeake Bay.[66]

The governor's benevolence seemingly extended to almost everyone, including the rebels whom Nicholson had so recently battled. Blakiston reinstated Mason as treasurer, discharged Clarke from his prison sentence and restored the attorney to the full enjoyment of his legal practice, and even granted a complete pardon to Coode, who had finally been captured, tried, and convicted. The governor declined to investigate actively the performance of duty by any local officer, in contrast to his predecessor, nor did Blakiston regularly scrutinize accounts and reports to detect any dishonesty or poor record keeping. The colony had a governor who would generally leave affairs in the hands of local leaders to conduct in whatever manner they wished.[67]

Blakiston summoned the last legislature elected under Nicholson to sit for two additional sessions. In the more relaxed atmosphere now prevailing in the province, these delegates interacted very cordially with Blakiston. The only incendiary aspect of the session of 1699 was a fire ignited by lightning that struck the statehouse, killed James Crawford, and seriously injured three others, while causing considerable damage. The fire was "Quenched by the Dillegence & Industry of his Ex^cy Nathaniel Blackistone," the journal of the lower house gratefully observed.[68] Similarly, the governor quenched any smoldering fires of rebellion. He asked little of this assembly and shrewdly compromised to obtain what was necessary in minimal obedience to his royal instructions.

The more favorable economic situation allowed Blakiston and the assembly to let some of the unpopular taxes expire and to keep public expenses low. The governor even suspended the public levy altogether in 1699 and paid the province's bills with the surplus that had accumulated in the treasury. The much disliked Act Against Divulgers of False News

66. Jordan, "Maryland's Privy Council," 78–79.
67. See particularly, *Archives*, 25:58, 75, 80, 103; Provincial Court Judgments, WT No. 3, fols. 4–5; Owings, *His Lordship's Patronage*, 157. Blakiston later boasted that "the Inhabitants here . . . have an universal Satisfaction of my endeavors since my arrivall . . . I am not sensible that any single person in the province is dissatisfyed." See Blakiston to Board of Trade, Apr. 5, 1701, CO5/715/III.
68. *Archives*, 22:334–35, 421 (quotation).

that had been used to prosecute Clarke was also allowed to expire without revival. In gratitude, the assembly voted Blakiston the usual three pence per hogshead duty traditionally given to governors, continued the additional duty of three pence passed in Nicholson's time, and awarded Blakiston a special gratuity of £250, while also waiving the three-year residency requirement to allow two of the governor's protégés to hold office immediately.[69] A final session of this legislature a year later proceeded just as smoothly, and Blakiston received another special gift of £200, which he could not resist from complaining was a reduction from their tribute of the previous year.[70]

The most noteworthy action of the assembly's last session in 1700 was repassage of an act to establish the Church of England. The Crown had indeed vetoed the revised statute of 1696 with its objectionable clause implying the extension of all laws of Parliament to the colony. Credit for a new law, minus the offending language, belongs less to Blakiston than to the tireless efforts of Thomas Bray, who had recently arrived as commissary general, and the assistance from Virginia of Francis Nicholson.[71] The former governor, still much concerned about the religious settlement of Maryland, worked closely with Bray and helped to devise a list of all the current delegates with a candid assessment of how each man might be expected to vote. The initial outlook was not very optimistic. "There are 19 of them supposed to be for passing the Law. Seven very stiff against it and twelve of them Dubious rather inclining to the Noes and easily carried away to the Lord Baltimore's Interest. Besides the Quakers have a great Ascendancy on many of the house," Bray learned from local officials.[72]

Proponents of the act soon discovered that the real challenge lay not in removal of the objectionable clause that had triggered disagreements in 1696, but in the thorny issue of establishment itself. As Blakiston later explained, "Those paragraphs which it contained of Contrary Nature did

69. Ibid., 285–582, especially 352–53, 354–56, 447–48.
70. Ibid., 24:1–124, especially 30, 107–8.
71. Carroll, "Quaker Opposition," 159–63. The best general studies of Bray are Bernard C. Steiner, *Rev. Thomas Bray,* Maryland Historical Society, Fund Publication No. 37 (Baltimore, 1901), and Henry Paget Thompson, *Thomas Bray* (London, 1954).
72. The list is a unique document for this period, because it contains the only extant breakdown of alignments in the assembly on any issue and in addition provides insightful characterizations of the individuals involved. Otherwise, the journals of the legislature rarely record how members voted or even gross totals. A List of his Majestys Council and the Burgesses . . . , Bray-Maryland Mss., fols. 226–27, Sion College Library, London; Bray to archbishop of Canterbury, Apr. 11, 1700, and Blakiston to same, Apr. 10, 1700, Fulham Palace Papers, Vol. 2, fols. 139–40 and 137–38; Nicholson to archbishop of Canterbury, May 27, 1700, in Perry, ed., *Historical Collections,* 1:117–21; Nicholson to bishop of London, Feb. 4, 1699/1700, Nicholson Papers.

seem unreasonable to most thinking persons and a Diminution to his Majestys just Prerogative which was carryed by some hotheaded people then [1696] in power here." Blakiston might have added that the most "hotheaded" person, Philip Clarke, who had actually drafted those paragraphs, had died the previous year and no one in the assembly continued his forceful position on combining temporal and spiritual concerns in the establishment act.[73]

The issue in 1700 became a new struggle for establishment itself. For several weeks before the convening of the assembly, Bray visited as many parishes and influential people as possible in efforts to persuade those men his confidential list described as "Dubious." He encountered frequent complaints that many parishes were without ministers despite payment of the church tax. To gain support, Bray promised to dispatch qualified candidates for these pulpits immediately upon his return to England. Ministerial supply comprised an important part of his responsibilities as commissary; his commitment to this task had led to his role in founding the Society for Promotion of Christian Knowledge in 1699 and was to be instrumental in his helping to create the Society for the Propagation of the Gospel in 1701. When the Provincial Court met in early April for thirteen days, Bray extended "much civil and chargeable hospitality," and later during the assembly itself, he tirelessly preached several well-received sermons, conducted daily prayers and even prepared the draft of the new bill for establishment.[74]

Blakiston's strategy with the assembly was less straightforward. In addressing the delegates, he disregarded the implications of the official letter from Whitehall concerning the disallowed act and even denied rumors then circulating in the colony that the act of 1696 had been "disassented to upon any other Grounds than it mentions; You having Clogged and Loaded it with things of Different Natures." Technically this was true, but there were also "other strong Objections" that had been registered against the statute, particularly by London Quakers lobbying on behalf of Maryland Friends, concerning the nature and power of the vestry, the implication that the use of the Book of Common Prayer would be required reading in all places of public worship, and the requirement for all dissenters to register baptisms, births, and

73. Blakiston to Board of Trade, May 28, 1700, CO5/715/I. Clarke had died by June 29, 1699.
74. Thompson, *Bray*, 36–42, 50–51, 62–63; Bray to Secretary of SPG, Mar. 24, 1704/05, in Perry, ed., *Historical Collections*, 4:55–56; *Archives*, 24:41, 65; "A Memorial Representing the Rise, Progress and Issue of Dr. Bray's Missionary Undertaking" (draft), Sion College Library (quotation).

deaths. The Board of Trade's letter to Blakiston had mentioned all of these complaints.[75]

Bray and William Dent, the colony's attorney general, were aware of these objections and in drafting a new bill quietly undertook to eliminate the grounds for most of them. Bray performed his lobbying tasks admirably, and the legislation eventually passed both houses with little difficulty. Moreover, the assembly awarded the commissary £50 for the parochial libraries he had sent to Maryland and appointed him as its special agent to gain approval of the act in England.[76]

"It is now washed and purged of all the Dregs that were the cause of its being dissented to, for it now contains nothing but what is essential to its own constitution," Blakiston proudly wrote of the statute to the archbishop of Canterbury.[77] "Impurities" did remain, however, and unfortunately for the advocates of establishment, the powers of this church's lobbyists in England were not sufficient to push the act through the Privy Council with these imperfections. Bray confronted an impressive opposition in the Quakers, who vigorously petitioned against the legislation. Representatives of each side literally raced to be the first to appear before the Board of Trade in the early autumn of 1700.

A brief but spirited warfare of petitions and pamphlets ensued. The "many pressing applications" of the Quakers eventually brought their partial reward, when Attorney General Thomas Trevor again objected to the law, citing the clause carried over from the previous act "that the Book of Common Prayer & Administration of the Sacraments . . . be solemnly read by all and every Minister or Reader in every Church or other place of Publick Worship within that Province." He ruled that this "may be lyable to be construed to extend as well to the places where any Dissenters from the Church of England meet together." The Quakers also had presented a catalogue of objections, which drew a sympathetic response. All of the Maryland acts had provided for an incorporated vestry of unspecified tenure with vacancies to be filled by cooptation. Each act since 1694 had also contained a provision that the vestry choose the two church wardens annually instead of holding full parish elections. The closed or "select" vestry had come under serious attack in England since the Glorious Revolution, and the later 1690s had brought several parlia-

75. *Archives*, 24:3–4, 7–8 (quotation); Quaker Memorial, Oct. 17, 1699, *CSP, 1699,* No. 868; Board of Trade to Blakiston, Jan. 4, 1699/1700, *CSP, 1700,* No. 11 (quotation).

76. *Archives*, 24:15, 31, 45, 69, 88–89, and for the text of the act, 91–99; Samuel Clyde McCullough, "Dr. Thomas Bray's Trip to Maryland," *William and Mary Quarterly,* 3rd ser., 2 (1945), 23–26.

77. Perry, ed., *Historical Collections,* 4:32; see also Blakiston to Board of Trade, May 28, 1700, CO5/715/I.

mentary attempts to change it in England and at least to remove control of parish funds from the hands of coopted vestrymen. The Quakers dwelled at length on these persisting aspects of the Maryland law.[78]

All interested parties attended a hearing on January 31, 1700/1, where Bray, the bishop of London, and the archbishop of Canterbury forestalled a complete defeat. Although the act of establishment was again disallowed in its present form, the lords of trade expressed a willingness to oversee the drafting of a new bill "with proper alterations agreeable to the toleration allowed here" and in the interim to let the disapproved statute continue in force in Maryland as long as it was not "put too vigorously in execution."[79]

Bray prepared several drafts before the lords finally approved a bill to be sent to the colony for official passage. A last, desperate appeal from the Quaker lobbyists failed, and Sir Thomas Lawrence, returning to Maryland, was entrusted with the acceptable text to present to the assembly. Mindful of earlier promises to the colonists, Bray dispatched on the same fleet six missionaries to fill vacancies in various parishes. "I found it necessary to obviate any other obstructing the bill," Bray explained to the Society for the Propagation of the Gospel in defense of his entailing such extraordinary expense for one colony.[80]

Blakiston laid the bill before the next regularly scheduled session in the spring of 1702. Since Bray's feverish efforts of 1700, a new election had been held, replacing the previous assembly that had already sat for the maximum three years. Twenty-five delegates who had voted for the establishment law in 1700 had gained reelection. Six of the twenty-one delegates not returned had died, and two others now held posts excluding them from eligibility. The replacements, by and large, were familiar figures who had supported church establishment in the past, including the influential William Dent.[81]

Blakiston's opening remarks apprised the assembly of the present status of its establishment legislation. "You'll find the Alterations, that are

78. Carroll, "Quaker Opposition," 165–66; Thompson, *Bray*, 56–57; Blakiston to Board of Trade, July 5, 1700, CO5/715/I; Perry, ed., *Historical Collections*, 4:34–40; Report of the Attorney General (quotation), CO5/715/II. For contemporary institutional developments in the mother country, see Sidney Webb and Beatrice Webb, *English Local Government* (London, 1906), 173–74, 247–51, and William E. Tate, *The Parish Chest* (Cambridge, Eng., 1946), 20.

79. Thompson, *Bray*, 59–60; *CSP, 1701*, Nos. 61, 83, 116 (quotation), 127, 132, 147, 175; Order of King in Council, Feb. 13, 1700/01 (quotation), CO5/715/III.

80. *CSP, 1701*, Nos. 237, 317, 329, 370, 406, 446, 468, 530; Bray to secretary of SPG, Mar. 24, 1704/05, in Perry, ed., *Historical Collections*, 4:55–56; Lawrence to Board of Trade, Dec. 8, 1701, CO5/715/V.

81. Papenfuse et al., eds., *Biographical Dictionary*, 1:35–36; Blakiston to Board of Trade, Dec. 10, 1701, CO5/715/V.

made but very little, and that such Visible Amendments to our Advantage being Corrected by so wise an Hand. We ought to be proud of the pattern in confirming it." He reminded the members of the previous assembly's request to the king to send an amended bill if he were unable to approve their submitted statute. After three days, the bill was referred to committee for close comparison with the former law. When the legislation finally reached the floor, the majority of delegates passed it in the recommended form rather than with the amendments some members desired.[82]

Despite continuing opposition from Quakers, the new monarch, Queen Anne, approved the much disputed act on January 18, 1702/3, and Maryland at last had a legally established church.[83] Major efforts ensued to implement the establishment. By 1715, all but four of the thirty parishes were staffed, although a single clergyman often served several neighboring churches. Congregations proceeded steadily to erect buildings, but the various parishes displayed an inconsistent institutional development. Some vestries became very active, whereas others seldom met. Some entered aggressively into disciplinary and charitable activities; others remained indifferent. Ministers dominated the proceedings in some places and in others were dominated themselves by the vestrymen. Whatever the pattern, the widespread complaint of both clergy and lay observers throughout these years continued to be the "universal disregard (a few only excepted) of holy things."[84]

Blakiston ended his harmonious tenure as governor in 1702 and returned to England for the stated reason of poor health. He met the assembly a final time for two days during his last summer in the province. News had reached Maryland of the death of William and the accession of Anne, and the governor thought it propitious for the assembly to send her an address. The previous session in 1701/2, upon learning of Blakiston's impending departure, had appointed him agent of the colony in England and voted him another special gratuity of £400. It is interesting that at the

82. *Archives*, 24:207–8 (quotation), 244, 247, 254, 265–73 (text of act).
83. Carroll, "Quaker Opposition," 167–69; Order of Queen in Council, Jan. 11, 1702/3, CO5/715/V.
84. Rightmyer, *Maryland's Established Church*, and Percy G. Skirven, *The First Parishes of the Province of Maryland* (Baltimore, 1923), provide excellent introductions to the early church in the colony. See also Rev. Samuel Skippon to Bishop of London, Jan. 19, 1714/15, in Perry, ed., *Historical Collections*, 4:72–73 (quotation). For examples of differences in activities and membership patterns among the various vestries, consult St. Anne's Parish Register, 1708–85; St. James's Vestry Minutes, 1695–1793; All Faiths' Vestry Minute Book, A, 1692–1720; St. Paul's Vestry Minutes, 1693–1726; King George's Vestry Minutes, 1693–1779, all available in manuscript or on microfilm at the Hall of Records. Gerald Eugene Hartdagen, "The Anglican Vestry in Colonial Maryland" (Ph.D. diss., Northwestern University, 1965), is also informative on this subject, as is Carr, "County Government," Text, 528–39.

same session, the delegates professed an inability to contribute the full £650 requested by the king as aid to New York. Blakiston typically did not press them on this matter and certainly did not publicly note the inconsistency of the assembly's denying an official royal request while rewarding him so generously beyond his already substantial salary.[85] English authorities perhaps noted that discrepancy, however. Instructions from the Board of Trade in 1703 for Blakiston's successor stipulated plainly that no governor or president of the council could consent in the future to any law providing for a gift, nor could he ever accept a present from the assembly "in any manner whatsoever" without incurring the Crown's displeasure and a loss of commission.[86]

Even without this restriction, it seems unlikely that John Seymour would ever have received such a gift. Certainly, he never enjoyed the same amicable relations as Blakiston with the Maryland legislature, nor did he win even grudging admiration as did Nicholson. Seymour arrived in early 1704 after a lengthy career in the army but without prior experience in colonial administration. Governors drawn from the ranks of the military had become commonplace; lacking much previous exposure to politics, however, Seymour possessed the particular rigidity of one accustomed to giving orders and having them obligingly obeyed. In day-to-day interaction with the colonists, he was to display little of the flexibility necessary for effective governance, a flexibility especially required in dealing with the increasingly assertive local political leadership.[87]

Other circumstances also put Seymour at a disadvantage. The resumption of war between the major European powers aggravated familiar economic, defense, and political problems. Like Nicholson, Seymour rejected many of the preferred local remedies and deplored the haphazard administrative procedures still followed by some officials. In contrast to Blakiston, this governor had numerous remedies of his own devising for curing the province's ills. But unlike Nicholson, Seymour never implemented very effectively his proposals through either executive action or legislative cooperation. His manner consistently antagonized the colo-

---

85. *Archives*, 24:205–81 (session of 1701/02), especially 207, 208, 220, 255–56, 283–309 (session of 1702).
86. Ibid., 329–30 (quotation).
87. On Seymour's governorship, see Charles Branch Clark, "The Career of John Seymour, Governor of Maryland, 1704–1709," *Maryland Historical Magazine*, 48 (1953), 134–59, and Jordan, "Royal Period," 201–315. Stephen Saunders Webb, "Army and Empire: English Garrison Government in Britain and America, 1569 to 1763," *William and Mary Quarterly*, 3rd ser., 34 (1977), 1–31, and *The Governors-General: The English Army and the Definition of the Empire, 1569–1681* (Chapel Hill, N.C., 1979) discuss the growing importance of military men among the colonial governors.

nists, and he attempted ever more arbitrarily to impose his authority and reforms upon the uncooperative Marylanders. Seymour's failures owed something to his temperament, his weaker administrative skills, and his inexperience in colonial affairs, but they also derived considerably from the development of a stronger and more independent assembly since Nicholson's tenure.

"I am an English Protestant Gentleman and can never equivocate," Seymour haughtily proclaimed in 1704. Indeed, whenever the governor perceived a possible encroachment upon royal prerogatives or detected any resistance to his favorite proposals, he became both stubborn and belligerent.[88] The members of the assembly, spoiled by Blakiston's indulgence and consequently more assertive of their current expectations, now represented more clearly a native or local interest that was no longer to follow unquestioningly the directives of any governor. Seymour might avow, as he did in 1704, that he possessed "no other ayme than the true Interest and Service of your Country," but he quickly put Marylanders on their guard when he also proclaimed that the colony's "Interest" could not "be Separate from that of the crown of England." As governor, he regarded it his solemn duty to uphold the prerogatives of the Crown and to prevent any separation of interests, an exceedingly difficult task by the first decade of the eighteenth century. As Seymour explained to the assembly gathered in April of 1706, "I have neither Lands nor Houses to loose here on any Suddaine fatall Insult, as you Gentlemen Freeholders have; yet my Reputation, which is dearer to me than anything in this World lyes at Stake."[89]

The colonists cared little about Seymour's reputation and intensely resented the fact that he had "neither Lands nor Houses" in the province nor any other attachments that might signify some closer identification with Maryland. The local population's concerns for their land, their homes, and their immediate personal interests greatly outweighed any deference to a governor's reputation and frequently even any fear of a distant monarch's displeasure. It was Seymour who invoked again and again the label of "Country" or "native" party to describe the sentiments and forces powerfully aligned against him, but this label, imposed initially by an outsider as a negative judgment, came eventually to be borne proudly by many Marylanders. Moreover, the appellation contained much truth. During Seymour's governorship native-born colonists did consistently oppose his programs and forcefully advocate policies di-

88. *Archives*, 26:46. Illustrative examples of Seymour's actions are provided in Perry, ed., *Historical Collections*, 4:57–63; *Archives*, 25:207; 26:44–46, 209–11; 27:179–221.
89. Ibid., 26:373, 524.

rected toward local interests that were separate from the concerns of the imperial bureaucracy.[90]

Seymour presided over the province for five years before his death on July 30, 1709. During that period, he convened eight sessions of four different assemblies, and each new election returned a less cooperative legislature.[91] Outward relations, though generally proper and cordial at the outset of Seymour's tenure, deteriorated steadily over these years, and even from the first meetings the lower house persistently declined to enact the legislation Seymour most ardently sought. Although differences extended over a wide range of issues, opposition coalesced most particularly around three disputes: the assembly's treatment of Sir Thomas Lawrence, the regulation of the economy, and the governor's greatly desired judicial reforms.

Nothing received more consistent attention from the assembly throughout the royal period nor aroused more heated controversy than did the continuous struggle over the powers and perquisites residing in the secretary's office. This bitter dispute, symbolic of more general differences regarding patronage and authority over officeholders, clearly replaced in importance the debates over the defense of the colony and the control of elections that recurringly dominated the legislative gatherings of the proprietary years. No other individual figured more prominently as the subject of the assembly's deliberations over this twenty-five-year period of royal rule than Sir Thomas Lawrence, who was secretary from 1691 to 1698 and again from 1701 to 1714, his son Thomas Lawrence, Jr., holding the post in the interim years.[92]

Lawrence always epitomized for Marylanders the alien placeman who never fully identified with local residents and who grasped for power and money without having any appreciable concern for the colonists' sentiments. The secretary's avaricious manipulations of county clerkships prompted the legislature's original passage of an act for the advancement of natives in 1694, and his unceasing demands for other revenues over the years kept the colony in a continual uproar. In the 1690s, Lawrence had successfully appealed to English authorities to redress the losses he had suffered under Copley and to nullify the statutes that Copley had endorsed to limit the powers and revenue of the secretary's office. By far

90. A provocative discussion of the new attitudes of and about the "country borne" in a neighboring colony is Carol Shammas's "English-Born and Creole Elites in Turn-of-the-Century Virginia," 274–96, in Tate and Ammerman, eds., *The Chesapeake in the Seventeenth Century.*
91. *Archives*, 24:325–423; 26:; 27:1–374, contain the assembly's journals for Seymour's tenure.
92. The following discussion draws extensively on Jordan, "Sir Thomas Lawrence, Secretary of Maryland," 22–44.

the most controversial revenues Lawrence claimed were the proceeds from licenses necessary to operate an ordinary in the colony. Lord Baltimore had traditionally bestowed this income on the incumbent secretary, and Lawrence always insisted it belonged permanently to his office. Under Nicholson, Lawrence regained briefly the rights to these fees and some other benefits as the assembly responded in gratitude for Lawrence's opposition to Copley and Blakiston and in acknowledgment of Nicholson's strong espousal of the secretary's claims. The legislation was temporary and depended upon the continuing good will of the assembly for its revival. At that moment, the delegates perceived the valuable assistance Lawrence could render as an agent and lobbyist in England, where he returned briefly in the mid-1690s. In this atmosphere of mutual advantage, the assembly at Nicholson's urging revised the law in 1695 and removed its temporary features.

Permanent acts could be easily undone, Lawrence soon regretfully learned, if the governor were willing to approve a law reversing the previous statute. Nathaniel Blakiston did just that in 1699. With his obliging concurrence, the assembly rescinded the "permanent" statute of 1695, once again made the granting of license fees to the secretary a temporary law, and in other legislation further reduced the income of that office. Local sentiment had swung decidedly against Lawrence or any other outside appointee, and the nativist or country party sentiment was rising. The opposing sides were poised for further battle when Seymour arrived in Maryland.

In the early spring of 1704, the governor convened for a final session the legislature first elected in 1701. He was uneasy about the authority of an assembly that had been sitting now for more than three years and through a change of monarchs and of governors. Without immediate legislation, however, Seymour would lose several months of revenue from export duties that belonged by law to the governor's office only during the period of Blakiston's commission. Seymour greedily eyed these funds and wanted a new act bestowing them on him as soon as possible. He did not anticipate any business other than this act and the necessary reviving statute for temporary laws.

The delegates had different ideas and immediately tested whether this chief executive would be as cooperative and pliable as his predecessor. The lower house proposed a new Act for Regulating Ordinaries that would transfer license fees from the secretary to use for public expenses. Lawrence vigorously protested that the assembly could not legally deny him those funds. The upper house divided 3 to 3 on the issue, but the representatives proclaimed that no tax of any nature could be levied without a "particular act of Assembly," that only the legislature authorizing the tax could determine its use, and that the present lower house wanted this revenue changed. As a compromise, Seymour recommended passage with a suspending clause while awaiting an indication of royal approval, but the lower house refused. It was abundantly clear that these men never intended again to bestow these fees on Lawrence or any other outsider. No act on licenses passed that session, and the previous law regulating ordinaries consequently expired. Among the few statutes emerging from this session was an act providing the new governor with his desired revenues.[93]

Seymour meanwhile issued writs for the election of a new assembly, which convened the following September. This body proved equally adamant and again passed a bill, without a suspension clause, allocating the disputed license fees "toward the Defraying the Charge of the County." The upper house and the governor surprisingly approved the act. Complaining of profits being "much lessened and Impaired," Lawrence requested permission to return to England, where he was to lobby actively over the next ten years to recover his lost revenue and powers.[94]

Whitehall officials endorsed Lawrence's claims and repeatedly instructed Seymour to have the license fees restored to the secretary. The governor obligingly brought the queen's directive before each successive meeting of the legislature, but time and again the delegates declined to honor her, or his, wishes. Most members accurately perceived that Seymour was technically complying with the Crown's request but scarcely exercising the full powers of his office to gain redress for Lawrence. Seymour obviously disliked Lawrence and like Copley coveted some of the secretary's revenues; the governor certainly conspired with William Bladen, an influential local placeman, to deprive the secretary of power and money in several maneuvers. Moreover, Seymour was unwilling to alienate the assembly and further jeopardize his own program and revenues simply to avenge Lawrence. He did only enough to justify his position in letters back to England, but that was sufficient to maintain the breach between him and the lower house. When the act of 1704 expired three years later, Seymour's instructions prohibited him explicitly from approving its renewal; the assembly circumvented this problem by passing instead an ordinance that did not require the governor's endorsement. This measure empowered county justices to grant the licenses and to regulate ordinaries pending royal approval. Seymour defensively explained to his superiors that he and the upper house "used our Utmost endeavors to persuade

93. *Archives*, 24:341–43, 350, 378–80, 403–5 (quotation, 404), 406, 407, 416–17; Seymour to lords of trade, May 23, 1704, CO5/715/VI.
94. *Archives*, 26:46, 48, 62–64, 65 (quotation), 304–9 (quotation, 305); 25:175 (quotation).

their Complyances" but added that Lawrence "seems to be the last person they are willing to oblige."[95]

Seymour was fast becoming a close contender of Lawrence for that dubious distinction. The governor could obtain the delegates' cooperation on little at all. For example, the Crown was pressuring Seymour for legislation establishing certain ports on each river where all ships would be required to load and unload. This would presumably facilitate enforcement of the navigation acts and assist, with other statutes, in improving the inspection and control of the quality and weight of exported tobacco. There had been an elaborate but abortive attempt to establish such ports in the 1680s, but only a few of the proposed towns ever materialized and even they remained quite small. Seymour undertook in 1705 responsibility for the passage of a new act, but he found the burgesses resolutely opposed to restricting the loading places to the mere five ports he suggested. Robert Quarry, Edward Randolph's successor as customs collector and now an itinerant member of the council, had expressed his doubts two years earlier on the willingness of either Virginia or Maryland legislators to enact voluntarily such measures, "for the Assembly consists of the Trading men in each river . . . for tho they know and are Satisfied that it would be more for a public good to have a fixed port, Yet unless each man's own plantation be appointed that place, they never will agree that it shall be anywhere else, & so it never must be by their consent."[96]

Seymour soon learned the accuracy of that observation and the wisdom of Quarry's recommendation that an act of Parliament be the solution. Such a strategy might also be necessary in other areas where local opinion was hardening against the Crown's wishes. Meanwhile, the governor sought permission to prevent by executive decree shipping from any but the five recommended places, should the assembly remain obstinate. He tried again in April of 1706, but the lower house responded with an act that fell far short of providing the features Seymour desired. The regulation extended only to the unloading of goods, and thus did not cover the loading of tobacco, and it encompassed many more sites. The statute was carefully framed to encourage settlement in the towns by traders, local merchants being favored over non-Marylanders.[97]

Persistent wooing in 1707 brought the assembly's half-hearted agreement to require the loading of tobacco in towns and ports, but the term

95. Jordan, "Sir Thomas Lawrence, Secretary of Maryland," 35–39; *Archives*, 27:335; Seymour to Board of Trade, Jan. 10, 1708/09 (quotation), CO5/716/IV.
96. Seymour to earl of Nottingham, July 3, 1705, CO5/721/I; Seymour to Board of Trade, s.d., CO5/715/VI; Quarry to Board of Trade, Aug. 4, 1703, *CSP, 1702–1703*, No. 993.
97. *Archives*, 26:522–23, 634–45 (act).

"port" was intentionally given such a broad definition in the resulting act that it proved virtually meaningless. The queen eventually disallowed all of the colony's feeble legislation on this subject. In the efforts to acquire even this weak concession from the assembly, Seymour had expended much good will and support, which he never possessed in any great abundance.[98] Meanwhile, Marylanders pursued their own solutions to the problems of the tobacco trade, including legislative provisions for a hogshead of a different gauge. Seymour battled repeatedly with the assembly over such acts, passed despite his objections, and over proposed laws on the cropping and defacing of tobacco. Again and again, the governor was caught between the demands of English merchants who secured instructions and orders from the Crown most benefiting themselves and the insistent demands of a contrary nature pushed by local planters and traders.[99]

Seymour reserved his greatest energies and resources, however, for his campaign to achieve a thoroughgoing reform of the province's judicial system. He regarded the local courts as a farce with unqualified judges and too broad a jurisdiction; even the Provincial Court he dismissed as "a mere Jest" with its justices "not knowing any Rules to guide their Judgment." Nicholson had tried to remedy judicial shortcomings by recruiting abler men, but Seymour considered the problem more deep-seated and he proposed to effect far-reaching institutional changes.[100]

Seymour's instructions from the Crown already directed him to limit the "extravagant" jurisdiction of the county courts, and he quickly formulated additional measures to combat what he regarded as a desperate situation. He envisioned making the Provincial Court a much smaller body, with four justices instead of twelve, and appointing the ablest men in the colony to this office. Like English assize justices, these men might then ride circuit and hear causes in the respective counties where Seymour hoped their example would have a positive influence on local members of the bench. Concurrently, he wanted to distinguish among these county justices with the introduction of two types of commissions; he proposed to appoint the six or seven most qualified individuals to a commission of oyer and terminer granting civil jurisdiction, but to extend to the usual ten or twelve justices only a limited commission without the accustomary

98. Ibid., 25:262; 27:159–68 (act); *CSP, 1708–1709*, Nos. 883, 904. In late 1709, the lower house defeated one last effort to secure a stronger law requiring tobacco to be brought to towns (*Archives*, 27:432).
99. See, for example, *Archives*, 26:331–32; 27:157–59, 182, 187, 212, 237–38, 395, 442, 465–67; *CSP, 1706–1708*, No. 1427.
100. Seymour to Board of Trade, June 10, 1707, CO5/716/II and the governor's followup letter of Mar. 10, 1708/9, *Archives*, 25:269. Almost all of Seymour's letters of this period speak disparagingly of the colony's courts.

authority to hear civil causes and lacking some other traditional powers. Finally, to improve the quality of law practiced before the courts, Seymour wanted a strict licensing of attorneys and more rigorous requirements for practicing before the Provincial Court.

Seymour could implement some of these proposed changes unilaterally, but other features clearly required the concurrence of the legislature, and all depended on the cooperation of the respective justices. Such a response was not forthcoming. The lower house and most local authorities guarded jealously the gains in jurisdiction and power acquired by the county courts in the 1670s and carefully maintained over subsequent decades. The local elite was loathe for many reasons to allow any diminution of this influence, and the delegates staunchly protected the independence of the current justices and the existing arrangements of the province's judicial system.[101]

Seymour launched his program in 1705, just a year after his arrival. Predictably encountering a negative response in the assembly, he proceeded administratively to introduce the dual system of commissions. The differentiations arbitrarily imposed upon sitting justices caused considerable trouble; some former members of the quorum found that their status had suddenly dropped, as new magistrates received appointments to the selective commissions of oyer and terminer with a greater prestige and power than that now held by many veteran justices. Individuals directly affected did not always share the governor's perception of who were the most capable men and who, if anyone, should lose power to hear civil causes. Furthermore, some men omitted from the superior commission were members of the lower house, a situation that did not bode well for the prospects of Seymour's other intended reforms. In addition, it undoubtedly did not help the governor's cause that his experiment with different commissions in fact revived a practice the Calverts had pursued before 1678, and a few delegates and justices could remember firsthand the proprietor's earlier distinctions among justices and his use of judicial patronage as a political weapon.

A number of offended justices refused to serve under the revised commissions, and spokesmen in the next meeting of the assembly demanded a return to traditional practices. Seymour held firmly to his course, however, throughout his tenure. At the first assembly after the governor's death in 1709, the lower house strongly advocated a single county commission with all justices having equal powers. By late 1712, the council

101. Carr, "County Government," Text, 133–43; C. Ashley Ellefson, "The County Courts and the Provincial Court in Maryland, 1733–1763" (Ph.D. diss., University of Maryland, 1963), particularly 24–83; and Smith and Crowl, eds., *The Court Records of Prince George's County*, especially xviii-xxii and xlv-lxiii.

and acting chief executive, Edward Lloyd, had completely abandoned Seymour's innovation; they reinstated the old-style commission "for the peace and for the trial of causes" but for the time being appointed a maximum of eight justices per county.[102]

Seymour's commissions in 1705 had also reduced the county court's realm of jurisiction, another objective accomplished solely by executive fiat. Outcries from all areas of the province forced a slight retreat, which he was willing to grant so long as the justices eligible to try the cases in question were limited to those men on the smaller commission of oyer and terminer. The assembly was still not satisfied. In December of 1708, noting that it cost twice as much and required a much longer time for the hearing of cases in the Provincial Court, the lower house requested new commissions with an expansion of the local justices' domain. In return for a reduction in the number of county court sessions from six to four per year, the governor and delegates reached a rare compromise. Once Seymour died, however, the representatives again successfully pressured the council into raising the maximum jurisdiction of the local courts and promising to lobby a new governor on his arrival to raise the minimum jurisdiction of the Provincial Court. The latter was accomplished a few years later during the administration of John Hart.[103]

The proposal for itinerant justices proved to be the most controversial component of Seymour's entire package. In 1692, 1694, 1701, and 1704 such an idea had surfaced in the assembly and on three of these occasions had been introduced by a member of the lower house, but the recommendation never received much support. Seymour failed to get a bill for assize justices through the elected chamber in 1706, but he soon received permission from the Board of Trade to implement this scheme administratively, just as he had the other reforms; if he followed this course, however, the justices would still be dependent on the assembly for their salaries. Seymour consulted the council and some trusted Provincial Court justices and lawyers on how he should approach the representatives again. Late in March of 1707, he reintroduced the reform as the queen's order and admonished the delegates "to remember our Royal Sovereigns' just commands are too Sacred to be trifled with or neglected." He proposed the establishment of four assize justices with an annual salary of £100 each and argued that this would result in substantial savings and an improved

102. *Archives*, 26:446, 533–34; 27:388–89, 390. Provincial Court Judgments, Liber B, fols. 410a-11a; Anne Arundel Court Records, Liber G, fols. 613–14; TB No. 1, fols. 17–19, 21, 45–46; TB No. 2, fols. 1–3, 89–90; Kent Court Proceedings, GL No. 1, fols. 480–82, 537–40; 1707–9, fols. 1, 114–15; Charles County Court Records, E No. 2, fols. 204–6.

103. *Archives*, 26:572; 27:243–44, 367–68, 390–91; 30:239–43; Carr, "County Government," Text, 142–43.

judiciary. Despite his prodding, the representatives refused to approve the plan.[104]

Seymour stubbornly proceeded without legislative sanction. In September, he revoked the existing commission for the Provincial Court and issued a new one to Thomas Smithson, William Holland, Thomas Smith, and Philemon Lloyd as assize justices; these men commenced sitting immediately. Holland and Lloyd were completely new appointees, but Smithson and Smith had been serving under the former commission. Since Seymour's arrival, his successive commissions for this highest court had dismissed a total of thirteen justices, only four of whom had subsequently gained an appointment to their respective county benches. These men resented their dismissals, and others deplored the fact that the new assize system abruptly ended the practice of drawing from every section of the colony twelve justices who were almost exclusively current elected members of the assembly. The four new itinerant justices came from just three counties, and only Smithson and Smith were current delegates. On the same day that Seymour issued the new commission for these assize justices, he also ruled by executive order that henceforth only men who had been members of the Inns of Court or of Chancery in England were eligible to practice in the colony's courts without first undergoing an examination of their "Capacitys honesty and good behaviour" by the governor and council. This move revived another of Charles Calvert's unpopular policies of the 1660s and threatened the livelihood of several individuals, some of whom were elected members of the assembly or influential individuals.[105]

Seymour discovered that it was one matter unilaterally to create courts, appoint justices, and disbar attorneys and quite another thing to obtain the necessary support for sustaining these actions. In 1708, freeholders returned a lower house highly disposed against his program. Half of the thirty new delegates had never received a judicial appointment from Seymour or had been dropped from the commission of oyer and terminer to the one for maintaining the peace only. Eight of the fifteen returning representatives were in a similar situation. In at least four cases, voters chose men whom Seymour had explicitly opposed in the recent months. He had expelled Thomas Brooke from the council, charged Joseph Hill

104. On past proposals, see Ellefson, "County Courts and Provincial Court," 116–18; *Archives*, 25:210; 26:605; Board of Trade to Seymour, Feb. 4, 1705/6, *CSP, 1706–1708*, No. 84. In his address to the delegates, Seymour stressed that "her Majesty designes you Judges borne within your own bounds, which is really so Indearing a condescention" (*Archives*, 27:4–5 [quotation], 11–14, 50, 58, 88, 114.

105. Provincial Court Judgments, PL No. 1, fols. 233–35; WT No. 3, fols. 612–14; WT No. 4, fols. 3–4, 165–67; TL No. 3, fols. 258–59; TB No. 2, fols. 65–67, 235 (quotation); *Archives*, 25:223–24 (quotation).

with complicity in an alleged conspiracy and contempt of the government, and had voiced his displeasure with Daniel Mariartee. In addition, the freeholders of Talbot had returned Thomas Smithson, whom Seymour had angrily dismissed as an assize justice a few months earlier for disregarding the governor's wishes concerning the treatment of a controversial lawyer. Smithson soon became the new speaker, a position held in the previous assembly by assize justice Thomas Smith, who was no longer a delegate. Seymour's support in the lower house was further diminished by the absence of his favorites, John Contee, Thomas Greenfield, and Samuel Young. Few delegates were forthright supporters of the administration.[106] Seymour attempted to increase that number slightly by extending representation to Annapolis and achieving the election there of two protégés, but the effort backfired when the lower house denied these men their seats and ruled invalid the executive charter bestowing representation on the capital.[107]

The governor's opening address to the new legislature did nothing to assuage the anger rising among the delegates. Asserting the Crown's interests over any local concerns, Seymour solicited the approval of laws requested by the queen to restore the income from the ordinary licenses to the secretary and to approve funding for the assize justices, noting that both of these were "repeated Instructions" from the monarch. "Let your concurrence therefore be hearty and chearful while its in your power and banish all flattering Whispers which advise you to swallow such a pernitious notion that you Gentlemen here Assembled are wiser than the vast Crowds of her other great Dominions who unanimously with open loyal Hearts run to obey and serve her sacred Majesty the Queen." Seymour followed this admonition with an unusually caustic attack on

> the many Immoralities of this unhappy deluded Country where Drunkenness Adultery Sabbath breaking and Forgery are a jest Murder Stiffled and the Malefactors Glory in it, Treason thought a Triffle and the Abettors caress'd Magistrates grow careless and the Offendors impudent till these things are in some measure amended by your Prudence and Example I have but slender hopes your debates can be successful but as we are willing to be called Christians let us in our several Stations Act like men who deserve that noble Excellent Character that the Heathens round about us may not continue to mock at our Hypocrisy and despise our Religion and let that Magistrate be

106. Papenfuse et al., eds., *Biographical Dictionary*, 1:38; *Archives*, 25:214, 237–38, 245; 27:41–47, 62, 114–18, 121, 125–26. Greenfield and Young had been appointed to the upper house.
107. Those elected were William Bladen, a close associate of the governor, and Wornell Hunt, a fairly recent immigrant and lawyer whom Seymour was actively sponsoring.

Stigmatized with Infamy whoever connives at or Countenances any Sort of Knavery or Athiesm.

The representatives ignored Seymour's priorities and launched immediately into their attack on the charter to Annapolis and refused to conduct any business until receiving satisfaction in that dispute. Consequently, Seymour angrily dissolved the body and called for another election.[108]

Any hopes for a favorable change in membership proved illusory. The new assembly convened two months after its predecessor's abrupt conclusion. Forty of the forty-eight members of the previous house had been returned, and the eight new members reflected no improvement in attitude toward the governor. The clear and unmistakable expression of popular support for the assembly's position forced Seymour to become more amenable. Only his reluctant concessions avoided another complete stalemate. A personal "indisposition," occasioned perhaps by the lower house's undisputed control of the situation, prevented the governor from sitting with the legislature for more than three or four days of the entire session. This meeting again denied Seymour's requests for funding for the justices, return of the income from ordinary licenses to Lawrence, and appeals for other legislation. The delegates successfully insisted that incorporation of Annapolis required legislative action and altered several provisions of the governor's earlier charter. The delegates from Annapolis continued to be denied a seat until an act of incorporation was passed and approved by Seymour. The lower house also declined to give the governor and council the power to license attorneys, but did compromise to allow the courts themselves to admit or suspend attorneys.[109]

Death intervened before Seymour could devise other strategies. The council thereafter did little to uphold his programs, except in support of assize justices, where the queen's instructions were quite clear. However, the lower house in 1709 again refused to appropriate funds for the salaries of these unpopular justices and after extended debate again in 1710 resolved "that the Country ought not to pay such Charge. That Constitu-

108. *Archives*, 27:181–221, especially 183–84 (quotations).
109. Seymour to Board of Trade, Jan. 10, 1708/9, CO5/727 and Mar. 10, 1708/9, and enclosures, CO5/716/IV. In notes appended to various laws passed by the assembly, Seymour said that the Act Ascertaining Fees to Attorneys "occasioned the hottest debates" because "this Assembly being many of them Justices of the County Courts and Extremely desirous to enlarge their Jurisdiction and Authority" had drafted the law to "discourage those [attorneys] who were most Capable to serve their Clyents from going the Circuits . . . and had they not been satisfied in the passing this bill they would have left the Temporary Laws Expired." *Archives*, 27:275–374, covers this entire session.

tion being very ill convenient to the Country and imposed upon them without their Consent."[110]

Seymour had also tried to battle the local opposition through the weapon of patronage. With the increasing sophistication of the freeholders and the elected branch of the assembly, such a strategy encountered greater obstacles than when it was adopted fifty years earlier by the Calverts, and it often backfired, as when voters embraced Thomas Smithson and Thomas Brooke after the governor turned against these men. In new appointments Seymour often looked beyond the emerging elite of ruling families to recruit an alternative political force, but this did not always work either. For example, the governor struck at the Brooke-Addison clique by replacing Brooke on the council with Thomas Greenfield, an old rival of Brooke, rather than with William Hutchinson, Addison's partner, who had long been a nominee. Seymour also extended commissions to Philip Lynes, who had married the governor's sister, and John Contee, a relatively recent arrival who had married the governor's favorite cousin. He swore in some of these men as councillors before the Crown approved their appointments. The strategy achieved little since Lynes and Contee died soon thereafter, and Seymour succeeded only in alienating further those whom he already distrusted. With the governor's own death on July 30, 1709, the emerging elite easily reestablished itself in the council as well as in the lower house and on the county bench.[111]

That particular group of dominant families oversaw the colony's affairs for the next five years without a governor in residence. Not until 1714 did the Crown dispatch John Hart as Seymour's replacement. During the interim, the assembly met annually for one session approximately two weeks in length, with Edward Lloyd, as president of the council, serving as the chief executive officer. The lower house asserted an equality in these meetings not previously achieved by always reconvening in its own chamber after Lloyd had prorogued the assembly and then conducting one last piece of business, its own speaker finally ending the session. This demonstration of independence and equality accompanied a growing insistence that the lower house play a superior role in interpreting the appropriateness of any legislation, for as the delegates strongly asserted

110. Provincial Court Judgments, PL No. 3, fol. 104; *Archives*, 27:397–98, 494 (quotation). Acts for assize justices finally passed years later after the royal period had ended but did not become a permanent feature (Carr, "County Government," Text, 143).
111. *Archives*, 25:226–27, 228–33, 239–40; Jordan, "Maryland's Privy Council," 79–80. As late as the 1690s, Nicholson had more success in such strategies. He remarked at the midpoint of his tenure, for example, that "the Sherifs being a place of profit is given to those who have done his Maj[y] Service in the House & to encourage others to do the like" (CO5/714/1).

to the upper house in 1712, "We cannot help your differing in Judgement from us but since you must own we more immediately represent the People than your Honble Board you must allow us to know more of their Oppressions and we offer the properest Remedies we can to relieve them." In the same session, the councillors, though disagreeing on some specific matters, did forthrightly admit to the members of the lower house that "you more readily represent the People."[112]

The disputes occasioning such exchanges were the delegates' desire to legislate in certain areas that the Crown had instructed the council to avoid or the Crown's desire for statutes that the representatives opposed. The members of the upper house often agreed in substance with their colleagues in the lower chamber but were still bound by a special oath to uphold the wishes of the Crown. The councillors tried to maintain a balanced position between these conflicting pressures. They attempted to restrict the primary business of each session to approval of the public levy and the revival of temporary legislation. No lower house would consent to a blanket authorization for levies that might render unnecessary an annual convening of the legislature. Lloyd dutifully reminded delegates at each successive session that instructions from the queen prohibited him from approving any act not "immediately necessary for the Peace and Welfare of the Province." Collectively, the upper house explained in 1711 that "tho we shall always shew a great regard for the Welfare of this Province (In which we have as great an Interest as any) and to you their Representatives, yet at the same time you must give Us leave to assert our Duty to her Majesty the Honour of this Board & our own Reputations." Nonetheless, the delegates often pressed the councillors to disregard those orders, to reinterpret their "Duty," and to broaden what they were willing to consider "necessary."[113]

The issues of Seymour's administration continued to occupy the attention of the representatives. In one battle in 1710, half of the delegates visited the upper house in an impressive display of determination and served notice that they would not proceed to any other business until the councillors agreed to limit the jurisdiction of the Provincial Court. The upper house acquiesced. Encouraged by this success, the delegates launched an attack the following year on the assize justices, pointing out especially that Philemon Lloyd was then serving both as justice and as

---

112. *Archives*, Vols. 27 and 29, contain journals for the assemblies during these years; see particularly 27:558 and 29:117 and 188–89 (quotation).

113. For example, ibid., 27:491; 29:3–4 (quotation), 26 (quotation); president and council to Board of Trade, Nov. 4, 1710, *CSP, 1710–1711*, No. 474; Lloyd to Board of Trade, July 15, 1712, CO5/717/III; and president, council and assembly to Board of Trade, Nov. 20, 1713, CO5/717/IV.

deputy secretary in Lawrence's absence from the province, and Lloyd was soon to join the council as well. The upper house defended the integrity of the justices and Lloyd's ability to be impartial despite conflicting interests, but they did agree that "to prevent the opinion of any one Justice being prejudicial, we think it advisable more be added to the Provincial Court." The representatives were only slightly mollified when the new justices turned out to be predominantly councillors who failed to restore the breadth of overlap between the lower house and the court before Seymour's reforms or the widespread representation from each county on that high court. Disputes would continue into the proprietary period after 1715.[114]

The lower house defeated another effort in 1709 for a stronger law requiring tobacco to be shipped from designated towns. The delegates also insisted on appealing to the Crown against the recent disallowance of acts on tobacco and tobacco packing. No councillor signed the petition that the lower house sent to England. Queen Anne subsequently allowed the act against the cropping of tobacco in return for the assembly's agreeing to abide by the standard size gauge used in Virginia. This compromise passed the legislature in 1711, although Lloyd reported that it "was Gained with great Difficulty."[115]

The representatives proved less amenable to any resolution of the Lawrence affair. They steadfastly declined to restore to him the ordinary license fee revenues. Again in messages to the queen not endorsed by the upper house, although many of its members shared similar sentiments, the delegates defended their position. Lawrence finally died in 1714, and a temporary settlement reached a few months later with the newly arrived Governor Hart provided for the disputed income to be applied toward the building of a new home for the governor. The delegates sensed this compromise to be a vindication of their persistent argument that the revenues were at the disposal of the legislature and not the inherent right of the secretary's office or of any other administrative authority, and they hastily passed the compromise proposal.[116]

Hart's arrival on May 29, 1714, finally ended a situation that had greatly disturbed Robert Quarry for five years. As the senior royal placeman in the Chesapeake area while Maryland was without a governor, Quarry had repeatedly beseeched the Board of Trade to send out a

114. *Archives*, 27:500, 502–7, 519, 522, 528, 541–42, 548–49, 559–61; 34:46; 29:17, 22–28 (quotation, 22), 52, 223–24, 292; Provincial Court Judgments, TP No. 2, fols. 329–30; VD No. 1, fols. 385–86, 626.
115. *Archives*, 27:182, 187, 212, 237–38, 395, 432, 442, 465–67; 29:5, 40; 38:128–30; Lloyd to Board of Trade, Jan. 25, 1711/12 (quotation), CO5/717/II.
116. Jordan, "Sir Thomas Lawrence, Secretary of Maryland," 39–40.

replacement for Seymour. "Maryland, which I allways took to be the most quiet and easyest Government of the Maine, the freest from all factions and partys, is now by the ill conduct of the late Governour run into as great extravagancy as any of the rest," he had lamented in late 1709. Quarry attended the assembly's sessions in 1709 and 1710 as a member of the upper house, and he urged the councillors to hold firm in their allegiance to the royal prerogative. The absence of the requested governor and crisis conditions of the economy during these years often overtaxed that allegiance. The councillors warmly welcomed Hart, for his arrival removed considerable pressure from their shoulders. It had been difficult to oppose so firmly measures with which these men often privately agreed.[117]

Hart had been recommended to the Crown by Benedict Leonard Calvert, the proprietor's son. The Calverts had become estranged in recent years, culminating in the son's conversion to the Church of England in 1713. Threatened by disinheritance, he applied successfully to the queen for financial support. The younger Calvert increasingly opposed his father by offering a different counsel on colonial matters and soon surpassed him in influence within the imperial bureaucracy, as evidenced by Hart's appointment.[118]

The new governor convened a meeting of the assembly just three weeks after reaching Maryland. Rescheduled in anticipation of the governor's arrival, this session was brief because the summer months were an inconvenient time for most members. Still, the presence at last of an official governor and the recent peace settlement concluded with France invited considerable activity even during a short gathering of the legislature. For example, Hart pushed for new legislation regarding the tobacco trade that would soon resume under more normal circumstances, but the delegates declined to oblige him. The assembly did pass five acts, including bestowal on the governor of the usual three-pence duty and an additional three-pence export tax for defraying public charges.[119]

The colony's depressed economy most disturbed Hart as he surveyed his tasks. There was abundant evidence of the province's suffering. In addition to long-standing problems, a serious drought since early 1714 had burned up practically all of the tobacco and other crops. Planters, much discouraged, were inclined to diversify their economy, which Hart

117. Quarry to [David Pulteney], Dec. 2, 1709, CO323/7, 1; *Archives*, 27:384, 503.
118. Jordan, "Royal Period," 316–47; Michael G. Hall, ed., "Some Letters of Benedict Leonard Calvert," *William and Mary Quarterly*, 3rd ser., 17 (1960), 358–70.
119. *Archives*, 29:345–446; Bernard C. Steiner, "Restoration of the Proprietary of Maryland," *American Historical Association Report 1899* (Washington, D.C., 1899), 235–44.

had been carefully instructed by English officials to prevent. Pervasive indebtedness characterized the colony, and Hart realized this had to be resolved if he were to abide by his instructions.[120]

When the assembly gathered again on October 5, a more leisurely time of the year for its members, Hart had extensive recommendations for the delegates to consider. High on his agenda was a complete revision of the colony's laws, an undertaking the Crown had been requesting for years. Only slightly less important was Hart's plan to revive the tobacco economy through "useful laws," in essence the same reforms earlier governors had proposed. The delegates had barely settled down to business, however, when unofficial word reached Annapolis that Queen Anne had died. Hart thought it prudent to suspend further business, with the exception of settling the public levy. Once that bill had been prepared and passed, he prorogued the assembly for one month to allow for confirmation of the report; if the queen were indeed dead, the assembly would automatically stand dissolved. Hart himself hastened to Philadelphia to verify the news and returned a few days later with the confirmation. Maryland commemorated the beginning of a new reign with a day of thanksgiving on November 25, while the governor effectively dealt with some Jacobite sentiment existing in the colony.[121]

A new legislature sat the following spring from April 26 through June 3 for one of the busiest meetings that any assembly in the colony had ever held. Almost half of the previous body had been returned. Eighteen of the replacements were taking their oaths as delegates for the first time, but most of them were young men whose fathers had similarly sworn oaths as assembly members. Indeed, few individuals in this legislature could not point to one or more direct relations who had served in earlier assemblies. The profile of the members gathered for this last assembly convened under royal authority attests clearly to the emergence of a distinctive social and political elite in the colony since the Calverts had been deposed in 1689.[122]

Hart again exhorted the delegates to initiate a complete revision of the laws and a wide-ranging program for economic recovery. The session was unusually productive. The body of permanent laws it enacted provided what one nineteenth century historian called "the substratum of the statute law of the province, even down to the Revolution; and the subsequent legislation of the colony effected no very material alterations in the

120. Hart to Viscount Bolingbroke, July 11, 1714, *CSP, 1712–1714*, No. 717; Perry, ed., *Historical Collections*, 4:77–79; Steiner, "Restoration," 244–45.
121. *Archives*, 29:449–82; 25:277–99, 327–36; Steiner, "Restoration," 246–48; The Humble Representation of Mrs. Mary Hemsley, n.d., CO5/720/III.
122. *Archives*, 25:293; Papenfuse et al., eds. *Biographical Dictionary*, 1:41.

system of general law then established." The legislature passed a total of forty-eight laws, many of them former acts governing the colony's political, judicial, economic, and ecclesiastical affairs in still further refined and improved language. Numerous statutes addressing various aspects of the same topics were incorporated into one law – for example, a comprehensive act regarding servants and slaves. Noteworthy new legislation considered the tobacco trade, land policy, and elections. Still other statutes might have passed, but business was again interrupted by unexpected news from England, this time word of the death of Charles Calvert, Lord Baltimore. Hart informed the council as well that the same packet of letters contained information that the Crown had restored the province to the Protestant Benedict Calvert, now the fourth Lord Baltimore. Since that news arrived in an unofficial report, he did not release it publicly.[123]

Hart did notify the assembly and the province at large of Calvert's death and indicated that the new Lord Baltimore had empowered the governor to serve as his agent in the colony. Hart encouraged the assembly to act promptly on the question of the proprietor's rents. The two houses hurriedly enacted a bill laying an impost of eighteen pence per hogshead, instead of the usual twelve pence, in recognition of the now larger gauges, to go to the proprietor during his natural life if he would accept payment of quit rents and fines, as his father had, in the form of tobacco at the rate of two pence per pound, a rate well above the current market price.[124]

Official word of the restoration of proprietary authority did not reach the colony until the end of the year. The unexplainable delays in communication between the lords of trade and Maryland officials had contributed much to the confusion and problems of recent years, and in the future such delays were persistently to undermine the efforts of those representing both the Crown and the proprietor in the colony. News of the disallowance of laws often reached Maryland three or four years after the initial passage of these statutes and a full two or three years after the Board of Trade received them. The assembly resented these delays as much as it did the actual disallowances when they occurred. A similarly frustrating delay attended the slow response of the imperial bureaucracy

123.   For the proceedings and acts of the assembly, see *Archives*, 30:1–355. The quotation comes from John V. L. McMahon's history of Maryland written in 1830 and cited approvingly by Steiner, "Restoration," 248. Hart to Townsend, July 30, 1715, *CSP*, *1714–1715*, No. 541, a letter of eleven pages, has the governor's account of the meeting. There appeared a few years later in England a printed volume of *Acts of Assembly, passed in the Province of Maryland from 1692, to 1715* (London, 1723), and in 1718 Andrew Bradford of Philadelphia had printed *Body of the Laws*.

124.   *Archives*, 30:77, 80–81, 204, 208–9.

to questions sent from Maryland. These problems of communication aggravated relations and spurred the representative assembly to assert a stronger local voice in addressing immediate problems.

Meanwhile, Benedict Leonard Calvert enjoyed his new title and restoration of proprietary authority for less than two months, for he himself succumbed on April 16, 1715. The fifth Lord Baltimore was Calvert's young son Charles, not yet sixteen years of age. Most decisions for some years were to be made by his guardian, Francis North, Lord Guilford, who promptly petitioned the Crown to continue Hart as governor.[125]

Through the confusing summer and fall of 1715 in Maryland, Hart delayed action on all but the most pressing business and awaited direction from England. When official word finally arrived, he hastily convened the council on December 27, despite "violent weather and deep Snow." He read the official instructions and immediately initiated the orderly tranfer of government, with business once again to proceed in the name of the proprietor and not the Crown. Public announcement occurred before noon on the following day at the courthouse in Annapolis with the province's dignitaries present. On the night before, Hart had dissolved the current assembly, "forasmuch as the said Assembly being called by His Majestys Writts of Election it wou'd not be Proper that they should Enact Laws in his Lordship's Name." The royal period of Maryland's colonial history was over.[126]

---

125. Jordan, "Royal Period," 337–43. As one condition of the restoration, the Crown retained the right of approval of governors.
126. *Archives,* 25:313–19, 322–26 (quotation, 326).

Epilogue: "Our Present Happy Protestant Constitution"

The Assembly of Maryland by 1715 little resembled the rudimentary gathering of freemen that had first met in the young colony eighty years earlier. Now, actual power underlay the rhetoric of legislative privileges and the claims to be the Parliament of Maryland. The central place of the assembly within the governance of the province was safely ensured, and within this now well developed institution, the assertive lower house with its elected membership had achieved a position as the equal of the appointed upper chamber and as the more legitimate representative of the people's interests.

This accomplishment had not come easily. The charter of Maryland, though calling for "the Advice, Assent and Approbation of the Free-Men" or their deputies in effecting "the good and happy Government of the said Province," had provided no definite design for the expression of that popular voice, and it had concurrently bestowed sweeping authority and power on the Lords Baltimore. The residents of Maryland battled almost a century before the proprietary family acknowledged that it could not keep the province frozen in time like a perpetual fourteenth century palatine of Durham or a subordinate sixteenth century Ireland. The charter's guarantee of a popular legislative voice always provided a potentially powerful instrument for freemen, and determined men eventually made it just that.

J. R. Pole has wisely observed that in the seventeenth century colonies the "governments started by being more popular than in England."[1] Certainly this was so in many ways in early Maryland. A greater equality initially prevailed among freemen, and all such men had a vested interest in the political affairs of the province and the new institutions that gradually emerged. The proprietor required a special cooperation from his colonists. It proved very important that the early assemblies were open to all freemen

1. J. R. Pole, *The Seventeenth Century: The Sources of Legislative Power* (Charlottesville, Va., 1969), 41.

and that for more than three decades these freemen enjoyed unrestricted eligibility to vote for the delegates who represented them in the elected legislatures that quickly evolved. This openness helped to forge new perceptions about the possible course of representative government.

This more "popular" concept of government persisted despite the property limitations imposed on the suffrage in 1670, the declining likelihood that ordinary householders might actually sit in the legislature, and the lamentable exclusion of Catholics and to a lesser extent Quakers from the political process in the years after 1689. Representative government as increasingly perceived by residents of Maryland depended upon a more assertive role by elected delegates in the assembly and a particular bond emerging between these men and the general population, both colonists who could vote and those who could not. Assemblymen articulated in 1692 this vision of government that had evolved over the previous fifty years. An act for publishing the colony's entire legislation remarked on the importance of every Marylander's familiarity with the statutes, since "all the Laws intend that every person in this Province is bound to take notice of what is passed in the Assembly, because every person is there present in their Representatives."[2] There is little evidence, however, that the voices of the colony's Indians, slaves, servants, free white females, or unpropertied free white males figured very importantly in the deliberations of the legislators or that these individuals were "present" in any reasonable meaning of that term. The representatives in actuality found themselves increasingly beholden to the freeholders who possessed the ultimate authority in their votes and seldom questioned their right to determine political issues theoretically if not actually in behalf of all colonists. The voteless Marylanders generally acquiesced, or at least no record survives of strong opposition to the course of representative government in the final decades of this first century.

This important aspect of popular sanction even began to affect the relations of the province to the mother country and the position of the local assembly with respect to royal or proprietary authorities in England. As Francis Nicholson remarked in 1698, the people of Maryland, as well as settlers in other colonies, "think no Law of England ought to be in force, and binding to them without their own consent. For they foolishly say, they have no Representatives sent from themselves to the Parliaments in England. And they look upon all laws made in England that put any Restraint upon them, to be great hardships."[3] Nicholson might have added that the people of Maryland and their representatives similarly

2. *Archives*, 13:467.
3. Ibid., 23:494.

resented any outside disallowance of laws properly enacted by the local assembly.

Through most of the years before 1715, however, the power of the proprietor and later of the Crown had easily dominated any popular voice in the governance of Maryland. Only gradually did the charter's provision for the role of freemen or their deputies acquire a greater meaning. The settlers first advanced their influence by exploiting critical religious and political differences within the infant colony and by successfully claiming the power to amend and to initiate legislation. They learned subsequently how to employ this legislative prerogative to draft statutes more suitable to their interests, to establish and then build upon precedents, to look beyond the simpler issues of the moment to lay a broader foundation for future victories. With the division of the assembly into two chambers, the lower house achieved a veto power over all proposed bills and the opportunity to develop a more independent political stance.

Long before the elected members could be confident of gaining legislation they ardently pursued, these representatives had become reasonably certain of defeating any bill they did not want enacted or of gaining valuable concessions in exchange for reluctant approval of such a statute. By the 1670s, the Calverts needed extraordinary patience and clever tactics to achieve their own legislative objectives, especially the necessary financial support of the government and endorsement of military expeditions. Proprietary recognition of the assembly's essential role in approving taxes gave the delegates the means for slowly ensuring other gains in power. A succession of lower houses over the next four decades shrewdly discovered how to control funding, to introduce conditions regarding the use of revenues, and to restrict in a variety of ways the independence of the governor and other officeholders. These advances, as well as a more sophisticated use of parliamentary tactics and temporary statutes, became effective weapons for bargaining with the nonelected authorities for still greater powers.

These steps toward a more truly representative government increased noticeably as the membership of the lower house came to include more individuals of education and legal ability and more members who had acquired valuable experience by serving repeated terms in the assembly. Finally, the emergence of a distinctive native elite in the respective counties provided a greater independence from the governor, as well as a stronger base of local support. None of these factors had characterized the political life of the Maryland assembly to any appreciable degree before 1689. Their mounting presence thereafter enabled the delegates to develop a more effective internal organization, to assert undisputed control over their own membership, to increase their skills as legislators, and to display the confidence and competence essential for accomplishing long frustrated legislative objectives.

These critical developments in Maryland mirrored a general process affecting the governance of most other New World colonies, a process that Jack P. Greene argues was making electoral politics at once "more settled, coherent and predictable" and providing the basis for a successful "quest for power" on the part of the representative branches of government. Elsewhere, as in Maryland, delegates were gaining the victories that had so long eluded them and making the assembly the significant forum for political action. Concurrently, voters were proving more discriminating in their ability to lobby persuasively and to render elected representatives more responsible to their constituents. The various colonies advanced along this process at different speeds, but by the early eighteenth century the elected chambers throughout British America had impressively reached the point at which "they could battle on equal terms with the governors and councils and challenge even the powers in London if necessary."[4]

The Assembly of Maryland clearly occupied this stage by the closing years of the royal period. With this maturing of legislative government in the province, the executive authority had lost, or found substantially restricted, one after another of the weapons it had once wielded so masterfully to keep the freemen and their deputies in an inferior position. The executive's power of the purse, power of patronage, and power of persuasion all diminished in influence as the assembly asserted its own preeminence in these areas. In 1700, one astute observer candidly acknowledged that "the Burgesses hold the purse in their hands or at least hold the Strings," and the repeated failures of John Seymour's administration similarly revealed the limitations of patronage and exhortation – either from the governor or the Crown – as effective means of attaining the compliance of delegates. Not many years later, another governor, Benedict Leonard Calvert, cogently underscored these impressive advances by the representatives when he noted that the colony's legislation now effectively circumscribed the fundamental powers of the proprietor and significantly limited what any nonelected official was able to accomplish.[5]

Lord Guilford, the guardian of Charles Calvert, the fifth Lord Balti-

4. Jack P. Greene, "Legislative Turnover in British America, 1696 to 1775: A Quantitative Analysis," *William and Mary Quarterly*, 3rd ser., 38 (1981), 442–63, especially 456 (quotation), and *The Quest for Power*, particularly 3–4 (quotation). Greene found a steady long term decline in turnover among members of the assembly in twenty-one of twenty-two colonies for the first eight decades of the eighteenth century.
5. Bray-Maryland Mss., fols. 226–27, Sion College Library, London (quotation); *Calvert Papers, Number Two*, 68–81.

more, personally acknowledged these changes when he notified the assembly in 1717 that "I do assure you nothing can be more welcome to my Lord Propry and me than the advice of our Assembly, it being so Vital a part of the Constitution and the best Counsell of the Province."[6] The second and third Lords Baltimore would never have made such an observation, but the assembly had indeed become by 1717 the central institution of provincial government, and Guilford, with all calculated flattery aside, realized the current influence and power of the legislature and, within that body, of the elected representatives.

The return of proprietary rule entailed no appreciable loss of that influence and power. New acts passed in the proprietor's name confirmed the fundamental advances made by the assembly during the royal period, and the young Calvert without hesitation approved these statutes. Despite the theoretical possession of powers almost identical to those enjoyed by the earlier Lords Baltimore, this proprietor and his guardian rarely attempted to exercise such a royal jurisdiction without regard for local attitudes. Calvert did veto legislation more frequently than the Crown had been accustomed to doing, but the assembly was now more assertive as well in promoting its own program and often more successful in obtaining the concurrence of the upper house in an interesting reversal of earlier roles.[7]

A veto had useful purposes from the proprietor's perspective, but it still could not compel the legislators to enact unpopular measures, and the representatives now bowed less frequently to executive pressure. In these years after 1715, statements from the Calverts, the governors, or the council often referred to prerogatives, but the lower house responded just as convincingly in language that repeatedly invoked its privileges. Each side gained an appreciation of the other as a formidable equal. Guilford aptly articulated this new arrangement of power in a message to the assembly of 1720. He observed that the governor should endeavor "to make the Interest of the Province & Proprietary One without either extending our Prerogative, or Lessening your Priviledge."[8]

Charles Calvert, who replaced John Hart as governor in 1720, envisaged the proper relationship as one in which the proprietor acted "as a

6. *Archives*, 33:8.
7. Ibid., 3–4; 34:67–68 and 200 detail some of these vetoes. Volumes 30, 33, and 34 of the *Archives* contain the journals and legislation of the early assemblies of the second proprietary period.
8. The governor was commanded "punctually to balance" the respective prerogatives and privileges (*Archives*, 34:62). Aubrey C. Land has aptly entitled a chapter discussing politics during this period "Prerogative and Privilege" (*The Dulaneys of Maryland*, 62–75).

bountifull Indulgent Father would towards a Dutifull Deserving Son."[9]
Paternalism had replaced the less mitigated authoritarian rule of the earlier Calverts with their "Monarchical Government." A further change was implicit, however, in the governor's analogy, whether he perceived it or not. The day would eventually arrive when the "Dutifull Deserving Son" might be expected to strike out and demand from the "bountifull Indulgent Father" ever greater degrees of autonomy.

Those days of ultimate challenge and independence were still five decades away, and the intervening years were to bring colonists in Maryland and elsewhere in America to an even fuller understanding and appreciation of the forms and substance of representative government. Meanwhile, the assembly would continue to consolidate its power and fulfill its acknowledged role in what it now liked to call "our present happy Protestant Constitution," a phrase that invoked the less tolerant religious consequences of the colony's own glorious revolution as well as the advances in representative government following upon that momentous event in 1689.[10]

9. *Archives*, 34:64.
10. Ibid., 33:495. For the transitional years between 1715 and 1776, see particularly Land, *The Dulaneys of Maryland*; Skaggs, *Roots of Maryland Democracy*; and Charles A. Barker, *The Background of the Revolution in Maryland* (New Haven, Conn., 1940).

Appendixes

Appendix A. Elected service in assembly

Terms of service	First elected 1637/38–60		First elected 1661–88		First elected 1689–99		First elected 1700–15		Total	
Elected, never served[a]	2	(2)	6	(4.4)	7	(6.4)	5	(3.7)	20	(4.2)
1	57[b]	(58.8)	71[c]	(51.8)	47	(42.7)	55[d]	(41)	230	(48.1)
2	21	(21.6)	27[e]	(19.7)	20[f]	(18.2)	23	(17.2)	91	(19)
3	6	(6.2)	19[g]	(13.9)	20	(18.2)	19	(14.2)	64	(13.4)
4	7	(7.2)	4	(2.9)	8[h]	(7.3)	15[i]	(11.2)	34	(7.1)
5	1	(1)	9[i]	(6.6)	3	(2.7)	4	(3)	17	(3.6)
6	1	(1)	1	(0.7)	3	(2.7)	4	(3)	9	(1.9)
7	1	(1)	0		0		4[k]	(3)	5	(1)
8	1	(1)	0		1	(0.9)	3	(2.2)	5	(1)
9	0		0		1	(0.9)	1	(0.7)	2	(0.4)
14	0		0		0		1	(0.7)	1	(0.2)
Total	97		137		110		134		478	

Note: Numbers in parentheses represent percentages.

[a] Includes men dismissed because of improper election or inability to meet requirements and those who never attended.

[b] Includes two men dismissed from assembly in this period who served in one assembly after 1660.

[c] Includes three men dismissed from a second assembly.

[d] Includes four men whose election to a second assembly was voided.

[e] Includes two men elected to a third assembly. One died before assembly met; one gained appointment to upper house.

[f] Includes two men. One was ruled uneligible to sit in a third assembly; the other died before third assembly met.

[g] Includes two men dismissed from two and three assemblies after 1692 as unqualified to serve.

[h] Includes a man discharged from a fifth assembly owing to improper election.

[i] Includes a man whose election to a fifth assembly was voided.

[j] Includes one man dismissed as unqualified to sit in a sixth assembly.

[k] Includes a man whose election to an eighth assembly was voided.

Appendix B. Appointive service in assembly

Terms of service	First appointed 1637/38–60	First appointed 1661–88	First appointed 1692–99	First appointed 1700–15	Total
Summoned, never served	7 (23.3)	0	0	0	7 (7.6)
1	7 (23.3)	9 (33.3)	4 (22.2)	1 (5.9)	21 (22.8)
2	3 (10)	9 (33.3)	2 (11.1)	5 (29.4)	19 (20.7)
3	2 (6.7)	6 (22.2)	7 (38.9)	0	15 (16.3)
4	2 (6.7)	2 (7.4)	1 (5.6)	2 (11.8)	7 (7.6)
5	4 (13.3)	0	3 (16.7)	0	7 (7.6)
6	1 (3.3)	0	0	2 (11.8)	3 (3.3)
7	2 (6.7)	0	0	2 (11.8)	4 (4.3)
8	1 (3.3)	1 (3.8)	1 (5.6)	1 (5.9)	4 (4.3)
9	0	0	0	1 (5.9)	1 (1.1)
10	1 (3.3)	0	0	1 (5.9)	2 (2.2)
11	0	0	0	1 (5.9)	1 (1.1)
12	0	0	0	1 (5.9)	1 (1.1)
Total	30	27	18	17	92

Note: Numbers in parentheses represent percentages.

Appendix C. Origins of assemblymen and councillors

	Date of first election or appointment				
	1637/38–60	1661–88	1689–99	1700–15	Total
Free immigrants, originally from Europe	104 (81.9)	103 (68.7)	49 (43.8)	23 (16.8)	279 (53)
Indentured servants	11 (8.7)	12 (8)	13 (11.6)	3 (2.2)	39 (7.4)
Free children or young adults transported by others, originally from Europe	1 (0.8)	11 (7.3)	4 (3.6)	6 (4.4)	22 (4.2)
Known natives of Maryland	0	3 (2)	22 (19.6)	71 (51.8)	96 (18.3)
Probably natives of Maryland	0	3 (2)	2 (1.7)	8 (5.8)	13 (2.5)
Known natives of other colonies	1 (0.8)[a]	8 (5.3)	8 (7.1)	6 (4.4)	23 (4.4)
Probably natives of other colonies	1 (0.8)	3 (2)	1 (0.9)	1 (0.7)	6 (1.1)
Unknown origins, probably free immigrants	4 (3.1)	7 (4.7)	13 (11.6)	18 (13.1)	42 (8),
Unknown origins, probably indentured servants	5 (3.9)	0	0	1 (0.7)	6 (1.1)
Total	127	150	112	137	526

Note: Assembly members include provincial parliamentary commissioners of 1654–57/58. Numbers in parentheses represent percentages.

[a] Nathaniel Utie sat with the upper house in 1658 but won his first election to the lower house in 1662.

A Note on the Sources

Michael Kammen directed historians' attention in 1969 to the dearth of scholarship on the beginnings of legislative assemblies in colonial America. In *Deputyes & Libertyes*, an introductory collection of source readings on this subject, he noted, "There is no systematic description and analysis of the seventeenth-century origins of representative government in British North America." In a "prolegomenon to such an inquiry," he reminded scholars of the exceptionally aggressive nature of these early legislatures and raised some important questions for any future study. That same year, J. R. Pole, in the seminal *Jamestown Essays on Representation*, focused briefly upon the sources of legislative power in the seventeenth century. Pole underscored "the high level of participation in the process of government" in the early colonies and the important advantages they enjoyed during their formative decades "to find their own way, to learn from the day-to-day handling of local problems how to organize themselves . . . singularly free from effective supervision, restraint, or external direction."

My study of the evolution of representative government in early Maryland attempts to address many of the questions posed by Kammen and the ideas suggested by Pole. Neither scholar paid much attention to the Calverts' colony in these brief essays, nor has the Assembly of Maryland figured very prominently elsewhere in the scant body of literature on seventeenth century legislatures surveyed by Kammen and others. Ironically, Maryland, possessing perhaps the best surviving records of any early assembly and of the society that it served, may ultimately provide the clearest story of how representative government developed in a British American colony.

Any systematic analysis such as Kammen invited must begin, of course, with a careful reading of those colonial documents, especially the records of the assembly itself. The journals for both the proprietary and royal periods through 1715 have, with a few notable exceptions, been published in the *Archives of Maryland* (Baltimore, 1882-), as have the equally important journals of the provincial council. Original or duplicate copies of all these records can be consulted at the Hall of Records in Annapolis or, for the years 1692 to 1715, at the Library of Congress or the Public Record Office in London.

The correspondence of provincial officials is an invaluable supplement to the journals. Again, most of this rich material is available to students in published form. Personal observations are rarer for the first fifty years of settlement in Maryland, but the surviving proprietary correspondence appears in *The Calvert Papers, Number One*, Maryland Historical Society, Fund Publication No. 28 (Baltimore, 1889). Letters from Catholics have been extensively reproduced by Thomas J. Hughes in his *History of the Society of Jesus in North America, Colonial and Federal* (London, 1907–17). Such personal commentary becomes more abundant with the increasing interest of the Crown and its imperial bureaucracy in the closing decades of the century. The bulk of official reports from governors, other officials, and the assemblymen themselves are kept at the Public Record Office in its Colonial Office Series but most have been excerpted in the many volumes of the *Calendar of State Papers, Colonial Series, America and the West Indies* (London, 1860-). The complete correspondence of one exceptionally observant official has been edited by Robert Noxon Toppan and Alfred Thomas S. Goodrich in *Edward Randolph: Including His Letters and Official Papers . . . 1676–1703* (Boston, 1898–1909). Many reflections on Maryland's government emerge from the papers of William Blathwayt and Francis Nicholson, microfilm copies of which are on deposit at Colonial Williamsburg's Research Library. Additional materials of this nature exist in the Fulham Palace Papers housed at the Lambeth Palace Library in London, many having been printed in William Stevens Perry's *Historical Collections Relating to the American Colonial Church* (Hartford, Conn., 1870–78). My footnotes throughout the chapters above cite other smaller collections of importance.

The student of early Maryland owes an enormous debt to the Hall of Records for its assiduous collection, preservation, and indexing of the voluminous religious, land, probate, and judicial records that have survived from the colonial period. Without such resources, the detailed biographical profiles of all the legislators, upon which I build so extensively, simply would not be possible. Archivists Leon Radoff and Edward Papenfuse have made this central repository a marvelous place to work. Helpful published guides to the records include Elizabeth Hartsook and Gust Skordas, *Land Records and Prerogative Court Records of Maryland* (Annapolis, Md., 1946), Morris L. Radoff, Gust Skordas, and Phebe R. Jacobsen, *The County Courthouses and Records of Early Maryland* (Annapolis, Md., 1963), and Phebe R. Jacobsen, *The Quaker Records of*

Maryland (Annapolis, Md., 1967). Only the judicial records appear to any appreciable degree in print, primarily in the *Archives*, and in Joseph H. Smith and Philip A. Crowl, eds., *Court Records of Prince George's County, Maryland, 1696–1699* (Washington, D.C., 1964). Elizabeth Baer, comp., *Seventeenth Century Maryland, A Bibliography* (Baltimore, Md., 1949), surveys other valuable resources.

In the pursuit of information on Maryland and the legislators, I investigated both published and unpublished records for England and other colonies. The manuscript and printed collections of the British Museum, the University of London Library, the Institute for Historical Research in London, and the Research Library of Colonial Williamsburg proved very helpful.

No historian works totally alone or isolated from what other scholars have written. The secondary literature on representative government extends back into the colonial period itself. Early studies for most legislatures, as indeed for the Assembly of Maryland, initially consisted of direct quoting and indirect paraphrasing of the journals themselves. Amateur and professional historians in the nineteenth century, men like John Leeds Bozman, John V. L. MacMahon, John Thomas Sharp, and Elihu Riley reproduced for their readers a narrative account with an occasional intrusion of analysis and bias, usually a prejudice for or against the proprietary family or on behalf of either Catholic or Protestant colonists. The publication of the *Archives* soon superseded these earlier accounts and, coinciding with the emergence of graduate programs in history, brought a new sophistication to the writing of this political history.

The preeminence of Johns Hopkins University, with its publication series in the historical and social sciences, brought a flowering of scholarship on Maryland early in this century. Newton D. Mereness's 1901 study, *Maryland as a Proprietary Province*, stood out from all other monographs and remains today a standard reference. Mereness typified the orientation of many in his generation, which was to forsake narrative history for more topically based analyses of an institutional nature, paying particular attention to political offices, especially powers and privileges and the time of their first appearance. Mary C. Clarke, from a more comparative perspective, gave important attention to Maryland's significant history in her *Parliamentary Privilege in the American Colonies* (New Haven, Conn., 1943). A few authors such as Bradley Johnson, Sebastian Streeter, Bernard C. Steiner, and Thomas J. Hughes did examine in some detail critical episodes and individuals in a more traditional approach. Few of these authors, however, drew on many sources beyond the official political records themselves.

For a period thereafter, many historians focused more immediately on social and economic aspects of early American life or on the imperial dimension of political history. It remained for a giant of this era, Charles M. Andrews, to pull together these various threads in his magisterial volumes, *The Colonial Period of American History* (New Haven, Conn., 1936). Andrews's account of proprietary Maryland remains the best study of its length and a beginning place for all subsequent scholars. A few years later, Wesley Frank Craven published the other "mainstay" treatment of the period, *The Southern Colonies in the Seventeenth Century, 1607–1689* (Baton Rouge, La., 1949).

Through the middle decades of the twentieth century, few historians studied colonial Maryland and most of them ignored the early assembly. A virtual reflowering of interest in the Calverts' colony has occurred, however, since the early 1960s. The fullest guides to this rich literature are Richard R. Duncan and Dorothy M. Brown's *Master's Theses and Doctoral Dissertations in Maryland History* (Baltimore, 1970) and the periodic updates on unpublished and published scholarship in the issues of the *Maryland Historical Magazine*. Thad Tate has admirably surveyed much of this new scholarship in his bibliographical essay introducing *The Chesapeake in the Seventeenth Century* (Chapel Hill, N.C., 1979). That volume and an earlier collection of essays, *Law, Society, and Politics in Early Maryland* (Baltimore, 1977), edited by Aubrey C. Land, Lois Green Carr, and Edward C. Papenfuse, presented to a broader audience the stimulating new work of Carr, Russell Menard, Lorena Walsh, Gloria Main, Paul Clemens, and Allan Kulikoff, among others, who were dramatically altering our understanding of the early Chesapeake and especially of Maryland. In tandem with the earlier pioneering work of Aubrey Land, these scholars overturned traditional ideas about the population, explored patterns of wealth holding, and poked into every nook and cranny of local life and institutions. Rarely, however, did they pursue explicitly political subjects, and when they did it was primarily to examine county government. Nonetheless, like their counterparts investigating New England towns and southern parishes and counties, these scholars had much to teach the student of provincial institutions.

Meanwhile, most political historians continued to focus more extensively on the eighteenth century, as Jack Greene, Bernard Bailyn, and a host of other scholars debated the characteristics of legislatures and the mindsets of assemblymen in the decades closer to the American Revolution. Greene's important analysis, *The Quest for Power: The Lower Houses of Assembly in the Southern Royal Colonies, 1689–1763* (Chapel Hill, N.C., 1963), filled an important gap but unfortunately ignored Maryland completely. A few historians still pursued the study of politics in the earlier formative decades, but these individuals tended to pursue a

broader inquiry from an imperial perspective, as had an earlier generation, but now often drawing quite different conclusions. David Lovejoy,
for example, in his comparative study, *The Glorious Revolution in America* (New York, 1972), espoused a neo-Whig interpretation in stressing
the colonists' spirited defense of their political rights and representative
assemblies against the designing assaults of the absolutist monarchs
Charles II and James II and their imperial bureaucrats. J. M. Sosin, in a
three-volume account of the years from 1660 to 1715, disputes the existence of any systematic imperial plan or well-coordinated assault on
colonial rights under the later Stuarts and, playing down any ideological
components of these power struggles, draws lines not so much between
the mother country and the colonies as between warring factions within
the colonies and within England. Stephen Saunders Webb, in *The
Governors-General* (Chapel Hill, N.C., 1979) and more recently in *1676*
(New York, 1984), emphasizes military considerations over commercial
or more narrowly political concerns in postulating a new conception of
empire emerging after the Restoration. John Murrin and W. A. Speck
suggestively survey the work of these men and other historians writing in
this area in historiographical essays that appear in Jack P. Greene and J.
R. Pole, eds., *Colonial British America* (Baltimore, 1984).

Meanwhile, a few individuals in the past few decades have directed
their attention more specifically to the political history of individual colonies and particularly to the early development of representative government. Much of this work originated in dissertations begun before the
explosion of new social history, often proceeded topically rather than
chronologically, and frequently resembled more traditional institutional
studies. The untimely death of John C. Rainbolt interrupted promising
work on Restoration Virginia. The posthumously published *From Pre-
scription to Persuasion* (Port Washington, N.Y., 1974) and several earlier
essays pointed in important new directions. Robert Wall completed a
dissertation at Yale in 1965 on the membership of the Massachusetts
General Court, 1634–86. Although he never integrated this important
research into a broader political study, his *Massachusetts Bay: The Crucial Decade, 1640–1650* (New Haven, Conn., 1972) did provide a suggestive model for a more ambitious work. Unfortunately, Martin H. Quitt
has also never developed further his 1970 dissertation at Washington
University: "The Virginia House of Burgesses, 1660–1706: The Social,
Educational and Economic Bases of Political Power." His approach bore
many resemblances to my own early work on the Maryland assembly,
and his data proved highly useful for comparative purposes. Warren
Billings, starting from a dissertation completed in 1968 at Northern Illinois, " 'Virginia's Deploured Condition,' 1660–1676: The Coming of

Bacon's Rebellion," has since written quite extensively on politics in the Old Dominion, but his published work has to date not addressed so directly or fully the colony's political history or the assembly's evolution. Jon Kukla has already advanced our knowledge of the Virginia assembly in its more formative years with his University of Toronto dissertation, completed in 1980, "Political Institutions in Virginia, 1619–1660," and several subsequent essays. Susan Rosenfield Falb made a fruitful start on the contemporary legislature under the Calverts in her 1976 dissertation at George Washington entitled "Advice and Assent: The Development of the Maryland Assembly, 1635–1689." Her approach was topical, but it too employed a biographical analysis of the assembly's membership. Falb has subsequently published only one essay on proxy voting drawn from her research. My own dissertation, "The Royal Period of Colonial Maryland, 1689–1715," completed at Princeton in 1966, had been the first political study of the seventeenth century Chesapeake extensively to employ prosopographical analysis and to incorporate an examination of the assembly into a general political narrative. *Maryland's Revolution of Government, 1689–1692* (Ithaca, N.Y., 1974), coauthored with Lois Green Carr, developed this approach more intensively for a brief critical period in the colony's history. Subsequently, I collaborated with others to prepare the two-volume *Biographical Dictionary of the Maryland Legislature, 1635–1789* (Baltimore, 1979–84), and in a series of essays cited throughout the chapters above I have attempted to lay the foundation for the general study that this book represents.

One sweeping study of a seventeenth century colony fully grounded in the new social history has appeared in these years. Edmund Morgan, in the highly provocative and influential *American Slavery, American Freedom* (New York, 1975), portrays a very brutal and exploitative Virginia society in which celebrated gains in political liberty and representation for the relatively few came at the decided expense of poor whites and enslaved blacks. Morgan strongly emphasizes class conflict and directly challenges traditional interpretations of the evolution of representative government, although he focuses his study less directly on the evolution of assembly than on social and economic developments. Others have questioned Morgan's arguments on Virginia and have questioned even more so the applicability of his thesis to other colonies. To the degree that Morgan is correct about Virginia, that colony may have more in common with British colonies in the Caribbean than with others on the mainland. His analysis, though often suggestive, seems less relevant in its extreme formulation to Maryland. Studies more focused on provincial politics in Virginia will be welcomed to test Morgan's conclusions, as will broader studies of Massachusetts and other early colonies.

No studies of seventeenth century colonial politics can safely ignore the rich scholarly literature on contemporary England, and this is especially true of the early legislatures and the development of representative government in British America. As previous pages try carefully to establish, the colonists possessed a surprising knowledge of parliamentary procedures, precedents, and current politics. I have relied heavily on the published primary and secondary literature regarding the Stuart period. In recent years, that scholarship has similarly enjoyed a creative flowering. Particularly helpful have been the many articles and books of G. R. Elton, Conrad Russell, Derek Hirst, and J. H. Plumb, all cited in the footnotes above.

Index

Adams, Henry, 74
Adams, Thomas, 30, 31n
Addison, family of, 154, 157–8, 222; John, 156n; Thomas, 156n
Allen, Thomas, 18
Alsop, George, 57, 65, 68, 74, 76, 87, 96
Andros, Edmund, 189–90
Annapolis, 144, 145, 165, 193, 230; assemblymen from, 150, 224–5
Anne, queen of England, 213, 228, 230; see also Crown of England
Anne Arundel, county of, 17, 65, 87, 113, 127, 208; assemblymen from, 73, 175, 176
Assembly of Maryland, eligibility to serve in, 21–2, 92–4, 164–5, 167, 185–6, 198; evolution of two houses of, 26–8, 31–3, 46–7, 53–4, 55, 57, 58; plans for, 1–7; writ of election to, 56, 57, 111–12, 121, 218, 225; writ of summons to, 19, 20, 21, 28, 32, 57, 89, 109, 115; see also assemblymen; clerk of the lower house; elections; speaker of lower house
Assembly of Maryland, sessions: of 1634/5, 19, 35–6; of 1637/8, 19, 20, 21–2, 29, 36–40, 42; of 1638/9, 20, 25–6, 29, 40, 42–4, 101; of 1640–1, 44–5; of 1641/2, 21, 30, 46–7; of 1642A, 26, 28, 46–7; of 1642B, 20, 30, 46–7; of 1644/5, 48; of 1646–46/7, 31, 49; of 1647/8, 22, 31, 50; of 1649, 52–3, 55; of 1650–50/1, 17, 21, 31, 32, 53–5; of 1654, 56; of 1657, 57; of 1658, 32–3, 57; of 1659/60, 32–3, 57–9; of 1661, 74, 76, 89, 90, 100; of 1662, 87, 100; of 1663–4, 102, 105; of 1666, 95, 100, 103–5; of 1669, 87–8, 93, 94–5, 105–8; of

1671–74/5, 93, 108–14; of 1676–82, 74, 86, 88, 89, 92, 93, 114–26, 128; of 1682–4, 71, 78, 88, 89–90, 126–31; of 1686–8, 71, 74, 78, 88, 131–5; of 1692–3, 92, 164, 177, 180, 183–9; of 1694–7, 143, 193–200; of 1697/8–1700, 176, 177, 200–11, 217; of 1701–4, 156, 212–14, 217–18; of 1704–7, 154, 159, 163, 215, 218–23; of 1708A, 163, 223–5; of 1708–11, 159, 163, 164–5, 221, 225–8; of 1712–14, 154, 228–30; of 1715, 154–6, 165, 230–2; of 1716, 166; Protestant Associators Convention of 1689–92, 135–7, 183–4
assemblymen, pay for, 24, 89; profiles of, 23–8, 69–80, 148–63; relations to constituents, 85–90, 94–6, 171, 180–1
Avalon, colony of, 1, 3, 12

Bacon, Nathaniel, rebellion of, 83, 85, 117–20
Baldridge, James, 18; Thomas, 18
Baltimore, county of, 65, 113, 171, 172n, 173n; assemblymen from, 109, 175
Barbados, colony of, 17, 23; assembly of, 32–3, 92, 102
Beale, Ninian, 153n, 156n, 158–9
Beard, Richard, 76, 92n
Bennett, Richard, 55–6; Richard, Jr., 78n
Berkeley, William, governor of Virginia, 108, 117, 120
Berry, William, 112
bicameralism, see Assembly of Maryland
Billingsley, Francis, 121
Bishop of Durham, palatinate of, 3–4, 17, 19, 20
Bladen, William, 153n, 192, 218, 224n